Contemporary British Theatre

Contemporary British Theatre

Breaking New Ground

Edited by
Vicky Angelaki

palgrave
macmillan

First published 2013 by
PALGRAVE MACMILLAN

Palgrave Macmillan in the UK is an imprint of Macmillan Publishers Limited,
registered in England, company number 785998, of Houndmills, Basingstoke,
Hampshire, RG21 6XS.

Palgrave Macmillan in the US is a division of St Martin's Press LLC,
175 Fifth Avenue, New York, NY 10010.

Palgrave Macmillan is the global academic imprint of the above companies
and has companies and representatives throughout the world.

Palgrave® and Macmillan® are registered trademarks in the United States,
the United Kingdom, Europe and other countries.

ISBN 978–1–137–01012–4

This book is printed on paper suitable for recycling and made from fully
managed and sustained forest sources. Logging, pulping and manufacturing
processes are expected to conform to the environmental regulations of the
country of origin.

A catalogue record for this book is available from the British Library.

A catalog record for this book is available from the Library of Congress.

Typeset by MPS Limited, Chennai, India.

For Paulina and Akis, spectators of the future

Contents

Foreword: Dramatic Developments

Liz Tomlin

By 1999, in the words of Aleks Sierz, 'in-yer-face theatre had become a new orthodoxy'[1] with the growing familiarity of once-shocking innovations suggesting that 'the tide was turning and that an era of confrontation had come to an end'.[2] In the same year, the very future of all dramatic playwriting was called into question with the publication of Hans-Thies Lehmann's *Postdramatisches Theater* (Postdramatic Theatre).[3] Although Lehmann's seminal text was not translated into English until 2006, the ideas it contained disseminated rapidly throughout Europe to question the continued value of the dramatic form of theatre. There had been, Lehmann argues, a 'retreat of dramatic imagination'[4] and 'disappearance of the dramatic impulse'[5] to the point at which '[d]rama and society cannot come together'.[6] He concludes that 'the dwindling of the dramatic space of imagination in the consciousness of society and of the artists seems, at any rate, indisputable and proves that something about this model is no longer in tune with our experience'.[7] If drama, as Lehmann consistently argues in this study, is no longer a valid form for theatre at this point in history, then one of three things must be the case. The first is that the playwrights and playtexts examined in this volume are relics of a bygone era, with no possible relevance to the twenty-first century. The second is that all such work can no longer be considered to be dramatic, an option that I will return to shortly. But I would like to begin with a third possibility that is rarely considered by scholars working within the rubric of Lehmann's postdramatic, which is that the historical notion of the dramatic as defined by Lehmann is no longer appropriate or relevant to the work being produced by significant numbers of dramatists at the turn of the twenty-first century.

Lehmann's definitions of the dramatic tradition consistently reference its classical Aristotelian origins, with an emphasis on its 'logical (namely dramatic) order', its 'unbroken, complete unity and wholeness', its 'mastery of the temporal progress', and its 'dialectic' which constitutes an 'implied teleology of history'.[8] He concludes that 'the complicity of drama and logic, and then drama and dialectic, dominates the European "Aristotelian" tradition – which turns out to be highly alive even in Brecht's "non-Aristotelian drama"'.[9] For Lehmann, these philosophical hallmarks are most clearly manifest in the representational world, or *'fictive* cosmos', of the pre-existing dramatic playtext that is already complete, in and of itself, and which then subsequently becomes the point of origin and authority for the theatrical production.[10] Speaking of the dramatic theatre, Lehmann argues that

> What is necessary [...] is the principle that what we perceive in the theatre can be referred to a 'world', i.e. to a totality. Wholeness, illusion and world representation are inherent in the model 'drama'; conversely, through its very form, dramatic theatre proclaims wholeness as the *model* of the real.[11]

The tendency of classical drama towards totality, closure and wholeness, makes the dramatic form, for Lehmann, ideologically regressive, in that it can only offer illusory representations of an even more illusory reality, enclosed within a pre-existing playtext which positions itself, again deceptively, as complete in and of itself. Thus it is only, according to Lehmann, the model of the postdramatic that can carry forward any radical potential in its *'self-reflection, decomposition* and *separation* of the elements of dramatic theatre'.[12] It is only by breaking the 'wholeness' of the model of dramatic representation (and thus implicitly the 'wholeness' of the reality it represents) through the fragmentation, deconstruction or decontextualization of its parts, that theatre in the postmodern era can escape complicity with the discredited philosophical notion of a singular, objective and authoritative reality.

Lehmann extends this ideological analysis of classical drama to models as diverse as Henrik Ibsen, Eugène Ionesco and Bertolt Brecht, on the basis that all of this theatre is text-driven and so 'remains pledged to the hierarchy that [...] ultimately subordinates the theatrical means to the text'.[13] He concludes unequivocally that 'the step to postdramatic theatre is taken only when the theatrical means beyond language are positioned equally alongside the text and are systematically thinkable without it'.[14] Thus, for Lehmann, there is no easy recalibration of the playwright as postdramatic. Under his terms, theatre in which the written text pre-exists as a given which then informs the development of the other theatrical vocabularies of the production (however significant these might become), must remain, within Lehmann's thesis, under the dramatic rubric and consequently bear the ideological weight of his analysis.[15]

The resistance to this unpalatable conclusion has led to scholars, including this author, attempting to circumvent the conflation of logocentric ideology and dramatic form in Lehmann's own analysis, by extraditing playwrights from the dramatic to the postdramatic over recent years.[16] This has been justified primarily on the grounds that writers such as Sarah Kane and Martin Crimp, the British playwrights most commonly assigned to the postdramatic, are themselves clearly engaging in precisely the activity that Lehmann describes as postdramatic – the '*self-reflection*, *decomposition* and *separation* of the elements of dramatic theatre'; yet such an argument does necessitate rejecting Lehmann's own imperative for the postdramatic to position the 'theatrical means beyond language [...] equally alongside the text'.[17] All attempts to conclusively categorize artistic forms, in any case, will inevitably be defeated by the vital and necessary resistance of artistic forms to totalizing categorization, but the choice of whether to prioritize Lehmann's definition of the activity of the postdramatic over his insistence that it must not be led by a pre-existing text or vice versa does, I will now suggest, hold implications which go beyond an analysis of the specific playwrights concerned. What has begun to concern me is the possibility that a continued recalibration of selected texts as postdramatic on the grounds outlined above will only serve to rescue certain types of individual texts or writers from Lehmann's ideological prosecution, whilst leaving the remainder of 'the dramatic' both narrowly conceived and ideologically stigmatized.

Re-configuring the dramatic

Lehmann's discrediting, on ideological grounds, of that which remains 'dramatic' – wherever the lines are drawn – inevitably serves to undermine the political efficacy of those dramatists whose innovations within the dramatic tradition might not neatly dovetail with the '*self-reflection, decomposition* and *separation* of the elements of dramatic theatre' that Lehmann envisages for the postdramatic, but who seek to address contemporary concerns with representation and illusions of wholeness by other means. Such an ideological analysis would appear particularly damaging to the broadly realist work of black dramatists such as Roy Williams and Kwame Kwei-Armah whose theatre might be argued to deconstruct and challenge, not primarily the dominant aesthetic form of the dramatic model, but the predominantly white and Eurocentric ownership of all its various manifestations throughout the most part of the twentieth century. The well-known postmodernist challenge to all realist representation on ideological grounds is well known, but it is worth posing the question, in more depth than has generally been considered and in more depth than is possible here, as to whether the representation of *an alternative* (not an illusory *the authoritative*) reality of marginalized communities, such as those offered by Williams and Kwei-Armah, might hold its own potential to confront and challenge the mass-mediatized representations disseminated about minority communities in Britain. Lehmann's preferred deconstructive aesthetic may well be the logical radical option for those artists (predominantly white and most often male) who are well embedded in the dominant culture, as their position lends itself most easily to self-reflexive critique of the ideological apparatus of which they are part, but we should be careful not to assume that such a position is universal. In his analysis of Jean Genet's *The Blacks*, Carl Lavery draws attention to the important preface that Genet wrote, but did not publish at the time of the play's first production. In this preface Genet makes explicit that his role as a white writer – in racial terms, therefore, a representative of the dominant cultural power – prevents him from speaking of the black experience, and authorizes him only to 'wound the Whitess [sic], and through this wound, to introduce doubt' to which end he stipulates at the beginning of the published text that it is written to be performed to white spectators only.[18] To represent the black race, Genet insists, must be the responsibility of writers of that race, who must find their own language and means to do so. Realist drama, seen through this lens, might well retain the capacity for progressive ideological impact when seeking to re-vision, from a minority or liminal perspective, representational worlds on the stage that have not historically been permitted to establish a cultural authority or spectacle, on their own terms, that is yet in need of deconstruction. Hal Foster's writing is often drawn on to support the ideological necessity of the deconstruction of realist representation, and is cited by Philip Auslander as proposing that 'the political artist today might be urged not to represent given representations and generic forms but to investigate the processes and apparatuses which control them'.[19] However, Foster actually advocates prior to this citation that '[t]o re-think the political [...] is not to rule out any representational mode but rather to question specific uses and material effects', which would precisely include consideration of the questions Genet raises about who is representing who to whom and in what context, rather than a rejection of realism as politically efficacious *per se*.[20] Thus, for the model of a broadly dramatic realism, when finally permitted to those whose race, in particular, has been most woefully under-represented in the modern drama canon, to be too easily dismissed as holding any political potential in the way Lehmann's analysis might suggest, does, to me, seem to risk an implicit cultural censorship of a deeply ideological nature.

To circumvent the potentially problematic consequences of Lehmann's ideological analysis, of which the above is only one example, a more productive enterprise might be to reclaim all playwrights as dramatists, as Lehmann's work proposes, but to then re-configure the definition of a contemporary, diverse and progressive notion of the dramatic, in line with what dramatists are now doing. Rather than recalibrating as postdramatic those whose work does not fit Lehmann's particular definition of the dramatic, why not ask instead how such work begins to redefine what we might mean by twenty-first century drama? I have argued elsewhere that work such as Howard Barker's Theatre of Catastrophe resolutely rejects the predicates of realism in its revisioning of a tragic poststructuralist dramatic; and even the broadly realist drama of the so-called 'in-yer-face' dramatists, often characterized by a distinctly postmodern dislocation, is again starkly different in form from the social realism of Roy Williams or the poetic realism of debbie tucker green.[21] To consider alongside these, and countless other, revisions and subversions of the classic realist model, the explicitly poststructuralist aesthetic of the more experimental texts by Kane, Crimp and Caryl Churchill, and the radical subversion of drama's invisible fourth wall in the theatrical innovations of Tim Crouch, enables us to understand contemporary drama as a much richer and more diverse field than the singular, logocentric and ultimately strategic 'other' to the ever-burgeoning field of the postdramatic. This acknowledgement of the plurality of the contemporary dramatic then enables us to ask more rigorous aesthetic and ideological questions about form and content in the context of each individual piece of work, as exemplified by the scholarship in this volume.

Such a manoeuvre, of course, requires crucially that those texts that do engage with the '*self-reflection, decomposition* and *separation* of the elements of dramatic theatre' are considered as dramatic, rather than postdramatic, texts, and to that end I will now propose a diachronic analysis that identifies the clear progression of drama's self-reflexive capacity throughout the canon of modern drama. I will argue that this capacity was, in fact, significantly more central to the developments within modern drama than Lehmann suggests when he acknowledges that '[t]his virtuality was present, though barely decipherable, in the aesthetics of dramatic theatre; it was contemplated in its philosophy, but only, as it were, as a current under the sparkling surface of the "official" dialectical procedure'.[22] Conversely, as Clement Greenberg argues, the imperative to self-critique has always lain at the very heart of modernism which, in drama as in all art forms, 'criticizes from the inside through the procedures themselves of that which is being criticized'.[23] This can be seen most explicitly within the broader field of theatre and performance in the ideological and aesthetic challenges to the representations of dramatic theatre launched by Antonin Artaud, Guy Debord, Allan Kaprow and Richard Schechner among many others, but it is no less present in the continuing trajectory of dramatic theatre itself where, in each successive movement (however impossible these are to conclusively define), we can see, as I will outline, what constituted the 'dramatic signifiers' of the previous period being critiqued, decontextualized or deconstructed in the 'new' drama of that time. When Lehmann argues that '*post*dramatic theatre [...] should [...] be understood as the unfolding and blossoming of a potential of disintegration, dismantling and deconstruction within drama itself', what seems to be overlooked is an acknowledgement of the capacity of the dramatic model, in its contemporary manifestation, to achieve precisely the same outcome, through self-reflexive critique.[24] Consequently, there is much to be gained by an examination of contemporary drama as a writer-driven model of contemporary theatre which is able to engage, in diverse ways, in the critique, deconstruction, revisionism or decontextualization of different aspects of a modern dramatic tradition that has, I argue, maintained strikingly similar questions throughout its history, despite the radical evolution of its responses. In this way, whilst I maintain Lehmann's own preference for all text-driven theatre to remain within the dramatic tradition, I will seek to overturn his suggestion that this negates the capacity of such work to engage in the poststructuralist deconstruction he assigns solely to the postdramatic.

Cracks in the framework

The realignment of the text-driven and the postdramatic most often occurs when the playtext in question is seen to explicitly reject the most commonly recognized attributes of the classical dramatic model: dialogue-driven characterization and the representation of, in Lehmann's terms, a coherent fictive cosmos. So when we are given a total absence of characters and place, as in Crimp's *Attempts on Her Life*, or Kane's *4:48 Psychosis*; or letters or numbers in place of character names, as in Kane's *Crave*, or Crimp's *Fewer Emergencies*; or seemingly 'real' situations which then collapse into ontological or linguistic ambiguity, as in Crimp's *The City*, or Churchill's *Blue Heart*, we are into the territory which is most often contested in relation to its dramatic or postdramatic status. The poststructuralist anxieties of our own age, and the form of the above dramatic models that have evolved to best address them, might seem far removed from the realist/naturalist dramas of Henrik Ibsen and Anton Chekhov which are too often taken as the standard bearers for a narrow and misconceived notion of the dramatic *per se*, as I have noted elsewhere.[25] For precisely that reason a synchronic analysis is most often undertaken that aligns the writer-driven models of Kane, Crimp and Churchill with the postdramatic ensemble or director-driven practice that shares its contemporaneous concerns with the critique of classical representation and a scepticism of 'the real'.[26]

Yet, in one important sense, contemporary drama's preoccupation with, and scepticism of, notions of subjectivity, representation and the real can also be traced back to the very beginnings of modernist drama. Modernism, after all, as Christopher Innes and F. J. Marker propose, was always propelled by 'a radically altered *Weltanschauung* born of a per-ceived loss of such values and beliefs as the rationality, purposefulness, and dignity of the human condition'.[27] As for the dramas of Ibsen and Chekhov, Raymond Williams argues that these constituted

> a repeated search for some means of defining the humanity that can-not be lived, in these well-ordered rooms [...] [t]he world of action, characteristically, is then the action of others; the world of con-sciousness is one's own. Out of this separation, and out of its terrible tensions, these men trapped in their rooms make their only possible, their exceptionally powerful, drama.[28]

If, at this point in history, the individual was most often pitted against a hostile environment or society that refused to accommodate the kind of ethical subjectivity the protagonist fought to uphold, then in August Strindberg's theatre, Williams argues, the environment itself was abandoned and the struggle resituated within the subjective tensions of the individual mind.[29] The person looking from the window of that trapped room is still there; but the room around them has gone, as have the other people in their direct dimension, and what they see from the window, now through their own eyes, is not the orthodox world but their own necessary version of it: a look from the window that is now, in essence, the dramatic form.[30]

In this way, Strindberg's expressionism begins to destabilize the relationship between the consciousness of the individual and the now-questionable reality of the external world, foreshadowing, in turn, the more radical deconstruction of character and reality embarked on by Luigi Pirandello. This was to undermine 'one of the fundamental conventions of Western drama' and ultimately destabilize 'the nature of theatrical representation'.[31] In Strindberg's work, the expressionist lens that distorted a recognizable or mimetic representation of the real was still most commonly secured within a rational framework which enabled the spectator to logically place the dramatic 'fictive cosmos' in relation to their own understanding of the real. In *A Dream Play*, for example, the very title asks the audience to view the action through the logic of a dream and, furthermore, the framing of the action by the divine quest of Indra's daughter also offers the framework of classical mythology which constitutes a logically coherent, if unfamiliar, world cosmos. *To Damascus* is most commonly interpreted through the lens of Strindberg's own subjectively re-mapped autobiography, and the narrative chronology and characterizations are, in fact, largely coherent and consistent throughout the three parts. Where there are significant ruptures, such as the halt to the passage of 'real' time that Strindberg spends at the banquet at the inn and in prison in Part Two, the events are recalibrated as a nightmare, rather than a breach in temporal logic. The same blurring of time and surreal encounters he endures in the asylum in Part One is recalibrated as a hallucination. Even when the seeds of poststructuralist thinking are explicitly discernible, it is ambiguous whether the reality of the world is merely unsettled by the distorted nature of the individual gaze that looks on it, or whether the possibility of the real itself is being put into question. This ambiguity is present, depending on whether or not the emphasis in delivery is placed on the 'you' and the 'your' when, in the final part of the trilogy, the Lady asks the Stranger, '[w]hat do *you* know of reality, child? It is not reality which meets *your* eye but the image of reality. And the image is only the appearance, not the thing itself. You fight for images and illusions.'[32] Either way, as Raymond Williams argues, there is certainly the impression with Strindberg's later work that 'the farthest developments of expressionism, and the fiction of special pleading, had converted all but one individual to illusion, but then *his reality was correspondingly emphasised*'.[33]

It was this expressionistic notion of solipsistic sovereign subjectivity that began to crumble under the vanguard attack of Pirandello's experiments in deconstruction; the early signs of a scepticism which was to characterize the end of the twentieth and beginning of the twenty-first century. For by the mid-twentieth century, as Williams continues, 'the work of art itself, maintained in those other forms by an emphatically personal consciousness, takes on more and more the quality of illusion, in its own mode' as the very possibility of an external reality, which the drama had always been charged to represent, begins to likewise give way.[34] Rather than offering the audience worlds which could still be rationally framed as nightmares, mythology or hallucination – thus leaving intact the notion of a reality that could be placed in opposition to such states – Pirandello's work locates the possibility of reality itself as illusion. In most of his work, contrary to much later twentieth-century developments, the questioning of reality does, however, remain firmly underpinned by the authorial voice, filtered through a character who frames the new parameters of the shifting dramatic framework. In *Henry IV* it is the protagonist himself who takes the audience through the philosophical basis of his performative act and in *Right You Are! (If You Think So)* it is Lamberto Laudisi who continuously explicates to the other characters the impossibility of a shared notion of 'the real'. At one point, alone on stage, he speaks only to his own reflection, thus elucidating Pirandello's philosophy explicitly for the benefit of the audience:

> Other people don't see you the way *I* see you! So what do you become! I can say that, as far as I'm concerned, standing here in front of you as I am now, I'm able to see myself and touch myself. But as for you, when it's a question of how other people see you, what happens to you? You become a phantom, my dear fellow, a creature of fantasy! And yet, do you see what these lunatics are up to? Without taking the slightest notice of their own phantom, the phantom that is implicit within *them*, they go haring about, frantic with curiosity, chasing after other people's phantoms![35]

Here we have the poststructuralist terrain mapped out before its time, but with the authorial voice as guide, to ensure that the ruptures in an otherwise coherent and logical narrative framework are rationalized by philosophical explanations of the metaphors of illusory identity which are isolated, in each play, to the characters of Henry IV and Mrs Ponza. Whilst the other characters are asked to reflect on the potentially illusory nature of their own reality, such a reality is not, within the fictive cosmos of the drama, in any actual sense disrupted.

Where Pirandello does begin to significantly pre-figure late twentieth-century poststructuralism is in *Six Characters in Search of an Author*. Here, despite the continued existence of the philosophical guide – in the guise of the Father – too much remains that is irreconcilable with logical or rational binaries of reality/illusion to fit into any previous dramatic model of 'wholeness' or 'completeness' as upheld by Lehmann. The deaths at the end of the play highlight the ambiguities throughout; if the boy and girl are fictional characters, how can they die at all? If they are real, how can they die within a fictional framework? And if the audience see real bodies in the characters, and a dramatic fiction that is clearly 'real' to those characters, then the real bodies of the actors, producer and stage manager and their own 'fictive cosmos' fall likewise into question, thus disrupting the illusory framework of dramatic representation, and implicitly unsettling the notion of its external referent of the real.

Ontological breakdown

This exposure of 'the real' as illusion was to drive the work of the mid-century existential dramatists, such as Beckett, Genet and Ionesco. Genet, in particular, is renowned for his use of metatheatrical frameworks which reject any straightforward distinction between the 'illusion' of the 'play within the play', and the 'reality' of the 'fictive cosmos' of the play itself. In *The Blacks*, the offstage execution is seemingly given credibility by the black actors playing the Court taking off their white masks to discuss the developments with those performers previously positioned as their enemies, thus marking the execution as a dramatic 'reality' that lies beyond the illusion of the 'play within the play'. However, as Carl Lavery argues, this shedding of masks also has the opposite effect by 'reinforcing the illusory quality of the performance that we are actually watching (their actions prove that nothing in this play is dramatically true)'.[36] In *The Balcony*, almost everything we are shown as dramatically 'real' is to be ultimately overturned as illusion. The 'reality' of the revolution that seemingly rips apart Irma's house of illusions, is itself thrown into question at the culmination of the play when Irma begins to explicitly re-set the stage, ready to 'start all over again'.[37] Her direct address to the audience reinforces the fact that the entire spectacle we have seen so far – the illusions of the brothel and the seeming reality of the revolution – have both been equally constructed for our benefit, thus breaking the dramatic contract of a closed and fictive cosmos in which the audience is expected to invest its belief. Furthermore, her closing words cast the same sceptical framework onto the audience's own 'reality', disrupting any conventional distinction between the spectacle of theatrical representation and its referent of the 'real' world beyond the theatre: '[y]ou must now go home, where everything – you can be quite sure – will be falser than here'.[38] The burst of machine-gun fire with which the play closes, serves to then ultimately undermine this notion of the whole play (and the world beyond it) as spectacle by the return of the 'real' of the revolution which has seemingly broken out of its fictive parameters to challenge the veracity of the authorial framework just offered by Irma.

If the ambiguity of Genet's metatheatrical structure displaces the more overt textual explication in Pirandello, then a key feature of the poststructuralist work which was to follow in the later twentieth and early twenty-first century is the continuing disintegration of the authorial framework, particularly expedited by the work of Samuel Beckett and Harold Pinter, which had helped to guide the audience through the otherwise tenuous worlds of Pirandello and Genet in the absence of the signposts, referents and philosophical certainties of previous dramatic models. Contemporary poststructuralist dramatists may appear to maintain an element of the authorial guide, often embedded within the characters' dialogue, as in Crimp's *The City*, where Clair's diary, found by her husband in the closing moments of the play, offers the audience a different lens through which to understand the 'reality' of the world they have been watching: 'I invented characters and I put them in my city. The one I called Mohamed. The one I called the nurse – Jenny – she was funny [...]. But it was a struggle. They wouldn't come alive.'[39] But in reply to her husband's question 'Am I / invented too?' Clair can only respond inconclusively '[n]o more than I am, surely', thus leaving her own ontological status – and consequently the validity of her explicatory framework itself – wide open to question.[40] Ultimately, as Elisabeth Angel-Perez discusses in her chapter in this volume, the deconstruction of language itself in the most formally experimental work of Crimp and Churchill removes the last vestige of authorial guidance, along with the very notion that any intended meaning might lie within the text. She concludes that

> the 'linguistic era' [...] has reached a conclusion and the pact with the spectator needs to be renegotiated. Language has failed [...] the text no longer contains its own truth, it becomes somehow contingent and therefore prone to being manipulated [...] Hermeneutics becomes vertical or paradigmatic, so to speak. (pp. 92–3, this volume)

In texts such as Churchill's *Blue Heart*, as Angel-Perez discusses, the audience are not even offered ambiguous or conflicting frameworks through which to make sense of the work, but are confronted with language games or 'constrained writing', which 'mean' nothing, in the old sense, but rather fill the space left by the absence of meaning with an invitation to play within new rules and perhaps reflect on the consequences of meaning's departure.

Whilst Pirandello and Genet, along with Beckett and Ionesco, offer the clearest evidence of the foreshadowing of an explicitly poststructuralist dramatic, the slide of language away from meaning was not only occurring in the absurdist or existentialist strand of modern European drama, but also informing and advancing the broadly realist tradition of British drama, most notably in the work of Pinter and Edward Bond. As Stephen Lacey observes, Bond always seemed to be recoupable within the realist tradition, yet attempts to do so tended to obscure 'the fact that he was, in several important respects, attempting to redefine realist languages and concerns'.[41] Most pertinently, in the context of the trajectory I am proposing here, Bond consistently denied himself, throughout his work, the implicit authorial guidance provided by the protagonists of Arnold Wesker or John Osborne, whilst also rejecting the construction of an authorial framework external to the narrative through which the action of the narrative might be critically read, as found in the 'complex seeing' of Brecht.[42]

In Pinter's early work the same absence of any guide to meaning was accompanied by the dislocation of seemingly recognizable realistic settings. Here, as Lacey observes, the otherwise familiar dramatic cosmos of the domestic rather becomes 'the sites of terror and fear, often when familiar, comfortable routines are wrenched from their associations and invested with newer, darker possibilities'.[43] Yet these possibilities are never conclusively realized, and the language that sketches them out explains nothing; '[i]t does not reveal the personality or explain the situation, nor does it necessarily clarify the "themes" of the play'.[44] Neither, as Mary Luckhurst observes, does Pinter's use of language enable the audience to locate his dramatic action, or offer the specificity that is commonly expected of the realist form.[45] As Lacey argues, once ideas remain suspended from representation in language, 'the chain of cause-and-effect that holds the realist narrative together is severed, and when these connections are broken, the "reality" that they construct loses its definition'.[46] In effect, as he concludes, 'Pinter's challenge to realism is a fundamental one, for it attacks the epistemological basis of the tradition.'[47] Contemporary descendants of such self-reflexive deconstructions of realism might include Crimp's *Play House* or Churchill's *Far Away*.

'A negative incommunicability'

Thus to trace the twentieth-century dramatic developments that criss-cross the existential, the absurd and the broadly realist is indeed to arrive at the most formally experimental work of Kane, Crimp and Churchill; the sites where character, understood in any former sense, is absent, and where language itself, the carrier of meaning throughout the dramatic tradition, can no longer communicate anything beyond its own arbitrarily selected and ever-shifting shapes and structures. This development was foreseen by Raymond Williams in his 1979 afterword to *Modern Tragedy* when he observed that

> [t]he fact and source of tragedy are now, centrally, the inability to communicate [...] [t]he skills of dramatic composition, within this dominant form, are now employed to render, that is to say produce, a negative incommunicability which is then presented to be overheard.[48]

Williams feared that this must inevitably lead to the nihilistic stale-mate that was first foreshadowed in the dramatic theatre of Chekhov; a tragic form which no longer bears any potential for either personal revolt or political change; a form which 'both reflects and builds a social model which is the last end of hope, for if we cannot, under any conditions, speak or try to speak fully to each other, that is the real end'.[49] Williams acknowledged, then, what is more explicit in much contemporary drama at the turn of the twenty-first century, that the total breakdown of any possibility of meaningful communication or fulfilling human relationships was not an existential condition, as it might be read in the work of Beckett, but 'an authentic condition of late capitalist or bourgeois society'.[50] Nevertheless, Williams is adamant that the mere reflection of such a condition will ensure that we remain 'indefinitely inside just such a society. It is not now the desperate but the wry end of hope.'[51]

The nihilistic stalemate feared by Williams at the dawn of the post-structuralist era is, however, reconfigured by Ken Urban who distin-guishes the historical notion of nihilism as 'a three-fold concept [...] a *philosophical problem* about value and meaning in a godless world, an *affect* of hopelessness, and an *ethical stance* where change comes from destruction'.[52] Urban argues that it is this last, the 'desire to transform annihilation into affirmation', which best characterizes the contempo-rary dramatic moment.[53] Williams himself acknowledges that, in the nihilistic philosophy of Nietzsche, the 'action of tragedy is not moral, not purgative [...] but aesthetic' and it is the affirmation of aesthetic invention as a potentially transformative antidote to the catastrophic collapse of both the Enlightenment narrative and the Emancipation narrative of communism (as experienced under the USSR) that most often characterizes the most radically poststructuralist dramatic texts at the beginning of the twenty-first century.[54] As Angel-Perez concludes:

> Martin Crimp and Caryl Churchill's theatres of the 'eternal return', though intrinsically playful, find a way of speaking out about the ethical disaster of our time: stepping out of the traditional contract that presupposes an adequacy between form and content – abdicating the grand romantic project, so to speak – stands out as a means of reinventing tragedy. (p. 93, this volume)

Comparable questions can be identified not only in relation to the more radically poststructuralist work of Crimp and Churchill, but also pertaining to those broadly realist dramatists first identified by Sierz as the 'in-yer-face' playwrights of the 1990s, who might be said to be most influenced by the earlier, ongoing extensions of realism in the work of writers such as Bond and Pinter. Whilst, for the most part, the use of language to communicate a more or less coherent dramatic narrative in a more or less recognizable world is maintained in the 1990s work of writers such as Mark Ravenhill, Jez Butterworth or Joe Penhall, the communication of explicitly ideological intentions, as had been the case in the 1980s political drama of Churchill, David Edgar, David Hare and Howard Brenton, was overwhelmingly rejected. In this sense, as observed by Luckhurst, it was not, in the main, formal innovations that marked out this new wave from its immediate predecessors, but the abandonment of the ideological framework of critical realism that had been dominant throughout the preceding decades (with the important exceptions of writers such as Pinter and Barker).[55]

This rejection of ideological authorial frameworks, already familiar, as we have seen, within existentialist drama, but not yet common within the realist tradition, caused many critics to suspect the new wave of drama might signal 'apathetic retreats from engagement with social issues'.[56] At worst, it was seen as guilty of 'a strong element of pessimism mixed with a strange sense of relish in the destructive and dehumanising worlds depicted'.[57] This combination of the absence of any authorial framework and the explicit and seemingly gratuitous brutality that was offered up in the vacuum was read by many as a 'voyeuristic glamorization of violence' which suggested a nihilistic attitude to the possibility, or even the desirability, of political or social change.[58] However, just as Angel-Perez contends that the poststructuralist work of Churchill and Crimp can offer its own redemptive possibilities, so this seemingly nihilistic new wave of broadly realist theatre can be differently understood. Dan Rebellato reads the representations of bodily pain and mutilation that characterize the 'in-yer-face' dramas of the 1990s as a revolt against the consumerist spectacles of global capitalism, arguing, as Graham Saunders and Rebecca D'Monté summarize, that such representations 'point to a desire within these characters to experience something genuinely *real* that is not in some form or another commodified'.[59] In some senses this extenuates the subliminal project that Rebellato identified in the earlier wave of British realism in the 1950s and 1960s which, he argues, sought to 'unit[e] a world of feeling with those of speech and action'.[60] More explicitly and self-consciously than previous dramatists had done, the theatre of Ravenhill's generation, Rebellato argues, 'offers an experience of discomfort that, in a sense, draws attention to experience itself'.[61] The same experiential turn in contemporary drama is explored by Chris Megson in his chapter in this volume. Here it is not bodily discomfort, nor the audience's empathetic engagement with it, but the transcendence of time itself, a shift into what Megson terms 'chronos time', that draws the character and audience into an awareness of an experiential 'here and now' that is 'grounded in the performative evocation of the moment, and which is constitutive of a reach for new values, new possibilities of living, beyond the grip of capitalism, religion and exhausted ideology' (p. 34, this volume).

Conclusion

The philosophical concerns identified above that permeate much contemporary drama – the deconstruction of language and the turn to the experiential – run synchronically to unsurprisingly comparable developments in the contemporary field of the ensemble- or director-driven postdramatic. The turn to the experiential can be explicitly seen in the work of body artists such as Franko B or the immersive performance of Punchdrunk; the attempt to capture time in an extra-daily sense occurs in the durational work of Forced Entertainment, or the extended and repetitive movement sequences of Goat Island, or the one-to-one performances of Adrian Howells, where the single spectator-participant is given the opportunity 'to take a really qualitative half an hour out of their lives, and to be very present and engage with themselves'.[62] Language games, whilst not as commonly pursued, for obvious reasons, by less text-driven models of performance, have always featured throughout the work of Forced Entertainment – an ensemble which has a highly accomplished writer as its artistic director – with particularly notable productions including *Speak Bitterness, Filthy Words & Phrases* and *Exquisite Pain.*

To read contemporary drama synchronically in this way, it is of most interest how different artistic driving forces and diverse distributions of authorship at play across the various models of writer-, director- or ensemble-driven processes might impact on the form, content and context of the artistic responses that follow. All have, after all, inherited the same philosophical trajectory, from modern drama and non-dramatic avant-garde performance, but simply choose to pursue what are ultimately similar questions through different models of theatre-making practice. To read contemporary drama diachronically as I have done here enables us, in addition, to see how the dramatic form itself has continuously questioned its own predicates, with a self-reflexivity that has enabled it to dismember the classical dramatic apparatus piece by piece, shape shifting into the absences that are left almost imperceptibly to form new structures that can accommodate the philosophical questions of the time. From the crumbling of external reality in Strindberg, to the deconstruction of reality itself in Pirandello and Genet, to the final disintegration of a language that communicates meaning in Crimp and Churchill, we can see a clear trajectory that is held in place by its own philosophical continuity and the text-driven vision of the playwright throughout.

I have responded at length elsewhere, to Lehmann's concerns about the logocentrism of the text-driven model, to argue, *pace* Foucault, that the 'author-function' does not disappear with the absence of the author, or playwright, and that any critique of the authorial voice of the playwright can likewise be levelled at the 'author-function' that takes its place, be that the director, the ensemble or the solo performance artist.[63] Furthermore, the evident fissures in the far-from-whole textual worlds of Kane, Crimp and Churchill – the absence of stage directions, characters, locations or ontological coherence – refutes the charge of the theological text as understood by Artaud and elucidated by Jacques Derrida, whereby the 'author-creator [...] keeps watch over, assembles, regulates the time or the meaning of representation'.[64] Rather the gaps in such texts pose innumerable challenges to theatrical representation, and call on the creative ingenuity and co-authorship of the directors, designers and performers, who are charged with positioning such texts within the entirety of the theatre event, and the audience, who are required to undertake their own acts of interpretation. That such work, when calibrated as postdramatic, is seen to undertake the '*self-reflection, decomposition* and *separation* of the elements of dramatic theatre' *despite* its reliance on the vision of the playwright seems to me to be missing the vital synergy between text-driven processes and the deconstructive imperative that Lehmann seeks in contemporary practice. For if one of the ultimate consequences of the sceptical project of poststructuralism is, after all, the implosion of meaning and the disintegration of communicative language, then who better, we might ask, to interrogate and transform such a potentially nihilistic dissolution, than those artists called dramatists, whose vision is driven precisely through their proven capacity to craft and manipulate language as best befits the philosophical challenges of their time.

Notes

1. A. Sierz, *In-Yer-Face Theatre: British Drama Today* (London: Faber & Faber, 2001), p. 248.
2. Sierz, *In-Yer-Face Theatre*, p. 249.
3. H.-T. Lehmann, *Postdramatisches Theater*, 2nd edn. (Frankfurt am Main: Verlag der Autoren, 2008).
4. H.-T. Lehmann, *Postdramatic Theatre*, trans. K. Jürs-Munby (London and New York: Routledge, 2006), p. 181.
5. Lehmann, *Postdramatic Theatre*, p. 182.
6. Lehmann, *Postdramatic Theatre*, p. 181.
7. Lehmann, *Postdramatic Theatre*, p. 182.
8. Lehmann, *Postdramatic Theatre*, pp. 39, 40.
9. Lehmann, *Postdramatic Theatre*, p. 41.
10. Lehmann, *Postdramatic Theatre*, p. 31 (original emphasis).
11. Lehmann, *Postdramatic Theatre*, p. 22 (original emphasis).
12. Lehmann, *Postdramatic Theatre*, p. 48 (original emphasis).
13. Lehmann, *Postdramatic Theatre*, p. 54.
14. Lehmann, *Postdramatic Theatre*, p. 55.
15. For an extended examination of the validity (or otherwise) of Lehmann's ideological analysis of the dramatic and postdramatic, see Chapter 2 of my book *Acts and Apparitions: Discourses on the Real in Performance Practice and Theory 1990–2010* (Manchester and New York: Manchester University Press, 2013).
16. L. Tomlin, '"And their stories fell apart even as I was telling them": Poststructuralist Performance and the No-Longer-Dramatic Playtext', *Performance Research*, 14.1 (2009), 57–64.
17. See among others D. Barnett, 'When is a Play Not a Drama? Two Examples of Postdramatic Theatre Texts', *New Theatre Quarterly*, 24.1 (2008), 14–23; K. Jürs-Munby, 'Introduction', in Lehmann, *Postdramatic Theatre*, p. 6; H. Zimmermann, 'Images of Woman in Martin Crimp's *Attempts on her Life*', *European Journal of English Studies*, 7.1 (2003), 69–85.

18. Written by Jean Genet in a preface to *The Blacks*, trans. C. Finborough, in C. Lavery, *The Politics of Jean Genet's Late Theatre: Spaces of Revolution* (Manchester and New York: Manchester University Press, 2010), p. 230.
19. H. Foster, *Recodings: Art, Spectacle, Cultural Politics* (Port Townsend, WA: Bay Press, 1985), p. 153, cited in P. Auslander, *From Acting to Performance: Essays in Modernism and Postmodernism* (London and New York: Routledge, 1997), p. 60.
20. Foster, *Recodings*, p. 143.
21. Tomlin, *Acts and Apparitions*, pp. 58–9.
22. Lehmann, *Postdramatic Theatre*, p. 44.
23. C. Greenberg, *The Collected Essays and Criticism*, vol. 4: *Modernism with a Vengeance 1957–1969* (Chicago: University of Chicago Press, 1993), p. 85.
24. Lehmann, *Postdramatic Theatre*, p. 44.
25. Tomlin, *Acts and Apparitions*, p. 53.
26. I undertake such an analysis in Tomlin, '"And their stories fell apart even as I was telling them": Poststructuralist Performance and the No-Longer-Dramatic Playtext'.
27. C. Innes and F. J. Marker, *Modernism in European Drama: Ibsen, Strindberg, Pirandello, Beckett* (Toronto: University of Toronto Press, 1998), p. x.
28. R. Williams, *Drama from Ibsen to Brecht*, 2nd rev. edn. (London: Hogarth Press, 1987), p. 338.
29. Williams, *Drama from Ibsen to Brecht*, p. 338.
30. Williams, *Drama from Ibsen to Brecht*, p. 339.
31. Innes and Marker, *Modernism in European Drama*, p. xiii.
32. A. Strindberg, *The Plays: Volume Two*, trans. M. Meyer (London: Secker & Warburg, 1975), p. 222 (my emphasis).
33. R. Williams, *Modern Tragedy*, 2nd edn. (London: Verso, 1979), p. 141 (my emphasis).
34. Williams, *Modern Tragedy*, p. 141.
35. L. Pirandello, *Luigi Pirandello: The Rules of the Game; Right You Are! (If You Think So); Henry IV*, trans. F. May (Harmondsworth: Penguin, 1969), p. 199.
36. Lavery, *The Politics of Jean Genet's Late Theatre*, p. 154.
37. J. Genet, *The Balcony*, rev. edn., trans. B. Frechtman (New York: Grove Press, 1962), p. 95.
38. Genet, *The Balcony*, p. 96.
39. M. Crimp, *The City* (London: Faber & Faber, 2008), p. 62.
40. Crimp, *The City*, p. 63.
41. S. Lacey, *British Realist Theatre: The New Wave in its Context 1956–1965* (London and New York: Routledge, 1995), p. 148.
42. Lacey, *British Realist Theatre*, p. 149.
43. Lacey, *British Realist Theatre*, p. 144.
44. Lacey, *British Realist Theatre*, p. 145.
45. M. Luckhurst, 'Harold Pinter and Poetic Politics', in R. D'Monté and G. Saunders (eds.), *Cool Britannia? British Political Drama in the 1990s* (Basingstoke: Palgrave Macmillan, 2008), pp. 56–68 (p. 62).
46. Lacey, *British Realist Theatre*, p. 145.
47. Lacey, *British Realist Theatre*, p. 142.
48. Williams, *Modern Tragedy*, p. 214.
49. Williams, *Modern Tragedy*, p. 215.
50. Williams, *Modern Tragedy*, p. 215.

51. Williams, *Modern Tragedy*, p. 215.
52. K. Urban, 'Cruel Britannia', in D'Monté and Saunders (eds.), *Cool Britannia*, pp. 38–55 (p. 44) (original emphasis).
53. Urban, 'Cruel Britannia', p. 45.
54. Williams, *Modern Tragedy*, p. 40.
55. Luckhurst, 'Harold Pinter and Poetic Politics', p. 61.
56. G. Saunders, 'Introduction', in D'Monté and Saunders (eds.), *Cool Britannia*, pp. 1–15 (p. 5).
57. K. P. Müller, 'Political Plays in England in the 1990s', in B. Reitz and M. Berninger (eds.), *British Drama of the 1990s* (Heidelberg: Universitätsverlag Carl Winter, 2002) pp. 15–36 (p. 15), cited in Saunders, 'Introduction', p. 7.
58. Saunders, 'Introduction', p. 7.
59. R. D'Monté and G. Saunders, 'Introduction to Part III', in D'Monté and Saunders (eds.), *Cool Britannia?*, p. 139 (original emphasis).
60. D. Rebellato, *1956 and All That* (London and New York: Routledge, 1999), p. 101.
61. D. Rebellato, '"because it feels fucking amazing": Recent British Drama and Bodily Mutilation', in D'Monté and Saunders (eds.), *Cool Britannia?*, pp. 192–207 (p. 193).
62. A. Howells, 'Adrian Howells', by British Council Arts Sg. (22 April 2010), http://www.youtube.com/ (accessed April 2010).
63. M. Foucault, 'What is an Author?', trans. J. V. Harari, in P. Rabinow (ed.), *The Foucault Reader* (Harmondsworth: Penguin Books, 1984), pp. 101–20 (p. 108), cited in Tomlin, *Acts and Apparitions*, p. 60.
64. J. Derrida, *Writing and Difference*, trans. A. Bass (Abingdon: Routledge, 2001, 2009), p. 296.

Acknowledgements

In 2010 I organized a conference on contemporary British theatre and was overwhelmed by the response to the call for papers, met with enthusiasm by established and emerging scholars alike. It was obvious that the need to attempt an account of the emerging phenomenon of powerful, unconventional theatrical representation in our time was shared. This was also the motivation behind this volume and I am extremely grateful to all contributing authors for bringing their exciting and provoking research to this book, moving debates forward and introducing urgent considerations. It has been a pleasure working with them.

I particularly wish to thank Chris Megson, beyond his groundbreaking chapter, for his support to this project since the very early stages, as well as for his incredibly valued and valuable encouragement and advice – I am immensely grateful. I am also very thankful to Liz Tomlin, not only for offering her expert opinion on the volume, but for taking the time to engage with the work thoroughly and with great integrity, producing a thrilling Foreword.

I thank my colleagues at the Department of Drama and Theatre Arts, University of Birmingham, as well as Paula Kennedy and Sacha Lake at Palgrave, for their support. I am grateful to the anonymous readers who contributed highly constructive and encouraging feedback at proposal and clearance stage and I thank Jo North for her copy editing work. I am very thankful to David Roberts at Birmingham City University for supporting the 2010 conference. Ursula Lutzky, Andrew Kehoe, Rob Lawson, Lesley Gabriel and, especially, Samantha Malkin, also at BCU, were great sources of encouragement around that time. I thank the BCU 2011 Class of Drama and English and particularly Cherrelle, Daryll, Kate, Mathew and Zoë, who also contributed to the conference, for their wonderful enthusiasm for new theatre.

The warmest 'thank you', as always, to: Vaso, Nikos, Manolis, Akis, Paulina, George and Deirdre. A very special 'thank you' to Dimitris for his faith and just about everything else, including, of course, coming up with this book's title.

Vicky Angelaki, 2012

Notes on Contributors

Vicky Angelaki is Lecturer in Drama at the University of Birmingham, UK. Her research is internationalist in its scope, with a specialism in modern and contemporary British and European theatre, translation, adaptation, spectatorship and citizenship, aesthetics and politics, as well as performance, critical/cultural theories and philosophy, with a focus on phenomenology. Her monograph *The Plays of Martin Crimp: Making Theatre Strange* was published by Palgrave Macmillan in 2012. She has published essays in edited collections and international theatre journals, subjects including Harold Pinter, Eugène Ionesco, Caryl Churchill, Howard Barker and the arts industry. Vicky Angelaki is co-editor (with Kara Reilly) of Palgrave Macmillan's series Adaptation in Theatre and Performance.

Elisabeth Angel-Perez is Professor of English Literature at the University of Paris-Sorbonne, France. She is a specialist of contemporary British theatre. Her publications include *Voyages au bout du possible: Les théâtres du traumatisme de Samuel Beckett à Sarah Kane* (Klincksieck/Les Belles Lettres, 2006), and, with Alexandra Poulain, *Endgame: Le théâtre mis en pièces* (PUF/cned, 2009). She has published extensively on Martin Crimp, Sarah Kane, Caryl Churchill and Howard Barker. She has also edited and co-edited a number of volumes among which *New British Dramaturgies*, *The European Journal of English Studies* 7.1 (April 2003), *Howard Barker et le Théâtre de la Catastrophe* (Editions Théâtrales, 2006), *Le Théâtre anglais contemporain 1985–2005* (Klincksieck, 2007), *Hunger on the Stage* (Cambridge Scholars Publishing, 2008), *Things on the Stage* (*Etudes Britanniques Contemporaines*, 2009), *Arcadias* (PUPS: Sillages critiques 13 (2011)), and, forthcoming, *Tombeau pour Samuel Beckett* (Aden, 2013). She has also translated plays and theoretical writings by Howard Barker, Caryl Churchill, Martin Crimp, Nick Gill and David Mamet.

Mireia Aragay is Senior Lecturer in the Department of English and German, University of Barcelona, Spain, and Life Fellow of Clare Hall, University of Cambridge, UK. Her research interests include contemporary British theatre, critical theory and film adaptations of literary classics. She has edited *Books in Motion: Adaptation, Intertextuality, Authorship* (Rodopi, 2005), co-edited *British Theatre of the 1990s: Interviews with Directors, Playwrights, Critics and Academics* (Palgrave Macmillan,

2007) and is currently co-editing *Ethical Speculations in Contemporary British Theatre* (Palgrave Macmillan, forthcoming). She was Principal Investigator of the three-year research project 'The representation of politics and the politics of representation in post-1990 British drama and theatre' (2010–12) and is now Principal Investigator of 'Ethical issues in contemporary British theatre since 1989: globalization, theatricality, spectatorship' (2013–15), both funded by the Spanish Ministry of Science and Innovation.

Marissia Fragkou is Teaching Fellow at the University of Birmingham, UK and holds a PhD in Drama and Theatre Studies from Royal Holloway, University of London. Her doctoral thesis examined the nomadic feminist politics in the work of Phyllis Nagy. Her current research focuses on representations of precariousness, witnessing and responsibility in contemporary British and European theatre and performance. Her recent publications include an article on debbie tucker green (*Performing Ethos*) and Rimini Protokoll (*Contemporary Theatre Review*). She is currently preparing a book chapter on Birmingham-based theatre company Stan's Cafe (for Methuen Drama).

Helen Freshwater is Lecturer in Theatre Studies at Newcastle University, UK. Her research focuses upon twentieth-century British theatre and contemporary performance, and she has published on censorship; audiences, participation and interactivity; archive theory and historiography; and British physical theatres. Her monographs *Theatre & Audience* and *Theatre Censorship in Britain: Silencing, Censure and Suppression* were both published by Palgrave Macmillan in 2009, and her journal articles have appeared in *Contemporary Theatre Review*, *Theatre Research International*, *New Theatre Quarterly* and *Performance Research*. She is a contributing editor to *New Theatre Quarterly* and *Performing Ethos*, and works as a dramaturg. In 2011 she was awarded a Philip Leverhulme Prize to support her latest research, which explores how contemporary theatre uses child performers and constructs the figure of the child through performance.

Lynette Goddard is Senior Lecturer in the Department of Drama and Theatre, Royal Holloway College, University of London, UK. Her research focuses on contemporary black British theatre, looking in particular at new writing by black playwrights and black productions and adaptations of Shakespeare and other canonical plays. Her publications include journal articles and chapters in *Contemporary Theatre Review*, and *Women: A Cultural Review*, and the monograph *Staging Black*

Feminisms: Identity, Politics, Performance (Palgrave Macmillan, 2007). She is currently completing *Contemporary Black British Playwrights: Margins to Mainstream* (Palgrave Macmillan, forthcoming), which examines the mainstream profile and politics of plays by Kwame Kwei-Armah, debbie tucker green, Roy Williams and Bola Agbaje.

Chris Megson is Senior Lecturer in Drama and Theatre at Royal Holloway College, University of London, UK. He has published widely on post-war British theatre, documentary/verbatim performance, and contemporary playwriting. His recent publications include *Get Real: Documentary Theatre Past and Present* (co-edited with Alison Forsyth, Palgrave Macmillan, 2009), *The Methuen Drama Book of Naturalist Plays* (Methuen Drama, 2010) and *Decades of Modern British Playwriting: The 1970s* (Methuen Drama, 2012).

Enric Monforte is Senior Lecturer in English Literature and Theatre Studies in the Department of English and German, University of Barcelona, Spain. He specializes in Caryl Churchill and contemporary British drama and theatre, film studies and contemporary critical theory, with a further focus on gender and sexuality. He has published studies on playwrights such as Churchill, David Hare, Mark Ravenhill and debbie tucker green, amongst others. He co-edited *British Theatre of the 1990s: Interviews with Directors, Playwrights, Critics and Academics* (Palgrave Macmillan, 2007) and *Ethical Speculations in Contemporary British Theatre* (Palgrave Macmillan, forthcoming). He is a member of 'Ethical issues in contemporary British theatre since 1989: globalization, theatricality, spectatorship', a three-year research project funded by the Spanish Ministry of Economy and Competitiveness.

Dan Rebellato is Professor of Contemporary Theatre at Royal Holloway College, University of London, UK. His books include *Theatre & Globalization* (Palgrave Macmillan, 2009), *1956 and All That* (Routledge, 1999) and *Contemporary European Theatre Directors* (co-edited with Maria Delgado, Routledge, 2010). He has written widely on contemporary theatre, subjects including David Greig, Sarah Kane, Suspect Culture, David Hare, Caryl Churchill, Katie Mitchell, Philip Ridley, theatre and violence, and theatrical representation. He has edited *Decades of Modern British Playwriting: 2000–2009* (forthcoming, Methuen Drama) and co-edited (with Graham Eatough) *The Suspect Culture Book* (Oberon Books, 2013). He is also a playwright whose work has been performed in the UK and internationally.

Elizabeth Sakellaridou is Professor of Theatre Studies at the Department of English of Aristotle University in Thessaloniki, Greece. She has published extensively on contemporary British and comparative drama and theatre in monographs, international journals and collective volumes from various perspectives, including gender, politics and cultural theory. Her more recent theoretical interests focus on phenomenology and performance and also tragedy, mourning and melancholia. Her current research project revolves around urban space as performance. Her latest book is *Theatre – Aesthetics – Politics: Traversing the British Stage at the Turn of the Millennium* (Papazisis, 2012, in Greek).

Liz Tomlin is a Lecturer at the University of Birmingham, UK. Her monograph *Acts and Apparitions: Discourses on the Real in Performance Practice and Theory 1990–2010* (Manchester University Press) was published in 2013. She is currently editing the third volume of *British Theatre Companies* (Methuen Drama, forthcoming). She was associate director of Point Blank Theatre from 1999 to 2009 and has edited *Point Blank* (Intellect, 2007), a selection of Point Blank Theatre's performance texts and critical essays on the company's work. Previous professional theatre productions she has written and directed have included *The Pool Game* (2012), *Roses & Morphine* (2005), *Operation Wonderland* (2004) and *Nothing to Declare* (2002). She is currently an associate editor of international journal *Performing Ethos*.

Introduction

Vicky Angelaki

In an article written in 2011 for *The Guardian*, theatre critic Lyn Gardner quotes playwright Simon Stephens, who, responding to an increasingly adverse funding climate for the arts, observes: '"I am fascinated to see the way playwrights throughout the country will use image and idea, irony, language, content and form to make sense of and dramatise this changed landscape."'[1] He is right, of course, but even though changes in art subsidy did become the centre of discourse in the field after the succession of Gordon Brown's Labour government by David Cameron and Nick Clegg's Coalition government in 2010, theatre in Britain had already been making a shift in its topics and representational methods in the previous years in ways that this volume aims to shed light on. Certainly, more key figures in contemporary playwriting, theatremaking and cultural management have come to the foreground in defence of theatre – and the arts more broadly – as well as of the need for the plurality of performance in the more recent period, and rightly so. In fact the debate seemed to reach fever pitch in late 2012 when Danny Boyle, whose Olympics opening ceremony still lingered in the collective memory, openly criticized the perceived lack of communication between practitioners and political authorities. Naturally, the monumentality of the Olympics as shared and unifying effort, in many ways like the arts themselves, also lingered, elevating not only Boyle's individual importance, but, more crucially, that of the point being made on behalf of the arts community. Boyle specifically drew on the fact, refuted by the Department for Culture, Media and Sport, that Culture Secretary Maria Miller had kept her distance from artistic directors at the forefront of UK state-subsidized organizations.[2] How, Boyle's comments suggested, is it possible to have an understanding of the landscape and the broader importance of arts institutions across

1

the country, when there has been no sense of contact with the very people representing the field?[3]

The conversation will most likely continue in print and electronic media as we attempt to establish the lay of the land. It is particularly important that such developments in the arts scene have come in the aftermath of major financial and social crises, as well as political tribulations, in the first decade of the twenty-first century. These critical events had already led to a general sense of the arts being tested both for their inventiveness in a climate of ever competitive funding and for their relevance against the intensifying challenges in contemporary society, not only in Britain but also further afield. Therefore, even if the current political moment, as demonstrated through comments such as those of Stephens and Boyle, has come to solidify the fact that a major test is at hand, the theatre had already entered a crucial stage. In the post-millennial period changes in theatrical representation had been building up, quietly beginning to simmer, reflecting, in their own way, social tensions. The theatre had been restless.

The flux that the arts as a creative industry have been experiencing finds its parallel in the flux emerging within playwriting itself – involved as they both are in a direct interrelationship with society, it could not have been otherwise. Playwrights had been actively engaging with the set of tools and parameters that Stephens singles out above. Theatrical representation in the United Kingdom had therefore been undergoing a period of redefinition from within, facing outwards to the audience, its plights and needs, and seeking new points of contact. It has been far from easy; for a cultural medium that thrives on topicality, it is difficult to remain urgent and convincing if it responds to today's challenges with the theatre equivalent of television's broadcast delay. It may still be a way, but hindsight is not necessarily the most apt means of providing resonant commentary. As Gardner notes, the communication between playwright, stage and audience is too often impeded by time and the conventional stages in the production process – it is prescience, she argues, that is of the essence.[4] The question, then, inevitably becomes: how many can attain this to avoid hyperbole and foster genuine interconnections between stage and society? It is a question followed by consideration for the kinds of calculated adventures expected, if not demanded, on the part of contemporary playwrights, or the leaps of faith expected from spectators. If the task for the theatre is to remain urgent without losing the plot, how can it manage sober social commentary without succumbing to mere chronographic accuracy and to what degree does formal experimentation play a role, not merely informing, but driving the effort?

The chapters in this collection, though diverse in their critical and theoretical enquiry, are equally driven by the need to account for how the challenge has been dealt with in the context of author-produced plays, which push the boundaries of visual representation, conceptual understanding and verbal exchange. The emphasis on this kind of performance piece is not neglectful of the major importance of ensemble work by companies working in the recent and contemporary period. Rather, it reflects the collective focus of the writers contributing to the collection, allowing a coherent and cohesive narrative to emerge through work that critically problematizes playwriting at a time when the role of the author has never been so strongly debated. The resulting narrative relies on discourse that strives to develop a model for the understanding of complex stage dynamics rather than a resignation to the inefficacy of the dramatic, as Liz Tomlin astutely observes in her Foreword, which sets the tone for individual and collective theoretical enquiries in this volume.

This collection, therefore, brings together distinct perspectives geared towards the same objective: to provide a rigorous and robust field of dialogue within which we may attempt, in turn, to locate the rigour and urgency of plays staged in UK theatres in our time through references to representative examples. There have been no geographical preferences in the attempt to account for the 'British' theatre that defies norms and expectations to arrive at novel representational schemata and avenues of inter-communication with the audience. If certain theatres, plays and playwrights emerge more notably in the ensuing discussion, this is because they and the kind of writing they represent have been strikingly ambitious, socially efficacious, remarkably innovative and ultimately essential points of reference. No attempt to account for an ever-growing field can be rigidly defined, or entirely complete, and the fact only reveals how much the theatre of our time has been reverberating with urgency. The dialogue continues.

For the purposes of this book, the essays are characterized by a shared focus on contemporary plays that have redefined dramatic representation, breaking new ground through form, content and the ways these interact with one another – not necessarily harmoniously. Authors pursue different routes to the understanding of the reciprocity and contingency between author, theatre, play and audience, while spectatorship remains a pivotal concept throughout: an action to account for leading to events experienced both privately and collectively. For all its critical and theoretical nuances, this volume is defined by the need to establish the spectator as the equally stable and mutable component *for* and *with* whom the performance must take place and *without* whom the text remains suspended, a potentiality on the verge, never fully materializing. The effort to account for his/her experience within the context of theatrical performance arises from this principle in all following chapters.

In 'Exit the Author' Dan Rebellato takes on one of the most enduring debates in contemporary playwriting: authorial intentionality and its centrality to the play. Through references to a range of pieces that enable the subtleties in different authorial methods to emerge, Rebellato shows why the intentionality debate needs to be drastically revisited so as to arrive at a more complete understanding of what we are dealing with today. Rebellato provides an engaging critical and theoretical framework that enables us to trace the ways in which the playwright's place may be seen as precarious, as well as why that is and how we may begin to move beyond the facile dismissal of the author as either irrelevant or overly dominating in relation to the text. The chapter reveals how the ground on which the relationship between playwright, play and audience is built has forever shifted to encourage a richer state of involvement in and responsibility towards the performance. It is not only a question of reinterpreting the playwright, but also of re-envisioning the spectator and the social resonance of the play.

In his chapter '"And I was struck still by time": Contemporary British Theatre and the Metaphysical Imagination', Chris Megson delves into a rigorous discussion of the complications arising in time and sense experience, as approached by playwrights in unconventional ways that function to redistribute the variables of the audience's perception. Through what Megson describes as the pursuit of the metaphysical in contemporary theatre, the chapter explores how, beyond questions of time and its suspension into a state of wavering yet heightened consciousness, playwrights have re-posited questions of faith, boldly engaging with the recesses of belief. Through this process, the chapter reveals, the entire relationship between form and content is reimagined, its tension manifesting a palpable dialogue not only between theatre and social context, but with ontological concerns and ideology as well. In the wake of such developments, theatrical representation is moving into new and unaccounted for territories, where the fractures to the text, as much as the quest for more – spiritually, dramatically – than is already there, set in motion a wave of theatre that negotiates enduring concerns through radical new perspectives.

'Politics for the Middle Classes: Contemporary Audiences and the Violence of Now' by Vicky Angelaki examines the ways in which contemporary playwrights have responded to the collective challenges of our time through drastic interventions on form and content. It proceeds from 'the middle class' as a ground for reinterpretation but also re-engagement, as the theatre moves away from placid reassurance and entertainment. The chapter argues that, though contemporary British theatre is far from reducible to trends and taxonomies, what we observe is essentially a consensus amongst innovative artists for a turn towards the deeper causes of our crises, simultaneously individual and collective. The chapter traces how these have been conceptualized as irrevocably linked to processes of withdrawal from the public and to the indulgent immersion in the capitalist ideal, whereby the individual is, from early stages in their development, pegged as the perennial consumer, both helpless and complicit. The chapter follows how authors capture states of everyday – often intangible – violence against the individual and highlight the importance of a possible dramatic, social and spectatorial emancipation. This involves imagining new ways of representing reality that move towards a more primal contact with the world. The style is further reflected in the distinctively unadorned, immediate dramatic language of these plays, which negate the barren conventionality of social but also artistic contracts from within, proposing an alternative for challenging audience perception.

In 'Language Games and Literary Constraints: Playing with Tragedy in the Theatre of Caryl Churchill and Martin Crimp' Elisabeth Angel-Perez turns to two of the most unapologetically unconventional playwrights of the contemporary period. She looks at representative examples from their dramatic oeuvre to argue for how language in their plays systematically defies set norms and typical expectations for dramatic discourse in order to arrive at an unprecedented level of potentiality and signification. Angel-Perez provides an insightful analysis of how verbal games in the work of Churchill and Crimp serve to deliver deep incisions to the body of the play. The chapter works to demonstrate how these extend beyond the level of artistic innovation. It goes on to establish a framework within which we may understand how such a relentlessly redefinable text opens the path towards a more perceptually involved, active state of spectatorship. Angel-Perez's examples clearly reveal that this comes to materialize as the texts playfully yet determinedly hinder not only their own unambiguous understanding, but also, and as a result, the gross categorization of the audience as a uniform, unidentified mass, predictable in its interpretations and reactions.

Mireia Aragay and Enric Monforte's 'Racial Violence, Witnessing and Emancipated Spectatorship in *The Colour of Justice*, *Fallout* and *random*' takes on an issue that has persisted in UK society's collective frame of perception, on occasion exploding into urgent resonance due to observed incidents. Focusing on representative work by Richard Norton-Taylor, Roy Williams and debbie tucker green, Aragay and Monforte create a dialogue between three different forms of theatre to arrive at an understanding of how racially motivated tension and/or urban violence have been given different outlets of expression in contemporary theatre. The authors probe the delicate balances emerging from the subject matter to concentrate on topical questions of ethics in dramatic representation. The aim is to work towards establishing how these materialize in correlation with the spectatorial empowerment fostered through the form and content of these plays.

In 'Old Wine in a New Bottle or Vice Versa? Winsome Pinnock's Interstitial Poetics' Elizabeth Sakellaridou identifies Pinnock as a representative case of the contemporary playwright who has defied gender and race categorizations to produce the kind of theatre that manages to transcend popular stereotypes. The chapter takes a penetrating look at Pinnock as a trailblazer ahead of her time who, through insightful and uncompromising work, metabolized the tensions in hybrid identities into a dynamic form of representation. Like all artistically ambitious playwrights, Sakellaridou shows, Pinnock undertook a long and challenging journey – one that, through the revisiting of forms, themes and discourses on national identities, reflects her maturation into a state of dialectical playwriting. It is the kind of work that emphasizes the importance of conversation and information, sometimes through its very shape and texture. Pinnock's theatre is seen as equally conditioned by an ever present past as facing forward and functions as an excellent case study whose relevance extends beyond the immediate references.

Marissia Fragkou and Lynette Goddard's 'Acting In/Action: Staging Human Rights in debbie tucker green's Royal Court Plays' concentrates on one of the most distinctive voices to emerge in the field in recent years. The chapter captures the intricacies of tucker green's playwriting, evidencing that we are dealing with theatre that is both diverse in content and powerfully driven by key preoccupations relating as much to the ideology as to the craft of writing for performance. What plays such as those discussed in the chapter unequivocally share, Fragkou and Goddard argue, is their instigation of a strong ethical process within the audience, one that constantly generates questioning. The authors proceed to discuss this within the context of a considerate textual, performance but also critical framework, drawing their primary examples from the playwright's not particularly prolific, yet undoubtedly influential work, including some of her most well-known texts.

In 'Children and the Limits of Representation in the Work of Tim Crouch' Helen Freshwater identifies the practitioner's controversial work as a suitably challenging case study through which to take on one of the most complex and topical subject matters in contemporary theatre. Being one of the main issues that accentuate the bond between theatre and society and the unsafe ground on which it is often constructed, the treatment and representation of children forms Freshwater's primary concern. She delivers an incisive discussion of the precariousness of childhood in the context of how plays or performance pieces – like Crouch's – that have selected this as their primary concern, have served the development of new forms to accommodate the sensitive content, arriving at work where the very viability of the play against public opinion hangs in the balance. Freshwater traces how the safety of children and their potential exposure to risk, as seen on the stage in work as provoking and seemingly malleable as Crouch's, serves to provide a hologram picture of our collective insecurities. This is in the context of an increasing compromise of innocence, both literal and metaphorical, for which childhood stands as the perfect representational vehicle.

As if to manifest that nothing could be taken for granted any more, not even in the most established of artistic organizations, the National Theatre's Nicholas Hytner made what would not be an overstatement to call a subversive choice for his end-of-the-year repertoire in 2012. It was a period when Britishness and the diverse images that it stands for today had been at the forefront of the global stage, dominating a year of events and showing the world the country's different faces. In many ways, these were captured in Boyle's ceremony. From the visceral realities of labour, the riches of creative imagination and the NHS, to youth culture, James Bond and the Queen, Britain was weaving its tapestry as the world was watching. It is interesting that the production selected for one of the capital's most high-profile venues – the Lyttelton auditorium – in the autumn following this explosive climax, was that of Howard Barker's 1980s play *Scenes from an Execution*. Few plays are as emblematic of the artist's struggle to capture the intermeshing narratives of history, society and representation as this – and with the world eagerly expecting the outcome, no less. The presupposition of failure to rise to the expectations is almost implicit. How could the artist possibly attack it? The answer came from Barker himself. Speaking to

The Guardian in the context of the new production, he defiantly declared that '[a] good play puts the audience through a certain ordeal [...] I'm not interested in entertainment' and went on to add 'I write from ignorance. I don't know what I want to say, and I don't care if you listen or not.'[5]

The presence of Barker's work, even in the form of one of his most accessible plays, at the National was no ordinary feat. In a way, the uncompromising dramatic past was firing a shot as to the unexpected dramatic future – an indication, perhaps, that nothing can be easily assumed any more about either the artistic establishment or the medium itself. If Barker's work (famously celebrated outside the United Kingdom but neglected within, despite its aficionados), a staple of the alternative, was set to entice the mainstream, there could not have been a better metaphor for the rules of the game publicly and permanently changing. Barker's comment should not be overlooked – the 'ignorance' he speaks of encapsulates the instinct of discovery and engagement that unifies groundbreaking contemporary authors, however differently they approach their craft. It is the same instinct that leads to new ways of showing, and new ways of seeing. In the pages that follow the idea echoes, as we focus on representative examples that will provide an understanding of how, without shortcuts, modern spectators have been equally challenged and encouraged by playwrights to take the journey into the new realms of the dramatic medium, not as passive bystanders, but as active participants.

Notes

1. L. Gardner, 'Theatre Doth Protest Too Little and Too Slowly', *The Guardian*, 1 February 2011, http://www.guardian.co.uk/ (accessed 2 February 2011).
2. C. Higgins, 'Danny Boyle Accuses Culture Minister Maria Miller of "Outrageous" Snub', *The Guardian*, 15 November 2012, http://www.guardian.co.uk/ (accessed 16 November 2012).
3. Higgins, 'Danny Boyle Accuses Culture Minister Maria Miller of "Outrageous" Snub'.
4. Gardner, 'Theatre Doth Protest Too Little and Too Slowly'.
5. M. Costa, 'Howard Barker: "I don't care if you listen or not"', *The Guardian*, 1 October 2012, http://www.guardian.co.uk/ (accessed 2 October 2012). An expanded version of the interview is published on Costa's website, http://statesofdeliquescence.blogspot.co.uk/.

1
Exit the Author

Dan Rebellato

The British theatre's first decade of the twenty-first century began and ended with the death of the author.

Six months into the decade in June 2000, the Royal Court Theatre Upstairs staged the premiere of Sarah Kane's last play, *4.48 Psychosis*, a play in which a British playwright foresees her death, written, it seems, in certain knowledge of her end, and performed in the shadow of her suicide. While we absolutely must not, as I and others have repeatedly insisted, treat the play narrowly or naively just as Kane's suicide note, it was evident, watching the play at the press night, surrounded both by the critics who hounded her and by her friends and family, that the play was written precisely to be experienced by this audience on that particular evening, to offer, in places, an account of her actions, and so was, in part, a sort of suicide note.[1]

At the other end of the decade, in late September 2009, the same theatre staged the premiere of Tim Crouch's play, *The Author*. In *The Author*, Tim Crouch plays an author, also called Tim Crouch, describing a play that he purportedly wrote but one which sounds pointedly more like it was written by Sarah Kane. Towards the end of the play, 'Tim Crouch' recalls slipping off to his computer, after a dinner party held to mark the success of the original show, and masturbating to an Internet video of a baby being sexually abused. His actions are discovered the next morning and perhaps in an act of shame, guilt or penance, he goes to a flotation tank for which he has been given tokens and cuts his throat. The stage direction reads: 'the death of the author'.[2]

Between those dates was David Greig's *San Diego* (Edinburgh International Festival, 2003) in which a thirty-something Scottish playwright called David Greig takes his first trip to the city of the title. Greig, appropriately enough, is the narrator of his own play and in the first

9

part of it serves as our guide through the world of the play, introducing its people and places to us. However, he is soon lost in San Diego and by implication, therefore, lost in his own play. While trying to get directions to the La Jolla Playhouse where one of his plays is being performed, he is stabbed in the chest by an illegal immigrant. Despite the efforts of two passers-by to save him, as the first of the play's four acts comes to an end, David's stage direction reads 'David is dead'.[3]

In the Introduction to his second volume of collected plays, published midway through the decade, Martin Crimp writes of the death of an author. The fourth of the 'Four Unwelcome Thoughts' promised by the introduction's title is called 'When the Writer Kills Himself'. It is a short description of a group of playwrights who are at first shocked and moved by their colleague's suicide but whose thoughts soon turn to how this changes their place in the pecking order until they start riding on this desperate act to boost their own careers, turning their envious eyes on each other. In some ways it foreshadows the pitiless satire of Mark Ravenhill's *pool (no water)* a year later, a play following the reaction of a group of artists when one of them – the most successful – nearly dies from jumping into an empty swimming pool ('Everything she thought was friendship was hate. Everything that was care was envy. Concern was destroy').[4] Crimp's is a prose piece of multiple deaths, silences and absences. The dead author is unnamed, uncharacterized, soon forgotten.[5] His death almost causes other deaths; on hearing of the suicide, one playwright is on the roof of a cathedral in Milan, in shock at the news, he stumbles and nearly falls, the description neatly and narcissistically drawing attention away from the actual suicide to the second playwright's imagined suffering ('The writer has killed himself! What a terrible thing! It's like being punched – right here – in the stomach!').[6] And there is a further authorial disappearance; the piece is written in the third person plural: the writer reacting to the suicide is generalized into 'the writers': 'they're up on the marble roof of a cathedral'.[7] It is somewhat like a hypertrophic version of using 'they' as a replacement for 'he or she' but further anonymizes these self-regarding auteurs. Crimp, meanwhile, gives us no direct sense of his relation to these writers. Is he one of them? Does he share in their cupidity and *schadenfreude*? Is it satire or confession? In his characteristically inscrutable way, Crimp the writer is absent from his writing.

If these playwrights are not dying, they are suffering in other ways. Gregory Burke is mocked and physically threatened in his own play, *Black Watch* (National Theatre of Scotland, 2006). A year later, in *Taking Care of Baby* (Birmingham Rep, 2007), one character tells the author,

Dennis Kelly, 'I think you are a parasite. I think you are a maggot. I think you are a piece of scum, something undigested and rotting, the lowest form of life, a monster, a vulture, a sickening little piece of shit and I can only pray that you get some kind of terminal illness like cancer', adding, perhaps unnecessarily, 'I hope I make myself clear'.[8] In *Come Out Eli* (Arcola Theatre, 2003), the writer Alecky Blythe spends much of the play trying to fend off the persistent sexual advances of one of her characters. In *The Power of Yes* (National Theatre: Lyttelton, 2009), a play about the banking collapse of 2008, David Hare places himself onstage as a character, frankly admitting his bewilderment, first economic then moral, at the behaviour of his characters. Hare has performed his own testimonial plays, but here, in an intriguingly perverse bit of casting, David Hare does not play David Hare; Anthony Calf plays David Hare, so the author is both present and absent in the play, both subject and object of the play's analysis, and not fully either of them.[9]

In considering these kinds of plays, we should acknowledge the earlier example of Paul Godfrey's *The Blue Ball*, an extraordinary play, years ahead of its time, which flopped disastrously at the Cottesloe in 1995; it concerns the space programmes of Russia and the United States and includes in its character list a playwright called Paul who is writing a play about the space programme. Through the play, Paul tries to find out from the astronauts he meets what it was like to go into space. He never gets an answer because, we come to understand, it is not something that can be expressed. At the end of the play – astonishingly, bizarrely – after watching the launch of the space shuttle, Paul the playwright, in an image of both astronautical transcendence and complete absorption in textuality, 'plunges upwards into the blue as if it were paper and vanishing from sight'.[10] Who was this playwright? asks an astronaut's wife: 'we never heard from him again; / perhaps it was a hoax?'[11] Sadly, after the critical mauling of *The Blue Ball*, the play was pulled from the National Theatre's schedules and this fine writer's career more or less disappeared into the blue.

These moments of literal and metaphorical death, of creative and structural self-harm, are, as I will show, part of a wider pattern of playwrights variously absenting themselves from their plays. These particular instances are only the most ostentatious examples of a wider phenomenon in which not just writing but authorship itself has become a key area of theatrical experimentation. Crouch's citation of the phrase 'the death of the author' recalls the famous essay by Roland Barthes.[12] It is tempting to think that Britain's famously – or, if you prefer, notoriously – writer-centred theatre has finally begun to adopt the principles of poststructuralism and that we are watching authors dissolve into their texts, yielding to the demands of the readerly text, deflecting to Jacques Derrida's principle of *différance*, abdicating from what Michel Foucault calls the 'author function'.

You may be able to tell from my authorial interventions in that last paragraph, inflating and parodying the rhetoric of the anti-intentionalists, that I am not convinced this is the right interpretation of what has been taking place. I will revisit the authorship debates that flared up in the 1970s and 1980s, inspired by Barthes's famous essay to suggest that the anti-intentionalist arguments as they are sometimes represented in theatre do not hold water – and indeed that no one, certainly not Roland Barthes, has ever seriously advanced them. Instead, I will suggest that authorship has become a ground for aesthetic and ethical questioning that stages the death of the author as a way of profoundly investigating theatrical meaning and our capacity for fundamental political change.

Against fiction

Nick Ridout, in a widely quoted article from 2007, remarks that the theatre is 'rubbish'. 'It happens in the evening, when there are more exciting things to do. It typically involves people dressing up and pretending to be other people, putting on accents and shouting too much.'[13] Ridout's claim is an elaboration, of course, of the old description of acting as 'shouting in the evenings', but it captures rather beautifully a striking characteristic of the last 10–15 years; that is, a profound distaste for fiction.[14] As I will suggest, this has a particular effect on the position of the playwright.

One example of this discomfort with fiction can be seen in a widespread cultural preference for documentary. One might point to the unprecedented critical and commercial success of documentary features like *Bowling for Colombine* (2002), *Fahrenheit 9/11* (2004), *Super Size Me* (2004), *An Inconvenient Truth* (2006), and perhaps even *March of the Penguins* (2005). It can also be seen in perhaps the most distinctive television format of the 2000s: 'Reality TV'. Prominent examples include *Big Brother* (1999–), *I'm a Celebrity ... Get Me Out Of Here!* (2002–), *Strictly Come Dancing* (2004–), *X Factor* (2004–) and *Britain's Got Talent* (2005–). Whether these were wholly in the spirit of documentary is hard to determine: many of them are structured and edited to produce fiction-like mini-narratives about their contestants, which seem to be part of the fun, though at the same time commentators are quick to point out instances of what they see as deception.[15]

Docudrama saw a major resurgence in the 2000s, with films and television shows as diverse as *Touching the Void* (2003), *The Deal* (2003), *The Queen* (2006), *The Road to Guantanamo* (2006), *United 93* (2006), *Frost/Nixon* (2008) and *The Damned United* (2009). A documentary feel crept into other fictional genres: witness the verité stylings of comedies like *Best in Show* (2000), *Curb Your Enthusiasm* (2000–), *The Office* (UK 2001–3, US 2005–), *The Thick of It* (2005–), *Summer Heights High* (2007), *Brass Eye* (1997–2001), *Curb Your Enthusiasm* and *Parks and Recreation* (2009–) as well as horror movies like *The Blair Witch Project* (1999), the *Paranormal Activity* series (2007–), *Cloverfield* (2008) and *The Bay* (2012). Channel 4 has specialized in a peculiar hybrid form of documentaries about real-life things that have not happened, including *Death of a President* (2006), *The Trial of Tony Blair* (2007), *The Execution of Gary Glitter* (2009) and *The Taking of Prince Harry* (2010). Although in all of these examples there are plainly or arguably fictional elements, the general impression of this type of work is that in the twenty-first century, we have preferred our fiction to be dressed up as documentary.

This has unsurprisingly also been felt in the theatre, which has attempted in various ways to get beyond 'dressing up and pretending to be other people'. One might look at a company like Rimini Protokoll, who have almost nothing to do with actors, as conventionally conceived, preferring to invite people with genuine expertise or experience in some area onto a stage to talk about their life and work. As one commentator puts it, 'they create an actual, extra-theatrical reality in the form of experts, as their biographies and documentary material are brought into the theatre'.[16] In a rather different way, some companies have produced work that seems to be attempting to avoid all theatrical pretence; for example, hoipolloi, in shows like *Floating* (2005) and *The Story of a Rabbit* (2007), wittily use a variety of theatrical devices to tell strange and fantastical stories, but continually explain how they are going to do it, thus, on one level, demystifying the theatrical magic.[17] The studied amateurishness of the performances by the New York City Players or the use of comically inept stage devices preferred by Forced Entertainment puts failure at the centre of the performance perhaps in an attempt to forestall any illusion of fiction.[18] At the beginning of his show *My Arm* (Traverse Theatre, 2003), Tim Crouch asks the audience for objects from their bags which he then uses in the show as props. None of the objects resemble visually the things that they are representing; it is unclear whether they 'represent' objects and characters in the fictional world or they merely stand in for them. Against that long semiotic tradition that everything on stage is a sign, these objects seem to resist symbolization and remain merely objects.[19]

A second example of this turn away from fiction is verbatim theatre. Verbatim, all too easily lumped together, mocked or dismissed, is as multiple and complex as any other form of theatre, as Alison Forsyth and Chris Megson's collection *Get Real: Documentary Theatre Past and Present* (2009) makes clear.[20] There is, however, a persistent strand of British verbatim work, associated principally with the Tricycle Theatre, which consciously seeks to exclude any hint of fiction from its theatricality. Most importantly for my purposes here, it is striking that playwrights have been edged out of the process. Playwright John McGrath collaborated on the first of these shows, *Half the Picture*, in 1994, but soon the texts were being put together almost entirely by journalists like Richard Norton-Taylor and Victoria Brittain, or indeed by the director, Nicolas Kent.[21] Playwright David Edgar argued in 2007 that British culture was pervaded with

> the idea there are certain subjects too important, too profound, too dangerous for writing (and painting, and performing, and even reporting) to touch. Behind that is an assumption that fiction writing in particular has no positive value, that it is a trivial pursuit, a luxury pastime which if it proves to be dangerous to its consumers should be suppressed for the greater good, like high-risk sports, keeping attack dogs, or eating meat off the bone.[22]

This belief seems to imagine that to fictionalize is always to trivialize and that playwrights, insofar as their work creates fictions, are therefore to be condemned. This view, however, is in part shared by a playwright like David Hare, who has spoken very strongly about the inadequacy of fiction to some of the most important events of our age. In the Holocaust Museum in Jerusalem, he reflects that the 'artworks [on display] seemed somehow to diminish their subject matter, to achieve nothing except to insert an artist's presence gratuitously between people's unbearable suffering and our own reaction to it'.[23] Hare's conclusion is not that fiction should be abandoned but that fiction must rise to meet the challenge of reality. It might be thought that his solo performances, which replace fiction with testimony, are therefore a sign of defeat, but Hare's feeling is that journalistic editing may be, in the present time, the highest and most appropriate form of art.[24]

At the more experimental end of playwriting, one might see the influence of Crimp and Kane in the spread of plays which present pure verbal construct and disavow any pretence at fiction altogether. In the case of Kane's *Crave* (Paines Plough, 1998), for example, we are presented with four speakers, named A, B, C and M; the play seems not to be constructing any clear or consistent diegesis. What we experience are voices from the stage rather than characters speaking within a fictional world. The same, in a somewhat different way, might be said of Crimp; in work like *Fewer Emergencies* (Royal Court, 2005) or the second act of *In the Republic of Happiness* (Royal Court, 2012) we attend to meticulously or satirically observed patterns of speech, but character is intentionally indistinct or mute. The precision of the language draws attention to its writerliness; the device is precisely what Hare wanted to efface – the insertion of an artist's presence between audience and stage – but the effect is the same, to prevent fiction from spilling out across the stage.

Playwrights in retreat?

A suspicion of fiction-making is not the only example of playwriterly withdrawal from their own plays. There are several perceptible dramaturgical shifts beginning in the mid-1990s characterized by writers abdicating from aspects of their plays that they formerly may have been expected to control.

The first and clearest example is the spread of playtexts that have a new kind of openness in them not found – or found very rarely – in British plays of the 1980s. The classic instance of this is Crimp's *Attempts on Her Life* (Royal Court, 1997), a playtext which does not specify time, place, character or indeed assign the lines to actors. Crimp has, in effect, transferred these decisions from the playwright to the production team. The same is true of Kane's *4.48 Psychosis*. Many of the playlets that comprise Ravenhill's *Shoot/Get Treasure/Repeat* (Traverse Theatre, 2007) have no character names assigned and, where they do, Ravenhill claims to have given them the blandest names he can think of so as to provide as neutral a sense of character as possible.[25] Simon Stephens's *Pornography* (Deutsches Schauspielhaus, Hamburg; Festival Theaterformen; Schauspielhannover, 2007) comprises seven sections of text and the author's note reads '[t]his play can be performed by any number of actors. It can be performed in any order.'[26] Caryl Churchill's *Love and Information* (Royal Court, 2012) is also divided into seven sections within which the scenes can be played in any order; there are additional scenes published at the back of the text that can be dropped into the performance at any point. On the whole, time, place and character are not specified, nor are the lines of dialogue assigned to particular speakers. In *Fewer Emergencies*, Crimp is unspecific in his direction: '*Time Blank / Place* Blank'.[27] In the introduction to my own play, *Chekhov in Hell* (Drum Plymouth, 2010), I admit to being unsure whether a character is black or white, even though the distinction seems important.[28] In the published text of *Far Away* (Royal Court, 2000), Churchill seems similarly haphazard in her directions for how many performers should take part in the 'parade' scene: 'five is too few and twenty better than ten. A hundred?'[29]

Secondly, it has become increasingly common for playwrights to withdraw from offering clear authorial commentary on the action of the play. Kane's *Blasted* (Royal Court, 1995) begins as a box-set naturalistic play before the blast of the title blows the set apart. This explosion is as much dramaturgical as it is narrative; the frame around the set that the blast destroys also seems to affect Kane's authorial presence in the play. Within the conventions of the naturalistic play, it seems easier to morally distinguish the characters; after the blast, Kane seems to be passing responsibility for judgement onto us. Ian begins the play as a monster; by the end of the play, it is hard for us to say what the author wants us to think of him. The play's first critics, used to plays with more explicit commentary, mistook her deliberate silence for irresponsibility. While authorial commentary is very hard to erase completely from a play – and, with hindsight, one can detect subtle forms of direction in the text – the deliberate authorial neutrality of many mid-1990s plays, like *Blasted*, *Shopping and Fucking* (Royal Court, 1996) or *Mojo* (Royal Court, 1995) had an influence throughout the 2000s in plays like Anthony Neilson's *Stitching* (Traverse, 2002), Dennis Kelly's *Osama the Hero* (2005) or Stephens's *Motortown* (Royal Court, 2006).

Principal among the means with which a writer can steer an audience's perception of a character or an action is irony and a turning away from irony is another detectable strand of British drama in the 2000s. In some more recent writers, I observe a note of weariness with irony, and instead a self-consciously naive sincerity. In plays like Kelly's *Love and Money* (Royal Exchange Manchester, 2006), debbie tucker green's *random* (Royal Court, 2008), Andrew Sheridan's *Winterlong* (Royal Exchange Manchester, 2011), Katie McCullough's *I Still Get Excited When I See a Ladybird* (Theatre503, 2011) or – most prominently – in plays by Stephens such as *Country Music* (Royal Court, 2004), *Harper Regan* (National Theatre: Cottesloe, 2008) and *Punk Rock* (Royal Exchange Manchester, 2009), the characters are given extraordinary moments of apparently artless fluency. Sometimes these comments are political; but unlike two generations before, the aggressive naivety of the comments, their lack of subtext, the curious evenness of style, make us doubt that the characters are mouthpieces for the author. Instead this kind of 'radical naivety' becomes oddly dislocating.

Mike Bartlett's *Earthquakes in London* (National Theatre: Cottesloe, 2010) is a recent example; its first four acts bring the characters to Waterloo Bridge, where Freya, a young woman who, finding herself pregnant, is thrown into confusion about the ethics of bringing another child into this world, jumps, or maybe falls, into the Thames. The fifth act is set in the year 2525 (probably) and Freya's speech has become the stuff of legend, a transformative moment in the history of humanity, a turn towards a new Enlightenment. 'She was young,' hymns the narrator:

> and so full of hope and truth that her speech, her words, the power and the light, was relayed, repeated, across the world, by radio, by television, by powerful rumour and written instruction to every man and woman on the planet and slowly, slowly, the tide turned. People listened and people changed. [...] And the people of the world were happy. They were saved and they rejoiced.[30]

This speech, with its messianic overtones and utopian dream of perfect communication, is a good example of the radical naivety I am describing. There is no sign that this is meant to be ironic; the play's focus on environmental politics gives some content to the message, but the sentiment is also so crazily guileless and unsophisticated that, hearing the speech in the theatre, I found myself wondering: Can this possibly be the meaning of the play? Are we supposed to take this claim seriously? Can this writer be that naive?

This tone, on a more personal scale, recurs throughout Stephens's work, as noted above. In *A Thousand Stars Explode in the Sky* (Royal Exchange Manchester, 2010), Roy returns with some ice creams. 'They're nice aren't they? Aren't the ice creams nice?' he says. 'I think they are. I think they're smashing and lovely.'[31] 'Nice' is a key word here. It is common to be warned off the word 'nice' in writing good English prose: it is an unsophisticated, bland word, which seems just to express approval without offering any precise account of that opinion, or offering any definition or colour to it. As *Punk Rock* opens, William asks Lilly where she's living. 'At the top of Broadstone Road,' she tells him. 'That's a nice street,' he replies.[32] In *Pornography*, a character promises another 'I'll have your tea ready for you. I'll cook you something nice. I'll go to the shops and get something nice to cook.'[33] In Stephens's work, 'nice' is almost always a guileless word of praise, a character artlessly affirming something about the world. (It is perhaps unsurprising that Stephens has written a play called *Country Music*, since country music is perhaps the musical genre that most fully devotes itself to plain and heartfelt expression of feeling without embarrassment.)

This tone is so complex because the characters are naive but we are given no reassurance that their authors are any less so. Only by deduction can we say that Bartlett, Stephens and others are such sophisticated writers of dialogue that, even if they were that naive, they could find ways of hiding their naivety. Instead, these moments produce a kind of suspension of intentionality, an authorial blankness, where insincerity is banished, but sincerity appears implausible. I call this 'radical naivety' because I think it is part of an experiment in authorship that has some political value. I shall return to this idea in the final section of the essay.

Of course, there are many theatre writers who still happily create fictional worlds, who write conventional stage directions, who employ irony to guide us through their stories, but I hope it does seem plausible to say that something distinctive has been going on in the tectonics of playwriting, a collective exploration of new attitudes to the making of playtexts. The question then is why this should be.

The death of the author

David Hare, in a 1989 lecture on Raymond Williams, explains why he came to dislike academics:

> Cambridge was flirting with something called structuralism, which downplayed the individual's imagination, and insisted that the writer was only a pen. The hand, meanwhile, was controlled largely by the social and economic conditions of the time. This depressing philosophy was not one to cheer the heart of a playwright. It was indicative of the way academics were once more turning their faces to the wall. The other day, one of the wittiest and cleverest structuralists in England, an ex-pupil of Raymond's, told me the whole thing was over. 'Oh, great,' I said. 'Does that mean I'm back in charge of my own work?' He looked at me a moment. 'Mostly. But not entirely,' he said.[34]

Let us set aside Hare's inexpert attempt to characterize the theoretical movement he is describing; he does, however, indicate clearly the sense in which the authority of the playwright has been seen to be in some sense compromised by theoretical arguments against intention.

If the anti-intentionalist argument is widespread enough to be known to someone as allergic to academia as Hare, it must have had considerable currency. Put loosely – because I think it has become rather loose as an argument – the anti-intentionalist argument states that the intentions of an author are entirely irrelevant to the meaning of a text. And in this rather vague form, it has been enthusiastically adopted by several groups of people in and out of theatre. Steve Waters, in *The Secret Life of Plays*, overstates the position only slightly: 'individual authorship in some theatrical circles has been imagined as inherently fascistic, patriarchal, phallocentric, phallogocentric – only collective creation is able to overcome such thought crimes'.[35]

Barthes's 'The Death of the Author' remains the most famous statement of the anti-authorialist position and, alas, once of the most badly read. It is held to have called for the complete irrelevance of authorial intention and the implication of the argument for theatre is a dethronement of the playwright. One of the first books to apply Theory – that is, post-war European cultural theory and philosophy – to British theatre was called *The Death of the Playwright?* as if the obvious corollary of Barthes's essay was to single out the playwright for execution.[36] As I have shown, Crouch cites the title of Barthes's essay as a stage direction in *The Author*; Greig is also familiar with the essay and it would not be extravagant to see *San Diego* as working with a poststructuralist logic, relinquishing authorial control to its characters: the three illegal migrants burst into the play near the beginning, one of them stabbing David, and immediately take control, giving each other new names, the borders they are crossing not merely being the American customs barrier but the border between author and text.[37] The play juggles a number of storylines and styles which bleed into one another intertextually. Towards the end of the play the illegal immigrants demand to see Paul McCartney, but bursting into his office they only find David Greig, and we might find a playful *jouissance* in the signifying chains that shuttle between two artists fictionally claimed to be dead.[38]

However, I think it would be false to read the authorial playfulness in *San Diego* and elsewhere as a demonstration of Barthes's anti-authorialism. I shall argue this on two grounds: first, the strong anti-authorialist claim is implausible; second, it is demonstrably not what Barthes is saying anyway.

First, can we dispense altogether with the idea of intentionality? To address this question, imagine a situation when you go to visit a relative, perhaps an aunt. When you arrive, she goes off to make you a cup of tea. You hear her call out 'How are you, lovely boy?'; you reply that you are fine. 'You're looking gorgeous', she replies. Perhaps confused by these fulsome compliments, you follow the sound of the voice and discover a room empty except for a parrot. I am confident that any reasonable person would immediately change their attitude to what had just happened: they would realize that they *thought* they were having a conversation but now they realize that they were not. They at first thought someone was enquiring after their health and complimenting them, but then discover that no one was doing so. In other words, the parrot's sounds can be heard in a certain way – we can apply our knowledge of English to them – but they are not meaningful in the same way they would have been if our aunt had said them. In that sense, what this tells us is that intention is not some external, separable set of facts that stand apart from the text. Intention is a precondition for a certain type of meaning to be derived at all.

An objection might be raised at this point: it may be the case that in ordinary speech situations, we rely on a notion of intentionality, but artistic uses of language are special and it is there that the author is able to be dispersed in language. There is some support for this reading in Barthes's essay. For one thing, he exclusively discusses literary authorship and does not consider ordinary language at all. For another, he remarks, very early in the essay, 'once a fact is *recounted* – for intransitive purposes, and no longer to act directly upon reality, i.e., exclusive of any function except the exercise of the symbol itself – this gap appears, the voice loses its origin, the author enters into his own death, writing begins'.[39] This might seem close to offering a distinction between ordinary and literary language based on aesthetic purposelessness; that is, in ordinary language use we are constrained by purposes and utility: we need to be understood to achieve certain practical ends. In literary language, however, there is no practical end as such – it is 'intransitive' to use Barthes's word – and language use may be unconfined, exploring both its own dynamics and a much wider range of allusion, connotation and resonance.[40] However, while I have a good deal of sympathy with this kind of distinction between ordinary and literary (or dramaturgical) language, it does not seem to me that intention sits solely on the 'ordinary' side of the line. Let us offer a different example; imagine that one of the famous monkeys at one of the famous typewriters did manage to produce a copy of *Hamlet*. While we would be able to use our knowledge of the English language to read it in a certain way, we would not want to say about it any of the things that we would say about *Hamlet* by William Shakespeare. It would be a curiosity, like spotting shapes in clouds, but not a work, barely even a text. If these small-scale thought experiments are correct, to eliminate intentionality *tout court* from texts would not merely strip away 'intended meaning' but pretty well *any* kind of meaning we characteristically derive from literary and dramatic texts.

Barthes does not address this kind of question, but I would suggest that this is because he is actually not making the absolutist anti-authorial case that is commonly ascribed to him. There are three reasons for believing this: first, in trying to show this move from author-centred *work* to the multiplicity of *text*, Barthes refers to a series of authors. Mallarmé, Valéry, Proust are all brought forward as exemplars of the modern style. 'For Mallarmé', he writes, 'it is language which speaks, not the author'. 'Valéry [...] entangled in the psychology of the ego [...] but led by a preference for classicism to conform to the lessons of Rhetoric, [...] continued to cast the Author into doubt and derision'.[41] Proust 'undertook to blur by an extreme subtilization the relation of the writer and his characters'.[42] In each case, let us note, Barthes is making statements about their psychological states, their intentions, their plan for what they were doing. Elsewhere he cites Flaubert, De Quincey and Baudelaire in his support – indeed, we cannot read Barthes's work in this essay, or almost anything written after it, and believe he is anything other than engaged in considering the things that authors do and intend to do.

Second, even when he is not naming authors, he uses characteristically intentional vocabulary to describe how writing happens: surrealism was 'striving to disappoint expected meanings', 'urging the hand to write as fast as possible', 'accepting the principle [...] of collective writing'.[43] Objects do not strive or urge or accept, only beings with minds and intentions do. He is again employing a vocabulary and a conceptual structure of intentionality to describe the change in writing. There is a somewhat respectable philosophical position called eliminative materialism that calls for the abandonment of our whole common-sense intentional vocabulary in favour of a purely naturalistic language of action; but Barthes, whose work from this moment on places 'desire' at its centre, is plainly not an eliminative materialist.[44] And nor one presumes are most of his supposed followers, since if they were they could not describe Barthes as having called for the death of the author, since 'calling for' in this sense is an intentional act.

Third, Barthes never actually dispenses with authors altogether. The rhetorical final flourish – 'the birth of the reader must be requited by the death of the Author' – should be understood in relation to the rest of the article.[45] Barthes speaks of a 'distancing' – in the Brechtian sense – of the author.[46] He talks of the author not preceding but being born at the same time as the text.[47] He favours a terminological change from author to *scriptor*, not something that has widely caught on.[48] Each of these preserves the idea that there is a figure, somewhat responsible for the texts they write. He says, in explanation of this: the author's 'sole power is to mingle writings, to counter some by others, so as never to rely on just one'.[49] In other words, the scriptor is the conduit for the multiple texts of culture, society, history. But to say someone has a sole power is evidently not to say that they have no power. Barthes is redefining the author's role away from the romantic solitude of biographical criticism to one where they are engaged, and to some extent constituted, in language, but where they still have agency.

One might perform a similar reading of the supposedly anti-intentionalist arguments of Foucault and Derrida. Foucault's essay, 'What is an Author?' tacks close to Barthes's in many ways, citing a similar group of early modernist authors – Flaubert, Proust, Kafka, Mallarmé – and promising to complete Barthes's project rather than fundamentally challenge it.[50] Instead, Foucault's project is to ask, given the author's absence, what was at stake in his or her presence, what social and cultural procedures were in place to constitute and separate out the author? Foucault is much more of an 'eliminativist' than Barthes and his sometimes technocratic vocabulary seems to be an effort to imagine a world of impersonal forces – structural, historical, discursive – rather than individual agency; in the essay, he coins the term 'author function', to designate the function assigned by a society to the writers of certain texts.[51] He seeks to show how the author function is constituted by attitudes to legal ownership, culturally specific principles of interpretation, and attitudes to psychology that are all implied in the attribution of 'authors' to texts. While Foucault's argument is provocative and compelling, it is by no means clear that it implies a radical detachment of authors from texts; to believe it does is to imagine we can stand outside discourse, breathing the purer air of ahistorical 'reality'. But in Foucault's terms, such a space is impossible, so it remains difficult to say how to turn his description into a prescription. We might also note that the 'author function' might just as easily be applied to theatre directors, who often describe themselves as the 'authors' of performance.[52]

Derrida's analysis, in 'Signature Event Context', of the complexities involved in trying to close off the meaning of any text hinges on the impossibility of assigning an 'original' or 'primary' context for that text, because words have 'iterability', that is, they are reusable tokens, designed to be used again and again in a variety of different contexts. And if no context can be logically prioritized over any other, it becomes difficult to claim that a text has been misread by being read 'out of context'. This in turn makes it difficult to insist that the intended context is the correct context for any utterance and so intention would seem to have limited authority over texts, which can be 'grafted' into unlimited new contexts. One might first observe that playwrights are very familiar with this structure: a play is an object designed precisely to be placed in a variety of new contexts generating new meanings and associations each time. Good plays, one might say, display maximal iterability. However, Derrida's argument might be susceptible to my claim that a sense of intentionality is essential for us to derive certain kinds of meanings from texts at all. Would texts display iterability if we did not think they were intentional objects? The Dada poem produced at random from words pulled from a hat is an intentional performance, but the poem thus produced is not interpreted and reinterpreted in multiple contexts, because we know it for what it is, a more-or-less arbitrary string of textual fragments. In any case, Derrida is not trying to deny intention or that texts can ever be said to 'mean' particular things. He is trying only to show that a certain instability lurks within – *and makes possible* – stability, that intention can only determine the meaning of texts by containing something that opens texts up to rival interpretations. 'Signature Event Context' does not imply the simple irrelevance of intention. 'If things were simple', Derrida remarked, 'word would have gotten around'.[53]

In other words, intention is not something that we can straightforwardly separate from a text and neither Barthes, Foucault nor Derrida believe that we can. Barthes's ringing final declaration about the death of the author proceeds from an historical story about the historical emergence of the modernist text, in all its fracture, its ambiguity, and its exercise of the sign. It is a story about the intensification of language as a ground for experiment, in which the figure of the author is centrally questioned. This seems to me the key for understanding what has happened in the last 15 years.

Playwriting and objecthood

In the mid-1960s, the art critic Michael Fried viewed minimalism with concern. His problem was that minimalist art – what he called literalism – introduces an unwelcome element of theatre to the experience of art.

Where the modernist artwork is to be prized for its autonomy, its internal play of form, surface and detail, minimalist art has no such detail and instead relies on establishing a relationship with the viewer to become interesting as art. This, he argued in his 1967 essay 'Art and Objecthood', brought visual arts into dangerous proximity with the theatre which is manifestly created for an audience and lives, so to speak, only in the presence of an audience.[54] A painting that is finished in a gallery is a completed painting, but a show at the end of rehearsal is still not quite the show until it is put in front of an audience. For Fried, this damaged everything that was important about art and artistic experience and he recommended that theatricality be expelled from the artwork.

Sadly for Fried, but happily for almost everyone else, this was probably the least successful critical intervention in post-war artistic history. Not only did people ignore him, but if anything the essay persuaded quite a few people that theatricality was an untried but potentially fascinating ground for artistic exploration. The article has been credited with encouraging the development of performance art, in which the basic dynamics of theatre were systematically taken apart, tested, challenged and played with. His attempt to keep art and theatre apart helped to create the opposite.

I suggest that these 'death of the author' plays stand in relation to the 'death of the author' thesis in the same way that early performance art stood in relation to Fried's objections. Just as Fried's critique identified a new area for artistic exploration, it seems to me that the effect of the attempts to expel the author from the theatre has generated a new attention on the artistic fertility of authorship itself as a means of generating complex theatrical effects. Indeed, what both minimalism and these experiments in authorship disrupt is objecthood. Minimalism disrupted the objecthood of the modernist artwork by introducing an element of theatre; these experiments in authorship disrupt the objecthood of theatre by complicating the self-present unity of performance.

It is important to note that, despite the rhetoric (in which I have participated) about the death of the author, none of the plays that I have discussed really amount to an author bowing out of their plays entirely. Crimp in *Attempts on Her Life* does indeed offer a considerable degree of freedom to theatremakers. In later editions, he also indicates an additional choice for the production team: that the first scene of the play may be cut.[55] But we should also note the subsidiary implication of that, which is that *no other scene may be omitted*. In other words, to relinquish some control is not to relinquish all control. One might even note that Crimp's dramaturgical innovation, remarkable though it is, is only an incremental change. While it may seem to the reader of, say, Ibsen's *Hedda Gabler* that a production can be immediately imagined from the text, it remains true that no playtext can exhaustively determine the productions that can be made of it. Language underdetermines the world and there are at least as many imagined productions of *Hedda Gabler* as there are readers. As a consequence, the playtext contains apertures that have to be filled by actors, designers, directors and audience. *Attempts on Her Life* is both a strikingly influential innovation in dramaturgy and the most typical play in the world.

Similarly, these playwrights all survive their deaths. Greig, as we have seen, reappears in Paul McCartney's office long after his demise on the streets of San Diego.[56] Crouch literally leaves his own play, announcing the death of the author, but he has, of course, written his own death and thus survived it. Writing stands as a kind of survival of death even in the most literal death of the author mentioned in this chapter, that of Sarah Kane; but even here *4.48 Psychosis* remains as a kind of witness to the ability of writing to cheat mortality. In the first edition of *The Author*, in any case, the death of the author is presented rather comically in the text, that stage direction immediately followed by 'Music and lights!' the jaunty exclamation mark undermining any sense that the author's death is to be taken wholly seriously.[57]

Because by placing themselves inside their plays to die, these playwrights draw attention to the writerly status of the texts. Despite his early demise, one cannot watch *San Diego* without asking questions of the place of David Greig in relation to his play. Much the same might be said of those plays where authorial control appears to have been relinquished; we should note that Kane's ostentatious lack of moral commentary on the action of *Blasted* encouraged her first critics to speculate precisely about her intentions. These tactical withdrawals from authorship in fact reassert and underline authorship; it is actually the mainstream tradition of new writing with its creation of coherent and transparent fictional worlds that keeps the author invisible.

Why is this significant? What is the value in drawing attention to authorship and disrupting the objecthood of performance? As I have argued elsewhere, a key context for understanding the politics of contemporary theatre is globalization.[58] By that I mean, specifically, the global extension of capitalism operating under neoliberal policy conditions. Since the 1970s, barriers to the free exchange of goods and services – and to a lesser extent, labour power – have been progressively lowered, creating an increasingly global market. While it is possible to overstate the completeness of globalization and there are good reasons to be sceptical about some of the claims made both by globalization's critics and its cheerleaders, the reach and power of global capitalism is unprecedented.[59] Even the 2008 banking collapse, which one might regard as a cautionary tale about the dangers of deregulated financial globalization, has become an opportunity for the market fundamentalists to insist that the only solution to recession is austerity: that is, market solutions to market problems.

Objecthood has a particular significance under globalization. Capitalism's development can be charted across two axes: the first is its *extensive* development, its restless geographical search for new sources of raw materials and labour, and new markets for its products; the second is its *intensive* development, seeking within its current territories for new things, experiences and relations that can be converted into opportunities for profit. In Marxist terms, this intensive development involves seeking out use-values and turning them into exchange-values, turning the fabric of our lives into commodities and those commodities into money. Use-values – say, friendship or fresh air – offer us multiple, complicated, shifting and playful rewards; exchange-values, however, are merely 'depositories of value' measured in terms of money.[60] As more and more of our life – even friendship and fresh air – is transformed into exchange-values, more and more of our life must be translatable into money. For these use-values to function effectively as exchange-values, they must acquire a certain objecthood: that is, they must become regular, bounded, self-contained. When we purchase a commodity, we are exchanging money for the commodity, an exchange that must be complete in both directions. The dazzling variety of life under global capitalism, then, has an underlying uniformity, in which everything must become an object with a monetary value. Theodor Adorno, writing in the 1960s, saw this underlying uniformity as the ever more pervasive experience of capitalism; its corollary in thought, he suggested, was what he called 'identity thinking', the insistence on every thing being neatly organized beneath its concept.[61] What commodities are to the form of money, objects are to concepts. Without any gaps between things and concepts, there is no space for the dialectic and thus the great process of human development towards utopia is threatened.[62]

Adorno's strategy is to search out and insist upon non-identity and he finds that most often in art. The value of art, for Adorno, is that art never totally resembles the world; it establishes a gap between the way the world is and how it might be: 'semblance is a promise of nonsemblance', he says dialectically.[63] Art's ambiguities, contradictions, complexities generate this double effect: '[a]n artwork is always itself and simultaneously the other of itself'.[64] While Adorno was a champion of modernist writers and composers, he may have seen the risks of Fried's view of the modernist artwork as contained, bounded and self-identical. Far preferable, perhaps, would be the theatricalized artwork whose edges are porous, that require supplementation by the viewer. Similarly, one might think that Adorno would consider with disquiet the idea the performance is complete, fully present and identical with itself.

The assertion of authorship multiplies and destabilizes the experience of the play in performance. It generates tensions between the performance and the play. In each of the cases I have discussed, the apparent withdrawal or death of an author makes the text more elusive and less fully established in performance. 'New writing' culture in Britain has the convention that the playwright has some control over the first production of a play; that is, writers have approval over casting and other key creative personnel, the right to attend rehearsal, and so on. This does not amount to saying that plays are performed according to the author's intentions; an author's intentions, properly speaking, are expressed in what they have written, and as I argued above, language cannot fully determine a performance; if the author has intentions as regards the performance, these might be expressed at rehearsal, but it is doubtful that anyone's intentions are sufficiently fine-grained to account for every aspect of a performance. It would be truer to say that, in conventional new writing theatre, plays are performed in a way that is broadly consistent with the playwright's intentions. Nor does this amount to saying that the first production is definitive, though the two thoughts have been known to blur into one another. In the case of a play like *Attempts on Her Life*, it is simply implausible to imagine that there ever could be a definitive production. The experience of this and the other plays I have discussed will always be provisional; this authorial intervention makes it impossible to 'impose a brake on it, to furnish it with a final signified, to close writing'.[65]

The instability of these texts makes them politically more questioning and radical, in Adorno's terms, because they insist that the world can be other than it is. They intensify the ambiguity and complexity of aesthetic experience and refuse the tidy objectness of fictional realism. The moments of authorial absence that they stage – the 'radical naivety' of Bartlett or Stephens, the moral neutrality of Kane or Kelly, the textual openness of Crimp and Churchill, the authorial deaths and resurrections of Crimp and Greig – are examples of playwrights discovering that authorship itself may be a key area for artistic experiment that offers the potential to ask questions about who we are and who we might be.

Notes

1. D. Rebellato, 'Sarah Kane: An Appreciation', *New Theatre Quarterly*, 15.3 (1999), 280–1; S. Gorman, 'The Mythology of Sarah Kane: How to Avoid Reading *4.48 Psychosis* as a Suicide Note', *Anglo Files*, 126 (2002), 35–42.
2. T. Crouch, *Plays One* (London: Oberon Books, 2011), p. 203.
3. D. Greig, *Selected Plays 1999–2009* (London: Faber & Faber, 2010), p. 39.
4. In M. Ravenhill, *Plays: 2* (London: Methuen Drama, 2008), p. 322.
5. As with the eponymous and fictional author in *The Author*, there are echoes of Sarah Kane. Although this anonymous author is referred to as 'him', we know that the dead playwright was young, with relatively few, short, imagistic plays to his name, and that these texts have 'sharp edges' and are resistant to explanation. At one moment, the text imagines the writers sleepless from jealousy. 'The writers look at the clock. Only 2AM', perhaps a sly reference to Kane's later hour of wakefulness in the title of her last play *4.48 Psychosis* (M. Crimp, *Plays Two* (London: Faber & Faber, 2005), pp. xi–xii).
6. Crimp, *Plays Two*, p. xi.
7. Crimp, *Plays Two*, p. xi.
8. D. Kelly, *Taking Care of Baby* (London: Oberon Books, 2007), p. 32.
9. Including *Via Dolorosa* (Royal Court, 1998), *Berlin* (National Theatre: Lyttelton, 2009), and *Wall* (Royal Court, 2009).
10. P. Godfrey, *Plays: 1* (London: Methuen Drama, 1998), p. 319.
11. Godfrey, *Plays: 1*, p. 308.
12. Roland Barthes's 'The Death of the Author' was first published in English in 1967, in French in 1968, and was included in his 1984 collection *Le Bruissement de la Langue*. See R. Barthes, *The Rustle of Language*, trans. R. Howard (Oxford: Blackwell, 1986). See also R. Barthes, 'La Mort de l'Auteur', in E. Marty (ed.), *Oeuvres Complètes II: 1966–1973* (Paris: Seuil, 1995), pp. 491–5.
13. N. Ridout, 'You, the Spectator', in D. Brine (ed.), *The Live Art Almanac* (London: Live Art Development Agency, 2008), pp. 17–20 (p. 17).
14. See, for example D. Hare, *Obedience, Struggle & Revolt: Lectures on Theatre* (London: Faber & Faber, 2005), p. 87.
15. There was an outcry in 2007 after the trailer for a BBC documentary about the Queen was misleadingly edited to make it look as if she was walking angrily out of a sitting with the photographer Annie Leibovitz. Later that year a string of minor deceptions came to light in a number of light entertainment and children's programmes, including *Blue Peter*. In 2011, a further row broke out over images from the wildlife documentary *Frozen Planet* which intercut shots filmed in the wild with those filmed in a zoo. It is unclear whether these had given rise to genuine public anger or were merely an opportunity for news corporations to attack the BBC.
16. M. Dreysse, 'The Performance is Starting Now: On the Relationship between Reality and Fiction', in M. Dreysse and F. Malzacher (eds.), *Rimini Protokoll: Experts of the Everyday* (Berlin: Alexander, 2008), pp. 76–97 (p. 83). Dreysse

goes on to argue that Rimini Protokoll's work in fact sets up a complex relation between reality and fiction. The theatre continues to frame and shape the real stories that give us aesthetic distance on the material being presented; as such we become aware – in a somewhat Brechtian sense – of the nature of fiction-making, which is itself a kind of unmasking of fiction, turning it into reality (pp. 85–6). One of the co-founders of the company, Daniel Wetzel, has noted the way that experts sometimes cannot help but turn into actors on stage and that ultimately 'in the end we really are not interested in whether someone is telling the truth, but rather how he [*sic*] presents himself and what role he is playing' (quoted in F. Malzacher, 'Dramaturgies of Care and Insecurity: The Story of Rimini Protokoll', in Dreysse and Malzacher (eds.), *Rimini Protokoll*, 14–43 (p. 38)).

17. Again, the real situation is much more complex. Both *Floating* and *The Story of a Rabbit* are narrated by 'Hugh Hughes' who is supposedly the creator of the shows; but Hugh Hughes is a fictional persona created by the artistic director of hoipolloi, Shôn Dale-Jones; Hughes's persona of childlike enthusiasm and wonder ensures that a sense of theatrical marvel continues to characterize the performance even as its workings are exposed.

18. See S. Gorman, *The Theatre of Richard Maxwell and the New York City Players* (Abingdon and New York: Routledge, 2011), pp. 30–49.

19. This idea is particularly associated with the Prague structuralists: J. Veltrusky, for example, declared 'all that is on stage is a sign' – see 'Man and Object in the Theater', in P. Garvin (ed.), *A Prague School Reader on Esthetics, Literary Structure, and Style* (Washington, DC: Georgetown University Press, 1964), pp. 83–91 (on p. 84), and J. Honzl insisted 'dramatic performance is a set of signs' – see 'Dynamics of the Sign in the Theater', in L. Matejka and I. R. Titunik (eds.), *Semiotics of Art: Prague School Contribution* (Cambridge, MA and London: MIT Press, 1976), pp. 74–93 (p. 74).

20. A. Forsyth and C. Megson (eds.), *Get Real: Documentary Theatre Past and Present* (Basingstoke: Palgrave Macmillan, 2009).

21. See C. Megson, '*Half the Picture*: "A Certain Frisson" at the Tricycle Theatre', in Forsyth and Megson (eds.), *Get Real*, pp. 195–208.

22. D. Edgar, 'From the Nanny State to the Heckler's Veto: The New Censorship and How to Counter It', *Contemporary Theatre Review*, 17.4 (2007), 524–33 (p. 532).

23. Hare, *Obedience, Struggle & Revolt*, p. 84.

24. See note 14. Hare observes that in wanting to write about the Israel–Palestine conflict he 'despaired of writing fiction which relied on conventional scenes' (*Obedience, Struggle & Revolt*, p. 78) and instead laboured to create what he insists was still a 'play' but one that sought to convey 'urgent sincerity' (p. 80) rather than artful fiction. He comes close to confirming Edgar's diagnosis of a cultural downgrading of fiction's importance when he writes, '[i]t was my contention that, in this case, when the subject of a work is so hotly contested, so open to argument, that the audience could best decide whether the witness were honest if the witness were willing to appear to before them' (p. 78).

25. Personal conversation, November 2012. *pool (no water)* does not assign characters to the dialogue. *Shopping and Fucking* perhaps draws attention to the artificiality of the very idea of character by naming everyone after members (and associates) of the boy band Take That.

26. In S. Stephens, *Plays: 2* (London: Methuen Drama, 2009), p. 214.
27. M. Crimp, *Fewer Emergencies* (London: Faber & Faber, 2005), pp. 5, 23, 39.
28. D. Rebellato, *Chekhov in Hell*, 2nd edn. (London: Oberon Books, 2011), p. 23.
29. C. Churchill, *Caryl Churchill: Plays Four* (London: Nick Hern Books, 2008), p. 132. To this, we might add the practice of writing 'impossible stage directions' about which I have written elsewhere (see D. Rebellato, 'Globalization and Playwriting: Towards a Site-Unspecific Theatre', *Contemporary Theatre Review*, 16.1 (2006), 97–113 (pp. 109–12)). This species of textual aporia marks both a withdrawal of explicit authorial control, and an aperture in the text that invites collaboration.
30. M. Bartlett, *Earthquakes in London* (London: Methuen Drama, 2010), p. 147.
31. D. Eldridge, R. Holman and S. Stephens, *A Thousand Stars Explode in the Sky* (London: Methuen Drama, 2010), p. 42. *A Thousand Stars Explode in the Sky* was co-written by David Eldridge, Robert Holman and Simon Stephens, and each section was worked and reworked by the trio, so it is not possible to say for certain that this line was specifically written by Stephens, though it sounds to me as though it was. It does not affect the broader argument, in any case.
32. In S. Stephens, *Plays: 3* (London: Methuen Drama, 2011), p. 311.
33. In Stephens, *Plays: 2*, p. 245.
34. Hare, *Obedience, Struggle & Revolt*, p. 164.
35. S. Waters, *The Secret Life of Plays* (London: Nick Hern Books, 2010), p. 184.
36. A. Page, *The Death of the Playwright?* (London and New York: Macmillan, 1992).
37. Greig, *Selected Plays 1999–2009*, p. 36.
38. The bizarre claim that Paul McCartney died in a car accident in 1967 and was replaced by a double took hold in the late 1960s and continues to circulate. See http://www.ispauldead.com/ for the preposterous details (accessed 17 October 2012).
39. In Barthes, *The Rustle of Language*, p. 49.
40. Barthes may have in mind his own earlier essay 'To Write: An Intransitive Verb' (*The Rustle of Language*, pp. 11–21), which sets out what he sees as the impact of structuralist linguistics on thinking about literature. There, while he appears to be talking about literature, he seems to see little distinction between literary and ordinary language. In the gap between these two essays, however, there is a perceptible shift from structuralist to poststructuralist thinking in Barthes's work and I am inclined to entertain the notion that Barthes's later essay is less committed to the idea that all language has the same underlying structure.
41. Barthes, *The Rustle of Language*, p. 50.
42. Barthes, *The Rustle of Language*, p. 51.
43. Barthes, *The Rustle of Language*, p. 51.
44. For a classic statement of the position see P. M. Churchland, 'Eliminative Materialism and the Propositional Attitudes', *The Journal of Philosophy*, 78.2 (1981), 67–90.
45. Barthes, *The Rustle of Language*, p. 55.
46. Barthes, *The Rustle of Language*, p. 51.
47. Barthes, *The Rustle of Language*, p. 52.
48. Barthes, *The Rustle of Language*, p. 52.

49. Barthes, *The Rustle of Language*, p. 53.
50. M. Foucault, 'What is an Author?', in *Essential Works of Foucault, 1954–1984: Volume 2 – Aesthetics*, ed. J. D. Faubion (London: Penguin, 1998), pp. 205–22 (pp. 206, 207 and 209).
51. Foucault, 'What is an Author?', p. 211.
52. Roger Planchon coined the term 'écriture scénique' to describe the work of the director (see D. Bradby, *Modern French Drama: 1940–1990*, 2nd edn. (Cambridge: Cambridge University Press, 1991), pp. 101–28, 132–41) and the term has been applied more widely, for example to the work of Robert Lepage (see P. Caux and G. Bernard, *Ex Machina: Chantiers d'Écriture Scénique* (Sillery: Septentrion, 2007)). Many directors have been acclaimed – and denounced – as 'auteurs' (see M. M. Delgado and D. Rebellato (eds.), *Contemporary European Theatre Directors* (Abingdon and New York: Routledge, 2010), p. 19).
53. J. Derrida, *Limited Inc* (Evanston, IL: Northwestern University Press, 1988), p. 119.
54. M. Fried, 'Art and Objecthood', in G. Battcock (ed.), *Minimal Art: A Critical Anthology* (New York: Dutton, 1968), pp. 116–47.
55. In Crimp, *Plays Two*, p. 202. The first scene, 'All Messages Deleted', takes the form of a series of answerphone messages to 'Anne'. The scene seems to have been intended to insist on the unity of the absent central character, and thereby to impose a unity on the play. Subsequent directors, notably Katie Mitchell, found that scene unnecessary and requested its omission (see A. Sierz, *The Theatre of Martin Crimp* (London: Methuen Drama, 2006), p. 198), which Crimp agreed to. It is striking that omitting the scene removes an authorial statement of the play's unity and thus further multiplies and complicates the sense of authorial presence and control.
56. Greig, *Selected Plays 1999–2009*, p. 105.
57. T. Crouch, *The Author* (London: Oberon Books, 2009), p. 59.
58. See Rebellato, 'Globalization and Playwriting: Towards a Site-Unspecific Theatre'; D. Rebellato, 'From the State of the Nation to Globalization: Shifting Political Agendas in Contemporary British Playwriting', in N. Holdsworth and M. Luckhurst (eds.), *A Concise Companion to Contemporary British and Irish Drama* (Oxford: Blackwell, 2007), pp. 245–62; D. Rebellato, *Theatre & Globalization* (Basingstoke: Palgrave Macmillan, 2009).
59. See P. Hirst, G. Thompson and S. Bromley, *Globalization in Question*, 3rd edn. (Cambridge: Polity Press, 2009).
60. K. Marx, *Capital: An Abridged Edition* (Oxford: Oxford University Press, 1995), p. 22.
61. T. W. Adorno, *Negative Dialectics*, trans. E. B. Ashton (London: Routledge, 1973), p. 149.
62. See Adorno, *Negative Dialectics*, p. 11.
63. Adorno, *Negative Dialectics*, p. 405.
64. T. W. Adorno, *Aesthetic Theory*, ed. G. Adorno and R. Tiedemann, trans. R. Hullot Kentor (London: Athlone, 1997), p. 283.
65. Barthes, *The Rustle of Language*, p. 53.

2

'And I was struck still by time': Contemporary British Theatre and the Metaphysical Imagination

Chris Megson

> I really remember the moment.
> Very intense.
> Of waking up – in the snow.
> That moment's where I start from. Now. New.[1]

David Greig's *Pyrenees* (Tron Theatre, Glasgow, 2005) tells the story of a man found unconscious in the snow on the mountainous pilgrims' route to Santiago de Compostela in Galicia. The Man (as he is designated in the text) suffers from severe memory loss and the play revolves around the mystery of his identity. The quotation above is taken from a conversation with Anna – the Man's contact from the British Consulate – as he recalls his feelings at the very moment of regaining consciousness. For him, this 'moment in the snow', unfettered by any recollection of a personal past, is analogous to birth and he describes how his self-awareness was at once fortified and disaggregated by this experience:

> THE MAN: I had an intense understanding of exactly who I was.
> ANNA: What do you mean?
> THE MAN: I was everything.
> Everything was me.
> There was no 'me'.[2]

Anna, in her response, likens his feelings to her own memory of the dissociated moments that book-end her epileptic fits. Immediately before and after a bout of epilepsy, her consciousness is overwhelmed by, as she puts it, 'an enormous intensity of sensation [...] A sense one has been made aware of another world.'[3]

Simon Stephens's *Pornography* (Deutsches Schauspielhaus, Hamburg; Festival Theaterformen; Schauspielhannover, 2007) is a play constituted in the torrential anger of disaffected speaking voices.[4] In one notable sequence, a woman is visited by a man after a period of absence and it becomes clear they are brother and sister. Their exchange unfolds in a brittle but intimate repartee that culminates in the brother's declamatory outburst: 'I love you so much it's like my body is bursting out of my skin and all I want is for you to love me in the same way and for it to be like this forever.'[5] He yearns for their moment of shared intimacy to be simultaneously frozen in time yet drawn out through eternity. At the end of the scene, their dialogue moves inexorably towards valediction. Given the social prohibition on incestuous desire, and their own corrosive sense of guilt, brother and sister acknowledge, hyperbolically, that '[h]undreds and hundreds and hundreds and hundreds of years' must pass before they can see each other again.[6] The idealized moment disintegrates and an encroaching infinitude of separation takes its place.

In Dan Rebellato's *Chekhov in Hell* (Drum Theatre, Plymouth, 2010), the playwright Anton Chekhov awakens from a long coma and embarks on a series of bizarre encounters with various eclectic characters from contemporary life.[7] The play's sardonic comedy is counterpointed by the repetition of a rhetorical trope in which speakers express a desire to rip a hole in the fabric of reality and step through the gap. This jolting semiotic of escape is expressed most forcefully by a troubled young character called Bob, who rhapsodizes about 'the perfect pause':

> Sometimes I want to stop everything. Like I wish there was magic so I could just stop everything, wherever it was. And when it was paused, and not like VHS (*wobbles demonstratively.*) but a perfect pause like a DVD pause (*he freezes.*), I would get a knife and cut a slash down the middle of everything and the lights would be bright behind it all and I'd step through and disappear. Shit I'm being intense again, aren't I?[8]

Introduction: British theatre's 'metaphysical turn'

Pyrenees, *Pornography* and *Chekhov in Hell* are three plays that extrapolate, in varying ways, the existential significance of moments in time. In the above excerpts, the moment is conceived, respectively, as the locus of subjective origin and awakening, the vertiginous site of encounter where present and eternity become mutually enfolded, and the utopic point of embarkation from crushing social realities into a more liberated personal imaginary. In all of these instances, the theatrical demarcation of the moment opens up, however fleetingly, numinous dimensions of experience that intimate the possibility of self-realization or transcendence within alternative worlds. Indeed, one of the striking features of new writing for British theatre over the past two decades is its arbitration of moments of dramatic intensity that 'pause', rupture or entirely reconfigure the flow of stage action.

In this chapter, 'metaphysics' is defined – following the Oxford dictionary – as 'the branch of philosophy that deals with first principles of things, including abstract concepts such as being, knowing, identity, time, and space'.[9] On this basis, the ensuing analysis identifies a 'metaphysical turn' in British theatre, grounded in the performative evocation of the moment, and which is constitutive of a reach for new values, new possibilities of living, beyond the grip of capitalism, religion and exhausted ideology. Throughout the 1990s and 2000s, a range of landmark plays have excavated momentary experience in such a way as to illuminate the pressures imposed on the human inhabitation of time by contemporary social organization. In so doing, these plays have often moved beyond systems of naturalist stage representation by calibrating a different experience of time – 'chronos' time, as I will proceed to define it. Moreover, it is from within such moments of dislocated temporality that these plays engender possibilities for ethical reflection.

The argument of this chapter is structured in three sections. The first introduces some of the current debates in the public sphere on religion, atheism and secularism in which theatre has been implicated. These debates address the perceived limitations of secular society and probe the viability of 'belief' outside the framework of religious doctrine and organization. In this section, I also set out a number of plays over the past decade that have engaged with 'belief' as a central problematic in ways that are distinct from their theatrical precursors. Following from this contextual account, the second stage of the argument traces the emergence in recent years of what has been termed 'atheist spirituality' and its attendant ethical injunction: 'fidelity in the absence of faith'. The focus of this section is the elaboration of the philosophical premises of chronos time, drawing on classical and contemporary sources. Informed by these conceptualizations, the final part of the chapter explores how 'living in the moment' has been foregrounded theatrically across a range of playwriting in order to galvanize an awareness of the interdependency of self and environment, and to situate the life of the human subject within a more cosmic teleology. In summary, then, the chapter argues a case for the 'metaphysical turn' in contemporary British theatre and, consequentially, sets in motion a discussion about theatre's engagement with the nascent discourse of postsecularism (as I shall explain).

'We don't do God'

The three scenes described at the start of this chapter draw on quasi-religious impulses and gesture towards the transcendence of individual identity and quotidian life. In this section, I want to show how these preoccupations resonate in the context of wide-ranging discussion in public life about the place of religion in contemporary culture and the perceived strengths and limitations of secularism in Western societies. These debates have gathered momentum over the past decade for a number of reasons.

In 2003, Alastair Campbell, then press secretary to Prime Minister Tony Blair, blocked an interviewer's question on the subject of Blair's much-publicized Christian faith: 'We don't do God', Campbell interjected.[10] The incident, which was widely reported, emblemizes the sensitivity that often surrounds discussion of religion in British public life, particularly the perception that a politician's religious beliefs might compromise their image and electability. Nearly ten years later, a different Prime Minister showed a similar circumspection when addressing religious matters. In December 2011, David Cameron, during a major speech in Oxford marking the 400th anniversary of the completion of the King James Bible, praised what he called 'Christian values' but was careful to qualify the terms of his own religious affiliation: 'I am a committed – but I have to say vaguely practising – Church of England Christian, who will stand up for the values and principles of my faith.'[11] To be 'committed' yet 'vaguely practising' sounds rather contradictory but Cameron's rhetoric strategically adheres to 'values' while downplaying his personal affiliation to actual religious practice.

During the 2000s, belief in Christianity amongst the UK population continued its long-term decline. A major report on Christian churchgoing, published in 2007, revealed that 53 per cent of the adult population identify themselves as Christian.[12] The report also confirmed that only 15 per cent of British adults go to church at least once a month, down from half the population 50 years ago, with statistics for churchgoing, irrespective of their mode of calculation, showing a consistent decline in attendance and an ever-increasing average age of congregants. The European Social Survey of 2002, quoted in the 2007 document, ranked Britain fourth from the bottom in church attendance across the continent while a *Guardian* report, published in 2008 and based on the Church of England's own statistics, forecast that church attendance would slump from current levels by a further 90 per cent by 2050.[13] What is more, during the same period, arguments for not doing God have garnered an increased profile in the first decade of the twenty-first century through the best-selling publications of so-called 'new atheists'. Pugnacious and incisive books by Sam Harris (*The End of Faith*, 2004), Richard Dawkins (*The God Delusion*, 2006) and Christopher Hitchens (*god Is Not Great*, 2007) assailed the truth-claims of monotheistic religion, targeting in particular creationism and evangelism in Christianity and fundamentalist elements within Islam.[14] For the 'new atheists', as one scholar puts it, 'secularization is understood as a kind of cognitive growing-up at the level of the species'.[15]

The continuing decline in Christian belief and church attendance, and the challenge to religion by atheist discourse, has coincided with widespread debate in the public sphere about the perceived merits and limitations of secularism. In the aftermath of 9/11, secularism as a mode of social organization has been upheld by some Western politicians in their attempts to legitimate the 'War on Terror', stoking heated arguments on security, immigration and human rights within and between Western nation states. There were forceful reminders during the 2000s, especially in Europe and the US, that secularism takes many contested forms and can place certain limits on rights of expression: for example, in 2004, the banning of specific kinds of Muslim dress in state buildings brought the French model of secularism (laïcité) into controversial focus. More recently, Cameron's colleague Baroness Sayeeda Warsi, cabinet minister and co-Chairwoman of the Conservative Party, wrote in *The Daily Telegraph* (in advance of a high-profile British delegation to the Vatican in February 2012) that 'militant secularisation', a 'rising tide of secularism', has 'taken hold' in Britain, causing religion to become 'sidelined, marginalised and downgraded in the public sphere'.[16] Within this fractious context, secularism, atheism and the religious practices of faith communities have been subjected to intense amounts of media scrutiny at a time when, according to theatre scholar Lance Gharavi, 'intersections of religion, politics and performance form the loci of many of the most serious issues facing the world today, sites where some of the world's most pressing and momentous events are contested and played out'.[17]

In July 2010, the influential current affairs magazine *New Statesman* (*NS*) published a special edition on 'secularism, atheism and belief' featuring contributions from various cultural and religious commentators. Other articles pertaining to these topics were published over the course of that summer. The following commentary draws on these articles because they identify specific kinds of unease about the perceived social impact of secularism and atheism in the UK at this historical juncture. For example, in an article published in *NS* in June 2010, Matthew Taylor, the Chief Executive of the Royal Society of Arts, argues that 'empathic universalism' should replace 'possessive individualism' as a way of countering the hegemonic 'logics' shaping British public life: '[t]he success of the Western post-Enlightenment project has resulted in societies such as ours being dominated by three logics: of scientific and technological progress, of markets and of bureaucracy'.[18] What is needed in the new century, Taylor suggests, is 'a more self-aware, socially embedded model of autonomy'.[19] Rowan Williams, then Archbishop of Canterbury, gave a thought-provoking interview to *NS* the following month which adumbrates these concerns: 'There are bits of human experience and suffering that have to go somewhere, and secular society simply doesn't have the spaces, the words or the rituals [...] where a person can feel related to something more than the sum of their own anxieties and their society's normal patterns of talk and behaviour [...].'[20] He asserts that an exploratory life of faith will become increasingly 'countercultural the more we settle for the customer as the basic model of identity'.[21] As Archbishop, of course, Williams was hardly a disinterested observer but his perturbations about the rising tide of economic materialism cut across many of the contributions to the *NS* special issue.

These interventions have dovetailed with a surge of recent scholarship that marks an attempt to reclaim 'spiritual' experience from organized religion, to understand what faith means outside of theistic conviction. This scholarship has constellated as part of the growing discourse of postsecularism:

[Postsecularism] typically designates a social or cultural consciousness – within a society deemed, or previously deemed, 'secular' – predicated on a certain scepticism or 'incredulity' toward the secularization thesis, and an awareness of the re-entry [...] of religion into public discourse. Defined thusly, postsecularism holds the possibility of a new and heuristic dialogue on religion and secularism in the twenty-first century.[22]

In his contribution to the *NS* conversation, the writer and philosopher Alain de Botton paid tribute to the nineteenth-century positivist Auguste Comte in terms that resonate with postsecular verve. Comte appeals to de Botton because he 'recognised that [...] a secular society devoted solely to financial accumulation and romantic love and devoid of any sources of consolation, transcendent awe or solidarity would be prey to untenable social and emotional ills'.[23] In his *Catechism of Positive Religion: Summary Exposition of the Universal Religion* (1852) and *Theory of the Future of Man* (1854), Comte sets out nothing less than an atheistic religion that embraces the infrastructure of church ritual while evacuating it of Christian content: he recommends that a calendar of special days be inaugurated to celebrate secular icons, with each month committed to honouring a field of endeavour (such as art or parenting), and that bankers should fund 'temples of humanity' focused on educational activities. Comte's vision led to the opening of the Chappelle de l'Humanité in Paris and, in 1878, Oxford don Richard Congreve opened the Church of Humanity in Lamb's Conduit Street in London (similar churches were opened in the US and Brazil from the 1870s). De Botton admires Comte for his attempt to create a social space for humanist reflection and regrets the lack of such a resource in contemporary society: '[Comte] identified a psychic space in atheistic society that continues to lie fallow and to invite resolution [...]. [He] attempted to rescue some of what is beautiful, touching, reasonable and wise from what no longer seems true.'[24] Pursuing his Comtean theme, de Botton's book *Religion for Atheists: A Non-Believer's Guide to the Uses of Religion*, published in 2012, argues for the value and utility of religion when shorn of antique systems of belief.[25]

Comte's and, latterly, de Botton's recognition of the philosophical insights and social benefits that even obsolete religion can bestow finds a perhaps surprising corollary in a polemical piece – titled 'God is behind Some of Our Greatest Art' – written, in 2008, by the playwright Mark Ravenhill for *The Guardian*.[26] In this article, Ravenhill mounts a defence of Christianity – or, more precisely, a defence of the impact of Christianity on culture – and criticizes the onward march of what he calls 'the Dawkins army'. He contends that the literature and art of Christianity, from the Bible to the Sistine Chapel, remain a source of inspiration and, in one of his more eyebrow-raising passages, suggests that Sarah Kane's *Blasted* (Royal Court Theatre Upstairs, London, 1995) and his own *Shopping and Fucking* (Royal Court Theatre Upstairs, 1996) 'wouldn't have been written without the Christian church'. The central part of his argument is worth quoting at length:

> Christianity is a myth. But it's a myth that has helped us – and continues to help us – ask searching moral and philosophical questions. Ours is an age in which a lack of belief, at least in secular Europe, is prized. Before, having one overarching belief was central to life, guiding our choices. But now we're all supposed to travel light, be supple, so that we can swap jobs, partners or political allegiances at a moment's notice. But this perpetual state of agnosticism, this lack of commitment, must surely be corrosive. Those who are able to locate, and to explore intelligently, a system of belief, be that religious or political, are surely making a valuable contribution to our times.

The reference to 'one overarching belief' echoes Robbie's eulogy to 'big stories' – 'The Powerful Hands of the Gods and Fate. The Journey To Enlightenments. The March of Socialism' – in *Shopping and Fucking*; it also chimes with Gharavi's observation, in his recent study of religion and theatre, that '[r]eligions may be cited for offering the grandest of grand narratives, whoppers dwarfing either those proposed by Marx's teleology or Enlightenment ideas of progress'.[27] The principal cause and symptom of 'travel light' postmodernity is, for Ravenhill, 'lack of belief': this apparent 'lack' triggers his rather melancholy assessment of the negative legacy of secularism. His wistful search for 'commitment' finds anchorage in the narratives and certainties of bygone faith and, in aesthetic experience, he senses the last vestige of the religious imagination. Ravenhill's conclusion is that religious art can inspire, that belief-systems (when 'explore[d] intelligently') can create value, and that aesthetics has supplanted belief as the gateway to philosophical truth.

The latter point is arguably the most contentious although similar perspectives have been put forward in recent historical and theological scholarship. The Oxford Professor of the History of the Church, Diarmaid MacCulloch, echoes Ravenhill when discussing his recently published *History of Christianity* (2009): '[i]f you ask me if I believe in Christianity, I'd have to say not in the sense that I believe in what I had for breakfast, but in the sense that I believe *Hamlet* is true'.[28] In other words, for Ravenhill and MacCulloch, Christianity can be approached, not as a system or object of empirically verifiable belief, but as an *aesthetic opportunity* to which one can be exposed, and from which one can benefit, without the freight of religious conviction.

The attempt to, in effect, aestheticize Christianity has attracted criticism for its sundering of belief from the experience of religious art. John Cornwell, the Catholic commentator and author of *'Newman's Unquiet Grave': The Reluctant Saint* (2010), makes a fierce counter-argument to MacCulloch's (and, by implication, Ravenhill's) views in an interview published in the *NS* about the life of his biographical subject, Cardinal Newman:

> One of the threats to Christianity in the 21st century is this idea that religion is best understood as a kind of aesthetic experience, and that you can get all your morality from that. [Cardinal] Newman saw that coming in the mid-19th century and said you can't do it that way. For a start, nobody has ever died for their interpretation of *Hamlet*. [...] [W]hat brings us certitude in faith is not logical argument – it's this great span of what [Newman] would sometimes call 'evidences', which involved imagination and all the rest of it.[29]

Cornwell holds that certitude in faith should be primary in the experience of religious art: aesthetics cannot surrogate belief. But he also contends that *belief* is an effect of *faith* and that faith draws on other kinds of 'evidences', including the imagination. This latter point is actually very important. The argument that belief and faith are different degrees of experience, requiring different kinds of 'evidences' for their validation, suggests that faith abides as a deeper order, or 'orientation', of experience than belief, and can even outlast it.[30] This observation takes on further significance in the context of the underlying argument put forward by a number of contributors to the *NS* special issue – namely, that British society is passing through a gargantuan crisis of belief. On this point, as we have seen, the views of the former Archbishop of Canterbury and Mark Ravenhill are in complete sympathy.

Turning to theatre, one might argue that the decay of belief has been the single most significant preoccupation of British playwriting through its entire post-war history. After all (indicatively) John Osborne, John Arden and Arnold Wesker traced the effects of Britain's imperial decline and the sense of disillusionment on the left in the 1950s; the 'state of the nation' plays by David Edgar, David Hare and Trevor Griffiths excoriated the bitter ideological compromises, political disaffection and institutional stagnation of the 1970s; while, more recently, Howard Brenton, Caryl Churchill and Ravenhill himself have articulated, in multifarious ways, the ideological tailspin following the fall of the Berlin Wall in 1989 and the subsequent implosion of the USSR. The reinvigoration of documentary, verbatim and other forms of fact-based performance from the mid-1990s has also been responsive to, in the words of Janelle Reinelt, 'a globalised world of indecipherable uncertainties'.[31]

More recently, however, there has been an extraordinary groundswell of plays engaging directly with themes of religious belief or upheaval. At the National Theatre in London, Canadian playwright Drew Pautz's *Love the Sinner*, staged at the Cottesloe in 2010, explored the personal impact of doctrinal fault-lines in the Anglican Church.[32] Ben Power's adaptation of *Emperor and Galilean*, Ibsen's epic study of religious faith and human emancipation, was directed by Jonathan Kent in a monumental production at the Olivier the following year.[33] Mike Bartlett's sprawling play *13* (also at the Olivier, 2011) sustained the apocalyptic tenor of his previous *Earthquakes in London* (Cottesloe, 2010). The central character in *13* is a Messiah-like figure called John who upholds belief as both constitutive principle of social life and antidote to a political culture riven by anxiety and compromise: the staging of the play in the aftermath of the August 2011 riots in English cities, and during the anti-capitalist 'Occupy' protests then encamped outside London's symbolic religious centre of St Paul's Cathedral, invested the production with arresting topicality.[34]

At the RSC, David Edgar's *Written on the Heart* (Swan Theatre, 2011) elaborated the creation of the King James Bible and its emergence from the Protestant and Puritan challenges to Catholic authority in England from the 1530s onwards, while Helen Edmundson's *The Heresy of Love* (Swan Theatre, 2012) takes its inspiration from the life of Sor Juana Inés de la Cruz, the seventeenth-century Mexican nun and writer whose creativity brought her into conflict with church patriarchy.[35] Over at the Royal Court, meanwhile, Richard Bean's *The Heretic* (2011) explored the volatile relations between religion and science ('I'm a scientist yeah. I can't allow myself to "believe in" anything', exclaims Ben, the student scientist in the play) and Alexi Kaye Campbell's *The Faith Machine* (2011) embraced the idea 'that we all need some kind of faith even if we can no longer subscribe to the dogmas of organised religion'.[36]

Other key plays include Abi Morgan's *27* (National Theatre of Scotland and Royal Lyceum Theatre, Edinburgh, 2011), which took both the tenacity and potential obsolescence of religious faith as its central theme, and Chris Goode's autobiographical *God/Head* (Oval House, London, 2012), which recounts a sudden, overwhelming and mystifying religious experience that shakes the premises of Goode's previously assured atheist self-identity.[37] Finally, mention should also be made of Jez Butterworth's award-winning *Jerusalem* (Royal Court, 2009), arguably the defining British play of the first decade of the new millennium.[38] Attempting to account for the play's appeal and his own extraordinary success in performing the central role of Rooster, the actor Mark Rylance commented in interview (in words that recall Ravenhill's comments quoted earlier):

> [t]he general story that people are told about the meaning of life at the moment is all logical and scientific and rational and economic [...] You have to spend every minute of your day paying your bills and thinking about them. [...] People are starving for deeper meaning and deeper stories in life because the church isn't really answering that any more. People are hungry for something in life to have more depth or sensation than the story they're told they have to worry about all the time.[39]

While 'crisis in belief', then, has arguably constellated as the defining trope in British playwriting for at least half a century, I want to argue that, over the past decade or so, there has been a perceptible shift in emphasis from the *objects and contents* of belief-systems (especially ideological belief-systems: their advocacy, contestation, the effects of their loss), to an exploration – often with metaphysical impetus – of the *existential dynamics and viability* of belief as a foundational premise for personal identity and action in the world. This latter point is exemplified in two recent plays, one by veteran playwright Howard Brenton, the other by relative newcomer Lucy Prebble.

From his earliest years in theatre, Brenton has examined the power of belief to motivate revolutionary action. These preoccupations have clustered around religious subject matter in his later work. For example, *Anne Boleyn* (Globe Theatre, London, 2010) presents the royal protagonist as a woman in the vanguard of the English Reformation: the religious schisms fermenting in Anne's world will lead eventually, as Brenton makes clear, to the English Civil War. In the closing moments, the ghost of the executed queen takes centre stage and surveys the audience with coquettish disdain: 'Dear demons of the future,' she says, 'what I can't tell ... what I can't tell is what you believe. You're so strange to me, as I must be strange to you.'[40] It is a moment resonant in irony: the source of Anne's 'strangeness' to a contemporary audience is not her manifestation as a ghost but the very fact of her religious conviction. With belief at the centre of her identity, Brenton's Anne Boleyn incarnates that lost value of 'commitment' that draws Ravenhill to religious art.

Brenton's earlier play *Paul* (Cottesloe Theatre, London, 2005) is note-worthy precisely because it establishes belief and faith as differential categories of religious experience. The piece recounts how the faith of Saint Paul endures even beyond his discovery that the fundamental tenets of Christianity are flatly untrue, including the resurrection of Christ.[41] Brenton's colleague David Hare describes this play as one of the most 'remarkable of the new century': 'Paul knew that perhaps Jesus hadn't risen from the dead, but [...] he wanted the idea of the resurrection to transform humanity.'[42] At the play's conclusion, in a kind of iconic theatrical condensation of the arguments of Cornwell outlined earlier, Paul's vision of – his *faith* in – an historical legacy of transformation through Christian teaching is seen to outlast his belief in the divinity of Christ.

In spite of its wholly different style and context, Lucy Prebble's barn-storming *Enron* (Royal Court Theatre, London, 2009) also anatomizes the collapse of belief.[43] Set in the high-rolling world of City finance, Prebble draws on real-life events surrounding the mesmerizing growth of the Enron corporation throughout the 1990s to the point of its spectacular bankruptcy in 2001. The play is important because it casts belief as the key alchemical agent within the citadels of global capital. In various onstage vignettes, Enron executives are seen to trade things that don't exist, their financial strategy is based on non-existent profits, and the rituals of business are choreographed, according to a stage direction, '*like a religious cult*': in the world of *Enron*, to be sure, the corporation has replaced the cathedral as the locus of fervent belief.[44] After the meltdown of the company, the City Analyst Sheryl Sloman steps forward to concede that the entire market economy depends on a projection of belief to the point of mass delusion:

> I believed in Enron. Everybody did. I told people again and again to keep buying that stock and I kept rating it and supporting it and championing it like it was my own child. And people say, how could you? [...] Well. You get on a plane, you don't understand exactly how it works, you believe it'll fly [...] Well, it's like that. Except. Imagine if the *belief* that the plane *could* fly was all that was keeping it in the air. It'd be fine. If everybody believed. If nobody got scared.[45]

Withdrawal of belief leads, inevitably, to the exodus of capital and the seismic collapse of the company.

The plays recounted above, and the arguments put forward by various public figures in the 2010 *NS* debate, establish 'belief' as a pressing and volatile site of epistemological scrutiny at the present conjuncture. In the next section, in order to frame my subsequent analysis of theatre, I turn to the French atheist philosopher, André Comte-Sponville, whose recent writing addresses a critical question arising from these debates: can an ethics of 'commitment' (as Ravenhill puts it) be resourced from a conception of faith pertaining 'beyond' belief?

'Atheist spirituality' and chronos time

Comte-Sponville's *Book of Atheist Spirituality*, published in 2006, is notable for its insistence on interpolating a notion of 'spirituality' within the parameters of atheist philosophy.[46] The most important chapter, 'Can There Be an Atheist Spirituality?', defines 'spirituality' against metaphysics as follows:

> we are finite beings who open on to infinity. It can now be added: we are ephemeral beings who open on to eternity, and relative beings who open on to the absolute. This 'openness' is the spirit itself. Metaphysics means thinking about these things; spirituality means experiencing them, exercising them, living them. This is what distinguishes spirituality from religion, which is merely one of its possible forms.[47]

The starting point for Comte-Sponville's analysis is his recollection of a momentous incidence of 'openness' that took place years ago, during a nocturnal trip with friends into the French countryside. This memory forms the autobiographical lynchpin of his analysis: '[m]y mind empty of thought, I was simply registering the world around me – the darkness of the undergrowth, the incredible luminosity of the sky, the faint sounds of the forest'.[48] Then, suddenly:

> What? Nothing: everything! No words, no meanings, no questions, only – a surprise. Only – this. A seemingly infinite happiness. A seemingly eternal sense of peace. [...] It was like truth without words, consciousness without ego, happiness without narcissism.[49]

His words ('consciousness without ego') recall those of the Man in Greig's *Pyrenees*, awakening in the snow. This epiphanic moment prompts Comte-Sponville to elaborate 'spirituality' as a particular quality of intense lived experience, a kind of embodied metaphysics. In a crucial passage, he turns to the classical philosophy of Stoicism because he sees his own experience reflected in a particular conception of time that the Stoics tried to analyse.

In their philosophical writings, the Stoics articulate two designations of time represented by the Greek words 'aion' and 'chronos'. Comte-Sponville defines aion as time 'that we can divide up and measure, waste and be wasted by': it is the etymological root of the word 'age' (via the Latin 'aevum').[50] Aion time, then, is conceived as an unending linear flow, often symbolized as a river. It is worth noting at this point that the word 'secular' originates from the Latin 'saecularis', meaning 'living in the world' or 'belonging to the state'.[51] Aion, then, is time experienced in saecularis – that is, time regulated by collective social organization (the state) which submits us to its discipline. Stoic metaphysics attest repeatedly to the total evacuation of the present in aion time, the relentless relegation of time into historical past and indeterminate future.

But there is another kind of time in Stoic philosophy that lifts human beings from the injunctions of saecularis and renders the present as replete and immanent. This is chronos time, which Comte-Sponville defines as 'concrete time that is the universe's present, the universe as presence'.[52] When we experience the 'presence' of chronos time, there is a 'dissolving of the ego' that awakens in the human subject a sense of interconnection between self and environment, of oneness with the cosmos, which the novelist Romain Rolland described famously as 'the oceanic feeling' – a term taken up by Sigmund Freud and critiqued in his *Civilization and its Discontents* (1930).[53] Comte-Sponville favours the term 'plenitude': '[m]oments when nothing is missing, when there is nothing to either wish for or regret and when the question of possession is irrelevant (because having is replaced by being and doing)'.[54] He notes how the promise of 'plenitude' has exerted a pull on Western philosophy from its origins: the Greeks aspired to 'ataraxia', or absence of disturbance, Lucretius writes of 'pura voluptas' – 'pure pleasure' (desire without lack), while Baruch Spinoza and Henri Bergson perceive time in terms of an expansive 'duration'.[55]

The Stoics were extremely attentive to chronos time because they perceived its focus on the present to be a stimulus for ethical action. Towards the end of the second century CE, Marcus Aurelius, the Stoic philosopher and Roman Emperor, writes in his *Meditations* of the transience of life: 'the swiftness with which all things vanish away: their bodies in the world of space, and their remembrance in the world of time'.[56] The sense of dismay one might feel at the inescapable prospect of entropy and death is countered by the human capacity to fully experience the moment and to create from it ethical value: '[t]o see the things of the present moment is to see all that is now, all that has been since time began, and all that shall be unto the world's end; for all things are of one kind and one form'.[57] By insisting on the potential of each moment to create this kind of transformation in outlook, Marcus Aurelius carries the baton forward from his Stoic antecedent, Seneca. In his treatise *On the Shortness of Life* (49 CE), Seneca defines the ideal state of life as firmness of mind, what the Greek philosopher Democritus termed *euthymia* (or 'tranquillity'), and it is the experience of *euthymia* that sets in motion an impulse to embrace others.[58] Indeed, Stoicism remains one of the staple theoretical foundations of modern cosmopolitanism: Seneca's moving *Consolation to Helvia* (42 CE), written in exile to his mother, is a testament to *euthymia* directed towards an embryonic cosmopolitan world-view – 'there can be no place of exile within the world since nothing within the world is alien to men'.[59] Marcus Aurelius expresses the same sentiment with a more grandiose flourish: '[t]he Mind of the universe is social'.[60]

For Stoics like Seneca, chronos time resists the expropriation of time in the worldly realm of saecularis. It thickens our experience of the present by opening up the moment to the bedazzling sublime. Comte-Sponville's espousal of 'fidelity' has its provenance in the peace, mutuality and 'plenitude' he experienced in the 'perfect pause' of the rural twilight. It is this inspiration that prompts him, in his book, to urge the abandonment of terms like belief and faith altogether. He contends, instead, that '[f]idelity is what remains when faith has been lost':

> Faith is a belief; fidelity, in the sense I give the word, is more like an attachment, a commitment, a gratitude. Faith involves one or several gods; fidelity involves values, a history, a community. The former calls on imagination or grace; the latter on memory and will.[61]

It is interesting to note the reappearance here of Ravenhill's word, 'commitment'. What separates atheistic 'commitment' or 'fidelity' from religious 'faith' is the former's insistence on 'values' that are actualized through discursive processes of 'history' and 'memory', rather than divine ordination or supernatural 'grace'. For Comte-Sponville, 'fidelity' emerges into the phenomenal realm via the agency of chronos time. In the final section of the chapter, I examine how a selection of plays has evoked a theatrical corollary of chronos time precisely in order to release 'fidelity' as an affect of performance.

'There's only now': chronos time and theatre

'In recent years,' argues Lance Gharavi, 'there has been a growing, though still nascent, energy in scholarship focusing on the intersections of religion and theatre/performance.'[62] This scholarship includes the launch in 2009 of the academic journal *Performance and Spirituality*, edited by Edmund B. Lingan, and the 2011 publication of Gharavi's ground-breaking collection *Religion, Theatre, and Performance: Acts of Faith*.[63] In this section, however, I want to focus on a particular aspect of the research over the past decade that has attended to the capacity of performance to incubate a sensorium of emotion proximate to the 'oceanic feeling': in her important 2005 book, for example, Jill Dolan sets out an argument for what she calls 'utopian performatives'.[64] These are defined as 'small but profound moments in which performance calls the attention of the audience in a way that lifts everyone slightly above the present, into a hopeful feeling of what the world might be like if every moment of our lives were as emotionally voluminous, generous, aesthetically striking, and intersubjectively intense'.[65] The upsurge of optimistic feeling described by Dolan brings the 'utopian performative' within the ambit of Stoic chronos time: indeed, the 'utopian performative' marks the *ostension* of chronos time into the domain of theatrical representation.

In terms of staging, the 'utopian performative' often signals a departure from the illusionist dispositions of naturalist theatricality. Classical naturalist theatre aspires to place the determining causes of behaviour and social phenomena under objective scrutiny. It is a scientistic form, influenced by the environmental determinism of Charles Darwin and the secular positivism of none other than Auguste Comte, with deep roots in the empirical epistemologies of the nineteenth century. While it is certainly the case that naturalist dramaturgy pushes into metaphysical territory, deploying a range of theatrical strategies in so doing, the pleasures of watching a naturalist stage production derive, in large part, from the audience's immersion in the spectacle of the observable world that is reproduced, often with photographic exactitude, onstage. Related to this, the emplotment of naturalist playwriting tends to follow the protocols of aion time (that is, socially regulated linear time) while the scenography of the naturalist *mise-en-scène* replicates the world of saecularis (the public and domestic spaces of actuality). In contrast, the heightened theatricality of Dolan's 'utopian performative' calls for an altogether different stage aesthetic that pushes beyond mimetic illusionism. As Daniel Gerould comments, in an insightful essay exploring *fin-de-siècle* Symbolism and its impact on modern theatre practices, '[t]he present-day return to the spiritual in art, characteristic of both the visual and performing arts in the first decade of the twenty-first century, is part of a recurrent pattern, a periodic need to go back to eternal sources and re-establish contact with the deepest well-springs of human creativity in the sacred, however that may be defined'.[66] In a number of contemporary plays, to a lesser or greater degree, the turn towards metaphysical or 'spiritual' content puts pressure on the apparatus of naturalist stagecraft where the exodus from naturalism reflects a drive to attune the temporal and spatial economies of theatre to the poetics of chronos time.

This arbitration of chronos time through the rupture with naturalism is exemplified in *A Thousand Stars Explode in the Sky*, jointly authored by David Eldridge, Robert Holman and Simon Stephens (Lyric Hammersmith, 2010). The play focuses on domestic life and is broadly naturalistic in style.[67] However, the apocalyptic premise of the play – that a so-called 'cosmic string' is exploding across the universe, as it did in the first thousandth second of creation – withdraws any prospect of a future from the characters, thus placing theatrical emphasis on the ever-depleting here and now. In his review of the Lyric production, Michael Billington describes the play, in a revealing formulation, as 'full of terminal stoicism and grace'.[68] He uses 'stoicism' in its colloquial sense – meaning patient forbearance in the face of adversity – but his comment captures the existential tenor of the play. The impending global annihilation forces a revaluation of individual and family life to the effect that past and present, self and universe, become harmonized in the play's image structure. One example of the implicit unity between micro- and macrocosm occurs when the eldest brother William (who is terminally ill) notes the serendipitous fact that the cosmic string resembles the Cava Filter that has been put into his own ailing heart.[69] In a later and more fantastical scene, the chronology of linear time is wholly up-ended when the youngest son, Phillip, cradles the infant baby who is, in fact, his mother.[70] The images of tenderness and reconciliation garner theatrical force at the end of the play when family members gather outside their homestead, move closer together, and offer words of gratitude as the stars across the night sky begin, finally, to explode.[71]

The experience of chronos time is also evoked in Dennis Kelly's *The Gods Weep* (Hampstead Theatre, London, 2010). The play is based on *King Lear* but set in a world of corporate infighting where economic competition and physical brutality have become indivisible, and where capitalist exchange has colonized the deepest levels of subjectivity.[72]

As rival factions attempt to seize power, the threats of ambitious executives like Gavin are constituted in the linear logic of aion time: 'Do not reject the realities of this time as it is the logical conclusion of previous times and I strongly advise you to begin to understand that. Now.'[73] Yet the dramatic trajectory of Kelly's play recalibrates the experience of what 'now' might mean outside of the temporal matrix of capitalist production. The Lear-like protagonist, Colm, is the formidable chief executive of a multinational company. He becomes marginalized in the escalating conflict and, as a result, his body is denuded of its corporate enigma (as his enemy, Richard, puts it: '[w]ithout the respect and fear we gave him he's just a sack of shit').[74] Colm's physical destitution causes his perception of time to become acutely concentrated – 'I feel like I've lived a thousand years in a single second' – until, finally, seeking shelter in the open countryside, he enters an uplifting state of tranquillity, or *euthymia*.[75] At this point, his language echoes that of Comte-Sponville when recalling his moment of 'openness' in the countryside:

> I began to realise that this tip, this piece of rock being pushed up through the hillside had once been the bottom of the ocean.
> And I was struck still by time.
> And I suddenly saw my infinitesimal place in it [...]
> And I felt such a peace, such a weightlessness, that I had never known since I was a boy.[76]

Colm's reverie of 'plenitude' contrasts with the emotional dysfunction of his alienated son, Jimmy. In a rhetorical tirade earlier in the play, Jimmy imagines using technology to preserve forever the moments he spends with the object of his infatuation, Beth:

> I began to fantasise about being cryogenically frozen so that this moment could last forever, and I began to think that this was potentially a great business opportunity, so you could stop time at this perfect moment and stay there, and all the pain that you've experienced since that moment had happened, the feeling that your soul had been sucked out by a vacuum cleaner and shredded into tiny pieces, the waking up in a panic and screaming, the feeling that you now had liquid shit for blood, those feelings might disappear and you might be able to stay in that perfect moment.[77]

Jimmy's breathless desire to eternalize the moment recalls the brother's forlorn declamation to his sister in *Pornography*, while his envisioning of the 'perfect moment' is a variation of Bob's 'perfect pause' in *Chekhov in Hell*. These impossible yearnings direct attention back to the social vicissitudes that all of these characters seek to escape: in Jimmy's case, the force of his frustration overwhelms the impulse to love, reducing it to a phantasmic 'business opportunity'. A similar thematic is evident in Ravenhill's *Shopping and Fucking* where emotions are routinely transacted or interpolated through commodities and cash. The violent drug dealer, Brian, for example, can only actualize his compassion by watching, as he puts it, the 'really terrific moment. Quite possibly the best moment' in *The Lion King*.[78] For a man who insists that the opening words of the Bible are 'Get. The Money. First', Disney is the singular portal to momentary and sentimentalized apotheosis.[79]

The quest for transcendence within scenarios of physical and psychological extremity is a recurring feature of the new writing for theatre that emerged in the 1990s. Sarah Kane's plays, in particular, demonstrate, in the words of Laurens de Vos and Graham Saunders, a 'predilection for the metaphysical over the material'.[80] Her work is populated with characters whose encounter with violence leads them to assert the integrity of the moment. In the opening sequence of *Blasted*, Cate states that she '[f]eels like I'm away for minutes or months sometimes, then I come back just where I was [...] Time slows down.'[81] She is referring (like Anna in *Pyrenees*) to her epilepsy but the remark also, of course, prefigures the temporal dissociation of the play, particularly in its apocalyptic second half. The explosion of the mortar bomb transforms the hotel room into a war zone, catapulting *Blasted* from the recognizable world of saecularis to a dystopic landscape where time becomes unquantifiable: the passing of time seems at once to accelerate (indicated by the series of snapshot tableaux of Ian's corporeal and psychological torment) and to consist in an unending, non-differentiable present that leads Ian, in exasperation, to pour vitriol on reassuring narratives of belief: 'No God. No Father Christmas. No fairies. No Narnia. No fucking nothing.'[82] Amidst this cornucopia of misery, Kane's stage directions imply that even the ultimate limit-experience of death is inexplicably reversible: Ian *'dies with relief'* but then, with rain falling on his head, he starts to speak again ('Shit').[83] The expressionist choreography of suffering in these moments bestows an atmosphere of redemption, of religiosity, on the closing scene. Indeed, the final line of the play – Ian's 'Thank you', addressed presumably to Cate – carries the trace of Stoic *euthymia*: it is a fledgling gesture of gratitude, of 'fidelity in the absence of faith'.[84] Kane's next play, *Phaedra's Love* (Gate Theatre, London, 1996) – a blistering and mordant reworking of Senecan

tragedy – concludes with the image of an eviscerated Hippolytus sur-
veying the corpses and body parts around him, before attesting '[i]f
there could have been more moments like this'.[85] Arguably, however, the
most quoted speech in Kane's canon occurs in *Cleansed* (Royal Court
Theatre, London, 1998) when Rod affirms his love to Carl: 'I love you
now [...] I'll do my best, moment by moment, not to betray you.'[86]
Rod's insistence that declarations of love are meaningful only in their
moment of exhortation is reiterated in a scene that follows shortly
after. Having endured torture and Carl's betrayal, Rod intuits love as the
quality of duration across an inexhaustible present: '[t]here's only now.
[...] That's all there's ever been.'[87]

Kane's theatre, with its image-repertoire of physical suffering, carries
the imprint of her theatrical precursor, Howard Barker. Barker's own
gravitation towards what he calls the 'art of theatre' from the mid-
1990s marks a similarly robust attempt to root metaphysical enquiry
in the spectator's experience of momentary time. The splintered and
stylized aesthetic of Barker's 'art of theatre' is intended to unlock
a quality of intensity in the spectator, akin to an act of erotic seduc-
tion, such that the awareness of time passing begins to fall away.
Reflecting on his approach in an interview in 2010, Barker comments
that 'the plays I write now have no time in them at all [... they] remove
time altogether as a concept in the evening'; this, he argues, allows the
performance to coalesce 'moment by moment' through an 'accumulation of scenes, maybe unrelated'.[88] The most ambitious example
of this approach is his millennial epic on metaphysical themes, *The
Ecstatic Bible: A New Testament* (Scott Theatre, Adelaide, 2000). Barker
describes his theatrical reimagining of the Bible as 'a testament not to
the presence of God in the universe but to his absence, consequently
a testament to the absolute solitude of Man' and it takes many hours
to perform, even in abridged form.[89] Barker's 'art of theatre', in this
respect, is an act of defiance against the subjugation of theatre to the
prescriptions of aion time.

Conclusion: 'remnant desire for another world'

In 1994, the Austrian film-maker Michael Haneke released his new film
71 Fragments of a Chronology of Chance. Haneke's work is renowned for
its disruption of narrative linearity, thus compelling the viewer to hunt
for connections between fragmented and apparently unrelated scenes
(such emphatic structural dislocation is also a feature of the new writing emergent in British theatre at this time). In conversation in 2005,

looking back on his extraordinary film, Haneke offers the following rationale for his approach to storytelling:

> In an era when God has ceased to exist, there's a remnant desire for another world. By another world, I don't mean Paradise, but another image of the world. And I believe you can only evoke it by avoiding its portrayal because otherwise it immediately becomes banal. And if you stimulate the desire for it, by pointing to what's false, you've found the best way to evoke it.[90]

It seems fitting to conclude with these comments because they parse the concerns of this chapter. At a time when public confidence in ideological and religious belief-systems has become increasingly embattled, the 'metaphysical turn' in theatre speaks directly to Haneke's 'remnant desire for another world'. As we have seen, this is evidenced in two principal ways: the explosion of new plays that negotiate religious content and/or which probe the ontology, contexts and viability of 'belief', religious or otherwise; and in a pattern of theatrical engagement with chronos time that gives putative expression to what Ravenhill calls 'commitment' and Comte-Sponville 'fidelity'. What emerges is a striking sense of British theatre attuned to the valences of postsecular discourse and well placed to shape this discourse in the years ahead.

Notes

My thanks to Vicky Angelaki, Karen Fricker, Lynette Goddard, Jake Poller, David Wiles and Marilena Zaroulia for their helpful feedback and/or conversation during the development of this research.

 1. D. Greig, *Pyrenees* (London: Faber & Faber, 2005), p. 40.
 2. Greig, *Pyrenees*, pp. 40–1.
 3. Greig, *Pyrenees*, p. 42.
 4. S. Stephens, *Pornography* (London: Methuen Drama, 2008).
 5. Stephens, *Pornography*, p. 32.
 6. Stephens, *Pornography*, p. 36.
 7. D. Rebellato, *Chekhov in Hell* (London: Oberon Books, 2010).
 8. Rebellato, *Chekhov in Hell*, p. 73.
 9. C. Soanes and A. Stevenson (eds.), *Oxford Dictionary of English*, 2nd edn., revised (Oxford: Oxford University Press, 1998, 2006), p. 1104.
10. See C. Brown, 'Campbell interrupted Blair as he spoke of his faith: "We don't do God"', *The Daily Telegraph*, 4 May 2003.
11. D. Cameron (2011) 'Prime Minister's King James Bible Speech: Commemorating the Version's 400th Anniversary', http://www.number10.gov.uk/news/king-james-bible/ (accessed 18 December 2011).

12. Tearfund, *Churchgoing in the UK: A Research Report from Tearfund on Church Attendance in the UK* (Middlesex: Tearfund, 2007).
13. J. Doward, 'Church Attendance "to fall by 90%"', *The Guardian*, 21 December 2008.
14. S. Harris, *The End of Faith: Religion, Terror, and the Future of Reason* (London: Free Press, 2004, 2005); R. Dawkins, *The God Delusion* (London: Black Swan, 2006, 2007); C. Hitchens, *god Is Not Great: How Religion Poisons Everything* (London: Atlantic, 2007, 2008).
15. L. Gharavi, 'Introduction', in L. Gharavi (ed.), *Religion, Theatre and Performance: Acts of Faith* (London: Routledge, 2012), p. 13.
16. Baroness S. Warsi, 'We stand side by side with the Pope in fighting for faith', *The Daily Telegraph*, 14 February 2012.
17. Gharavi, 'Introduction', p. 4.
18. M. Taylor, 'The 21st-Century Enlightenment', *New Statesman*, 21 June 2010, 20–3 (p. 22).
19. Taylor, 'The 21st-Century Enlightenment', p. 22.
20. 'There is a Universal Human Nature', interview with R. Williams, Archbishop of Canterbury, by J. Derbyshire and J. Macintyre, *New Statesman*, 19 July 2010, 30–3 (p. 33).
21. 'There is a Universal Human Nature', p. 33.
22. Gharavi, 'Introduction', pp. 14–15.
23. A. de Botton, 'Not the Messiah', *New Statesman*, 19 July 2010, 40–1 (p. 40).
24. De Botton, 'Not the Messiah', p. 41.
25. A. de Botton, *Religion for Atheists: A Non-Believer's Guide to the Uses of Religion* (London: Hamish Hamilton, 2012). On a related note, see also political philosopher Simon Critchley's historical study *The Faith of the Faithless: Experiments in Political Theology*, also published in 2012, which offers a powerful identification of the religious energies that have imbricated leftist political structures through history. S. Critchley, *The Faith of the Faithless: Experiments in Political Theology* (London: Verso, 2012).
26. M. Ravenhill, 'God is behind Some of Our Greatest Art', *The Guardian*, 14 April 2008. Subsequent quotations are taken from this article.
27. M. Ravenhill, *Shopping and F***ing* (London: Methuen Drama, 1997), p. 64; Gharavi, 'Introduction', p. 10.
28. Quoted by J. Cornwell, 'The Books Interview', *New Statesman*, 14 June 2010, 49.
29. Cornwell, 'The Books Interview'.
30. The Christian scholar Harvey G. Cox argues this point in an insightful Buddhist–Christian academic dialogue published in 2009 (the year before Cornwell's intervention): 'faith as a way of life is becoming more important than belief [...] Belief hovers near the upper, cognitive stratum of the self. It can come and go. [...] But faith locates itself in a deeper dimension. It is a matter of fundamental life orientation.' H. G. Cox and D. Ikeda, *The Persistence of Religion: Comparative Perspectives on Modern Spirituality* (London: I. B. Tauris, 2009), p. x.
31. J. Reinelt, 'The Promise of Documentary', in A. Forsyth and C. Megson (eds.), *Get Real: Documentary Theatre Past and Present* (Basingstoke: Palgrave Macmillan, 2009), pp. 6–23 (p. 13).
32. D. Pautz, *Love the Sinner* (London: Nick Hern Books, 2010).
33. H. Ibsen, *Emperor and Galilean*, adapt. B. Power (London: Nick Hern Books, 2011).

34. M. Bartlett, *13* (London: Methuen Drama, 2011); M. Bartlett, *Earthquakes in London* (London: Methuen Drama, 2010).
35. D. Edgar, *Written on the Heart* (London: Nick Hern Books, 2011); H. Edmundson, *The Heresy of Love* (London: Nick Hern Books, 2011).
36. R. Bean, *The Heretic* (London: Oberon Books, 2011; the quotation is from p. 80); A. Kaye Campbell, *The Faith Machine* (London: Nick Hern Books, 2011; the quotation is from Michael Billington, 'The Faith Machine – Review', *The Guardian*, 1 September 2011).
37. A. Morgan, *27* (London: Oberon Books, 2011); C. Goode's *God/Head* is unpublished.
38. J. Butterworth, *Jerusalem* (London: Nick Hern Books, 2009).
39. M. Brown, 'Jerusalem Fans Queue All Night as the Final Curtain Comes Down', *The Guardian*, 13 January 2012.
40. H. Brenton, *Anne Boleyn* (London: Nick Hern Books, 2010), p. 115.
41. H. Brenton, *Paul* (London: Nick Hern Books, 2005).
42. D. Hare, quoted in 'Howard Brenton: "All writers are ecstatics, which is why we can be seduced by the siren calls of addiction or extremism"', interview by A. Dickson, Review Section, *The Guardian*, 10 July 2010, 10–11 (p. 11).
43. L. Prebble, *Enron* (London: Methuen Drama, 2009).
44. Prebble, *Enron*, p. 58.
45. Prebble, *Enron*, p. 98 (original emphasis).
46. A. Comte-Sponville, *The Book of Atheist Spirituality*, trans. N. Huston (London: Bantam Books, 2006, 2008).
47. Comte-Sponville, *The Book of Atheist Spirituality*, p. 136.
48. Comte-Sponville, *The Book of Atheist Spirituality*, p. 156.
49. Comte-Sponville, *The Book of Atheist Spirituality*, pp. 156, 158.
50. Comte-Sponville, *The Book of Atheist Spirituality*, p. 172.
51. See http://www.etymonline.com/index.php?allowed_in_frame=0&search=secular&searchmode=none (accessed 7 May 2013).
52. Comte-Sponville, *The Book of Atheist Spirituality*, p. 172.
53. Comte-Sponville, *The Book of Atheist Spirituality*, p. 150. Also, S. Freud, *Civilization and Its Discontents*, trans. D. McLintock (London: Penguin Books, 1930, 2010).
54. Comte-Sponville, *The Book of Atheist Spirituality*, p. 164.
55. Comte-Sponville, *The Book of Atheist Spirituality*, pp. 164, 172.
56. Marcus Aurelius, *Meditations*, trans. Maxwell Staniforth (London: Penguin Books, 1964, 2004), p. 15.
57. Aurelius, *Meditations*, p. 68.
58. Seneca, *On the Shortness of Life* [includes *Consolation to Helvia* and *On Tranquillity of Mind*], trans. C. D. N. Costa (London: Penguin Books, 1997, 2004), p. 73.
59. Seneca, *On the Shortness of Life*, p. 45.
60. Aurelius, *Meditations*, p. 55.
61. Comte-Sponville, *The Book of Atheist Spirituality*, pp. 21, 22.
62. Gharavi, 'Introduction', p. 1.
63. Also: in October 2010, the scholars Joshua Edelman, Kim Skjoldager-Nielsen and Farah Yeganeh announced the foundation of a new working group, 'Religion and Performance', at the International Federation for Theatre Research (IFTR); the group held its first meeting at the IFTR conference in

Osaka, Japan, in 2011. A one-day symposium titled 'A Make Believe World' was held at the Chelsea Theatre in London on 13 November 2010, organized as part of the theatre's SACRED season. The publicity for the event echoes the comments quoted earlier from Sheryl Sloman in *Enron*: '[t]he current financial crisis has revealed how the system upon which we supposedly all depend is itself dependent upon how much we believe in it. Value is an expression of belief: if we believe that such and such a company, or bank, possesses the assets it purports to possess, then, in effect, those assets exist. The moment we stop believing, the value of the company or bank collapses, and the assets in question cease to exist.' See http://www.chelseatheatre.org.uk/index.php?pid=104/ (accessed 25 October 2010). A two-day conference on 'Performance and Mystical Experience' took place on 16–17 May 2013, hosted at Queen Mary, University of London, by the Theatre, Performance and Philosophy Working Group of the UK's Theatre and Performance Research Association (TaPRA).

64. J. Dolan, *Utopia in Performance: Finding Hope in the Theater* (Ann Arbor: University of Michigan Press, 2005).
65. Dolan, *Utopia in Performance*, p. 5.
66. D. Gerould, 'Return to Tradition: The Symbolist Legacy to the Present-Day Arts', in Gharavi (ed.), *Religion, Theatre and Performance*, pp. 172–84 (p. 172).
67. D. Eldridge, R. Holman and S. Stephens, *A Thousand Stars Explode in the Sky* (London: Methuen Drama, 2010).
68. M. Billington, 'A Thousand Stars Explode in the Sky', *The Guardian*, 13 May 2010.
69. Eldridge et al., *A Thousand Stars Explode in the Sky*, p. 6.
70. Eldridge et al., *A Thousand Stars Explode in the Sky*, p. 46.
71. There is some evidence of a concurrent move towards spiritual, apocalyptic and eschatological subject matter in contemporary art house cinema: for example, in *Melancholia* (2011, written and directed by Lars von Trier, Zentropa Entertainments), a fraught family gathering is set against the impending collision of a planet with the Earth, while *Tree of Life* (2011, written and directed by Terrence Malick, Plan B Entertainment) intersperses the story of a family's loss of a son with cosmic sequences of creation and destruction in the universe.
72. D. Kelly, *The Gods Weep* (London: Oberon Books, 2010).
73. Kelly, *The Gods Weep*, p. 85.
74. Kelly, *The Gods Weep*, p. 81.
75. Kelly, *The Gods Weep*, p. 107.
76. Kelly, *The Gods Weep*, p. 162.
77. Kelly, *The Gods Weep*, p. 42.
78. Ravenhill, *Shopping and F***ing*, p. 6.
79. Ravenhill, *Shopping and F***ing*, p. 85.
80. L. De Vos and G. Saunders (eds.), *Sarah Kane in Context* (Manchester and New York: Manchester University Press, 2010), p. 3.
81. S. Kane, *Complete Plays* (London: Methuen Drama, 2001), pp. 10, 22.
82. Kane, *Complete Plays*, p. 55.
83. Kane, *Complete Plays*, p. 60.
84. Kane, *Complete Plays*, p. 61.
85. Kane, *Complete Plays*, p. 103.
86. Kane, *Complete Plays*, p. 111 (italics in original).

87. Kane, *Complete Plays*, p. 142.
88. H. Barker interviewed by D. I. Rabey, 'TheatreVoice', 10 May 2010, http://www.theatrevoice.com/ (accessed 18 December 2011). Subsequent quotations from Barker are taken from this recording.
89. H. Barker, *The Ecstatic Bible: A New Testament* (London: Oberon Books, 2004), p. 7.
90. Interview with M. Haneke, *71 Fragments of a Chronology of Chance*. Dir. Michael Haneke (Wega Film, 1994; DVD release, 2009). The interview with Haneke is part of the DVD 'Extras'.

3
Politics for the Middle Classes: Contemporary Audiences and the Violence of Now

Vicky Angelaki

In a statement when her tenure as the new artistic director of the Royal Court Theatre, succeeding Dominic Cooke, was announced, Vicky Featherstone observed: '[t]hese are challenging times. Now more than ever we need places where reflection, question and visceral experience can elevate the daily and the private and remind us of our humanity and universality'.[1] She added: '[t]he fearlessness and skill of our playwrights, [... along] with our complex and thrilling contemporary culture is a powerful combination'.[2] Further to the key staples of the perspective she brings to a seminal new writing venue within the United Kingdom but also further afield, responsible for fostering the careers of many major playwrights of the recent and contemporary period, Featherstone used her early statement to reinforce the very significance of the playwright. At a time when debates relating to heavily mediatized performance and presumed tensions between playwright and director auteur are raging on, Featherstone allowed no ambiguity as to where she positions herself artistically. Through her words she emphasized that the Royal Court is not scared to advocate and support the primacy of the author. 'It is the playwrights who find a story, form and structure [...] and who breathe the life into ideas, thus demanding their urgent work be realized for an audience', Featherstone continued.[3] The sentiment, reinforced by her first event announcement, the playwright-driven season *Open Court* in the summer of 2013, may seem like stating the obvious, as though Featherstone is not postulating anything controversial, but this is not the case. We know that there has been an unusual kind of conflict imposed on the terms drama and performance in contemporary theatre studies and the emergence of non-text focused forms of representation has sometimes functioned to establish an artificial binary between the two. Still, surely the goal is to trace how they work together, rather than against one another; to conceptualize them not as irreconcilable opposites, but as allies in the process of achieving richer signification and deeper layers of meaning, leading to more avenues of involvement for contemporary audiences. This chapter asks how today's theatre might work to engage and challenge us, not coercing us into perceptual participation but activating it intersubjectively through ambitious languages – spoken, visual and sensory – of representation. It also traces how, as playwriting has redefined itself, these languages may have the capacity of being both complex and intuitive, establishing immediacy and contact with the individual spectator.

Featherstone was not alone in reasserting the strongholds of the Royal Court, but rather follows in a tradition of similar recent statements, arguably aiming both to realign and defend the theatre's artistic mission. For the purposes of this chapter the Royal Court acts as vehicle for the argument, but the proposition is less exclusive to the specific theatre than a means of gauging what new writing venues have been gearing themselves towards; which territories artistic directors have been keen to both defend and cultivate. In 2007, Cooke, himself recently announced as the new artistic director of the Royal Court, argued for the importance of not turning a blind eye to the fact that it is 'liberal middle-class' spectators that typically form the average audience member of his institution, but also of theatres more broadly.[4] The statement was firm and powerful, but at the same time gave rise to different interpretations. Cooke's tenure has been somewhat haunted by the statement, for two main reasons: on the one hand, it seemed to propose a drastic detour from working-class lives, with which the Royal Court had been unambiguously associated in the modern stage of its history, post-1956.[5] On the other hand, Cooke's words appeared to legitimize the primacy of privileged experience, instating an orthodoxy of the status quo, which the repertoire would in turn placate on stage.

Cooke has been repeatedly reproached on this early statement in press and scholarly discourse, but more than anything it was the range of plays performed at the Royal Court during his term that did the talking most convincingly. Further to the subversive energy of many of the pieces concentrating on middle-class lives, Cooke stresses that work by Bola Agbaje (*Gone Too Far!*, 2007) or Roy Williams (*Sucker Punch*, 2010), as well as the Theatre Local scheme, also affirms the importance of staging the working-class experience.[6] What such creative decisions achieve, I would argue, is to broaden the audience base and attempt to educate what constitutes the larger portion of the Royal Court's spectatorship. As Cooke notes, '"[t]he liberal position is often a very simple and uncontested position because most liberals only mix with other liberals"'.[7] Cooke also underlines the significance of a play like David Eldridge's *In Basildon* (2012), which concentrates on '"the world of the lower-middle class, the skilled working-class Tory, [which] has not been on stage that much"'.[8] It is also worth mentioning that the remainder of Cooke's original statement alluded to the fact that this turn towards middle-class experience was actually neither aimed at reassuring that specific portion of the audience that they were not being neglected, nor at playing it safe. It was, rather, a hint that the plays commissioned would deliver a resonant depiction of middle-class lives, so as to instigate a ground of interrogation.[9] At the Royal Court, but also further afield, this needed to entail a sensory and thought process that would materialize in a sphere other than that of quiet condoning of accepted practices and ideologies. This act of challenging the spectator would carry the potentiality of a revisiting of the individual experience, along with own decisions and (in) actions in the social realm. As Cooke later qualified, it seemed essential to him '"to build audiences in different sectors from the traditional middle class"'.[10] This implies the questioning of what *middle classness* connotes today, a diversification of the spectatorship, and catering for the different spectators comprising an audience in a nuanced way, beyond facile acts of equating audience with an unidentified mass, functioning at the level of a common denominator. Within each assumed group there is the seed of individuality, as much undoubted as it has been neglected.

If the action of enhancing spectatorial experience by instigating new acts of perception is key, the theatre space as a premise (in both senses of the word) needs to be conceptualized much more broadly than simply the space of enterprise – however implicit a material transaction may be – or a host that performs its part but fails to establish a sense of enduring connection. If the theatre is aiming for the full experience, the total act of embedding itself in the audience's consciousness, then it must also find more immediate and practical means of forging that connection. 'We no longer live in the days when playwrights wanted to explain to their audience the truth of social relations and ways of struggling against capitalist domination', writes Jacques Rancière in the context of addressing the formal innovations that have encouraged spectatorial questioning and involvement.[11] It is an attractive thought, not necessarily entirely applicable to all that we see on UK stages today, but it captures the right sentiment. It is the notion of fostering exposure to a performance that will not be one-sided, but will engage us in the act of evaluating our lives without pretending to occupy a moral ground higher than what constitutes the everyday. It is reductive to talk about one 'political theatre' and more purposeful to trace how new 'political theatres', emerging from the work of playwrights of the recent and contemporary period, some of whom are discussed in this chapter, have seemed cognizant of the imperative Rancière's text discusses. This is the ground on which symbiosis materializes – it is where and how the audience ultimately becomes part of a theatre's life narrative and vice versa. The theatre, as space and cultural forum, ought to foster the debate – to feel not as a closed up entity but as the flexible ground of intercommunication, to which it is always worth returning.

For Cooke, such questions involved forging a deeper physical connection between spectator and the space of performance, the building itself as vessel of the radical. A point he makes about the Court resonates for many of the venues we visit: it '"can be an intimidating building and people need to feel they belong there"'.[12] Intimidation of course, inflicts not only physical but also conceptual and emotional barriers; until the point where a given theatre infuses itself into our lives, our relationship will remain tentative. Any theatre that boasts cutting-edge relevance must work hard to break the façade between itself and the spectator. This is even more important considering that the act of theatre watching is still ridden with the paradoxes of the audience's privileged perspective, though they are, at the same time, immersed in darkness and lulled into a state of passivity. Nor is theatre-going, even today, free from the remnants of social privilege and upper/middle-class humanism. The act of establishing relationships rather than transactions, of allowing ourselves, as spectators, to become convinced that the theatre has the right, authority and perspective to tell us something about our lives today hinges on a reciprocal commitment. It demands the willingness on the part of the organization to appreciate and respond with dare to the different tissues in our constitution of viewing and reacting. Similarly, it expects us to abandon the safety of convention and venture into the unknown territory of active seeing, which harbours many eventualities. The questions that emerge strongly are how the theatre can achieve this, encouraging the spectators into a genuine state of interconnection, even if the path to it involves potentially dangerous acts of watching and whether there is a kind of play that is best positioned to meet this imperative.

The unpredictable theatre

We know that intention and outcome do not always meet in the theatre – authorial intentionality has been widely attacked by writers and audiences alike, also because the play is a living beast that may feel ferocious on the page but tame on the stage (and vice versa). It is helpful to consider Dan Rebellato's reflections on recent Royal Court plays in the context of Cooke's statement, especially as the list of plays staged during his term is characteristically diverse, representing drastically different types of theatre, from the mystifyingly surreal to the unapologetically popular.[13] As emerges from Rebellato's text, the line, on the one hand, between middle-class critique through a play that reflects middle-class mores and, on the other, middle-class placation through a play that over anything achieves middle-class entertainment, is very thin; sometimes imperceptible even for the playwright. The question becomes all the more pressing: how can we be satisfied that a given play commissioned by a leading new writing venue – whether or not their artistic directors made any statements similar to Cooke's – can achieve resonance beyond a shared grin and nod?[14] If theatre-makers and spectators share the need for more than a brief moment of self-reflection, it seems that beyond producing acquiescence or shock, contemporary artistic expression should possess the affective power that can encourage active perceptual recognition that at least bears the potential for change.

Thus we could move to more aware states of watching and begin to partake in our own emancipation as theatre audiences. The term 'emancipation' has been at the forefront of theatre studies largely due to Rancière's seminal work. It signifies the process we ought both to pursue and submit ourselves to as aptly as few other words could. Rancière defines emancipation in performance as 'the blurring of the boundary between those who act and those who look; between individuals and members of a collective body'.[15] Rancière's position echoes the phenomenological emphasis on intersubjectivity, which I have discussed elsewhere – a negation of assumed antagonisms that will result in the collapse of unworkable binary constructs, such as stage/audience, personal/collective, aesthetic/political in our everyday and performance experience equally.[16] Beyond staging effects that generate momentary unease, perceptual questioning in the context of art has the potential of becoming holistic, with the play operating on the level of affect so as to produce a fuller sensory and intellectual reaction, causing barriers between the real and imaginary to collapse. In this chapter I will consider examples of plays that deliver an enduring affect in diverse ways, functioning to establish a point of raw contact with the audience through intermixing, even conflicting variables. The shared narrative in the work of the playwrights considered is a drive towards conceptual and/or formal experimentation. It does not always succeed; sometimes an experiment can hover mid-air in performance, in that indeterminate territory between burgeoning impact and failure to launch. It is fascinating, though, to follow what transpires when experimentation does yield results, obliterating the stage–auditorium distance and causing the old familiar binary of performer/spectator to collapse. These are the plays that, as Rebellato writes, submit 'middle class life to unflinching scrutiny in a way [...] very uncomfortable for its audience', the very certitude of that life 'violated, captured and questioned'.[17] This is not to say that a play needs to be radically unconventional to accomplish results but rather to suggest that with conventionality come a set of limitations that double up as risks. Rebellato relays an anecdotal remark by a playwright whose work formed part of the recent Royal Court era: '"I'm beginning to think I've written a boulevard comedy"', s/he admits.[18] Popular theatre is not a villain in this scenario – appealing to a wide base of spectators means the play can transcend barriers that other theatre forms stumble upon, to set up a process of exchange with the spectator. However, the issue remains that a 'boulevard' play may not necessarily possess the full set of triggers that will stir our collective civic and spectatorial conscience, propelling us into a process of self-questioning. The anecdote also underlines the fallibility in anticipating not only audience response, but the behaviour of the play itself the moment it evolves from text to public event.

The uncertainty and frustration that follow initial surprise at mispredicting audience reaction are also vividly documented by playwright Dennis Kelly. He recounts his own experience when, as an artist/citizen disillusioned with his government's position in the War on Terror he felt compelled to produce a play like *Osama the Hero* (Hampstead Theatre, 2005):

> I was angry. [...] I wrote it into the play, [...] I didn't really know what I was doing, but I did my best. [...] I knew that once people saw my argument, things would change. [...] I fully expected a withdrawal from Iraq and Afghanistan by the end of the year.[19]

Kelly reveals his dismay at the failure of the work's direct and immediate impact with compelling honesty, not only in connection to the specific text but also with references to other timely plays driven by the need to make a strong statement. When Kelly discusses *Love and Money* (Royal Exchange Manchester, 2006), his formally ambitious and textually potent attack against the materialist and consumerist frenzy that set the stage for the major financial collapse of the late 2000s, he becomes even more explicit:

> This, I thought, will change everything. This must mean something. But in 2008 the credit crunch happened and now we're all fucked. If only you bastards had listened.[20]

Certainly *Love and Money* is the kind of prescient play that occasionally happens as if to confirm a sixth sense that might be unique to theatre as artistic form and forum. Still, in any way predic(a)ting audience response is a major challenge for practitioners and scholars alike. This relevant comment by Helen Freshwater is worth quoting at length:

> although it is possible to speak of 'an audience', it is important to remember that there may be several distinct, co-existing audiences to be found among the people gathered together to watch a show and that each individual within this group may choose to adopt a range of viewing positions. [... A]wareness of these differences requires that statements about audience response be framed in careful, conditional terms, sensitive to tendencies to generalise about audiences and to judge them without evidence.[21]

The difficulty, also voiced in Kelly's comment, is unquestionable. What I propose is that in attempting to address how urgent pieces of theatre interact with spectators, we take into account the shared mental, social, textual and physical spaces likely inhabited by the audience during performance. A form of social consensus established on the givens of a historical moment may act as compass towards a plausible framework on reception and interpretation, especially if a consideration of the techniques and affects of the play as text and performance piece figures in the analysis. This ought to hinge more on what the play enables than what the playwright envisioned.

Material crutches of the middle classes

Love and Money would have been more likely in 2010 (and beyond) than 2006. Once the dust of the financial crisis had begun to settle, its full extent of repercussions became plainly visible. Today Kelly's play is painfully resonant in terms of its content. Meanwhile, its episodic form does not yield to expectations, nor does it allow for reduced speed in its dizzying countdown to the innocent start to a couple's life that never materializes into happiness. The play brutally stages self-destruction with verbal and emotional violence that bursts through the seams, depicting its characters' awkward hunger for human contact on the same scale as their incessant craving for material possessions. The latter sharply contrasts with their moral emaciation. In seven scenes/episodes the utter devastation of Kelly's characters, never likeable yet entirely plausible, becomes a deluge that holds the power to overwhelm the collective conscience. It may be difficult to speak of what each audience member makes of the play in performance, but this is not a piece of theatre that one can easily ignore. It is a text that takes a peering look at contemporary modes of cynical object, emotion and corporeal consumption, without falling in the trap of cynicism itself.

Cynicism, Kelly adds, is not the point, so it is not surprising that there is a sense of helplessness and need for compassion emanating from multiple directions throughout the play.[22] The act of consuming is broached as another form of addiction; a battle that is always more easily lost than won. Kelly is cognizant of the sensitivities involved when he unequivocally states that social change can originate in the theatre, affecting lives on an individual and collective basis.[23] However, he clarifies, dramatic impact does not necessarily lead to drastic actions; this is not how the spectator's involvement in the concerns explored in the play should be measured.[24] The question of how we may conceptualize the imprint of a play on the spectator, if not on such terms, finds its answer in the writer's own responsibility towards the audience. Memorably accounted for in, among other texts, Howard Barker's *Arguments for a Theatre*, this responsibility rests not with reassuring the spectator, but with putting him/her through paces that may appear relentless, but ultimately encourage a more honest engagement with the text/performance piece.[25] If honesty does justice to the audience, it is also key for the playwright, who, as Kelly notes, must be fully invested in the process of attaining it in theatrical representation.[26] To take on the big issues affecting local and global communities at a social, political and historical crossroads is a noble cause, but it needs to translate across the stage; it must spark a truthful and enduring connection with the audience.

Kelly's play presents, in reverse chronological order, human crises articulated on a financial basis. The second scene features a young woman's grief-stricken parents, identified only as 'Mother' and 'Father' in a way that evokes their ordinary, generic status. We hear them negotiate mourning in unlikely terms, as they recount their daughter's burial.

Without forcing the issue the text conveys early on how materialist obsessions have seeped through to the very core of things, as even death becomes a commodity to be assessed, like any other:

> FATHER: [...] I mean it's two thousand five hundred pounds for the plot alone for the space, for the dirt that you put your daughter inside.[27]

This line is the culmination of a memorable digression in the dialogue, where the couple recall the amounts they have had to spend on their daughter's grave, including VAT.[28] Conversation soon moves to their income and whether it even afforded them the luxury for such extravagance. Their exchange eerily recollects neoliberalist allegiances to profit: '[e]arly eighties, eight-bedroom house' the Father recalls.[29] The suggestion is made that it was the failure to sustain a certain lifestyle that caused their daughter's, Jess's, emotional dissatisfaction to escalate. When the Mother laments not having 'the killer instinct' she regrets the decision to move from that house; this act, synonymous with sliding down the property and social ladder, also 'broke her [daughter's] heart'.[30] Jess went on to develop a shopping addiction and receive treatment for it though she eventually succumbed, in a way consumed by her habit: after ingesting pills, in what we may take as desperation prompted by buyer's remorse, she is found unconscious by her husband, David. Rather than attempt to save her, he decides to induce her death, forcing her to consume vodka. The motive behind the act is neither disdain nor pity, but the realization that once Jess has died her colossal debts will evaporate. The text eradicates any suspicion that David is driven by anything beyond self-serving materialism: earlier on in this opening scene we learn about him coveting an expensive car – one that he would now be able to afford.

Kelly's play captures the human liabilities of applying VAT on lives and emotions. As individual life stories become irretrievably fractured, the one grand narrative that survives dismantling is the shared history of debt, imprinted on consciences exactly as it is recorded on bank statements and credit scores. Spending and debt are the two factors permanently conditioning the characters' responses to life, as well as to one another. When Jess witnesses a crime on Oxford Street, David's primary concern is not the event itself or his wife's state of shock, but demanding an explanation as to why she was in Oxford Street in the first place, if not to shop. The insights into Jess's state of mind are those moments in performance that abundantly prove Kelly is not taking a detached approach to his subject matter. In the play's final, climactic scene, depicting the moment when Jess has agreed to marry David, we are offered such an unadulterated account. In the midst of personal happiness, Jess is debating the meaning of life in a long monologue, where she contemplates

> JESS: [...] maybe it's about more than just I have this pot of stuff here and that's got more in it than your pot of stuff over there [...] a world that is more than numbers and quantities and saving [...] a world that is flesh and bone.[31]

In a moment that merges naivety with profound clarity, Jess reaches a state of perception more astute than David's problematic rationalization of personal value on the basis of financial capacity. Of course, Jess is not blameless: even here, when her desire for David and their shared life enables her to reach an almost transcendent state, the sum of her wishes is eventually subsumed under a broader scope of lust, this time over 'things':

> JESS: Not saying I don't want things though.
> [...]
> I want things for us. [...]
> I want it to be a little like it's supposed to be, [...]
> a bit like it is on the telly.[32]

If artistic directors have aimed at bringing middle-class spectators to the theatre, re-presenting their realities in ways that would actively encourage them to invest their attention, then plays like Kelly's were crucial to such efforts. *Love and Money* directly reflects its context: the flurry of lifestyle and/or property television programmes in the late 1990s and early 2000s, the excesses of product placement and the gradual idolization of certain living standards as presented to the viewing masses. This was accompanied by systematic acts of establishing, through such programmes, artificial needs at the centre of the individual's existence; of rendering it impossible to recollect a state when designer clothes or furniture did not form part of everyday lives. *Love and Money* could have been a comedy, feeding off consumerist frenzies and incessant buying as a cure of personal and collective neuroses in the thriving capitalism of the late twentieth and early twenty-first century. Though the play does have its humorous moments, it never treads anywhere near the space that Rebellato writes about – that tacit transition of the witty, society-focused play into boulevard comedy. What Kelly achieves with this play is significant: a seamless complementation between form, content and the contemporary, experiential sensation of human lives, where balances are continuously threatened by the same principles societies had built lives on. The play creates a dialogue that audiences can feel part of, without relying on a traditional narrative: it both involves spectators and disallows empathy.

Love and Money was written in the years before the markets crashed, when personal spending habits were still causing individuals and households to spiral out of control, albeit without yet reaching their full public implications. Today it is as common to speak of shopping addictions and the vicious circle of overspending habits as the legitimization of coveting designer products, elevated to (pseudo-)ideology in itself, had become a few years earlier. In a study published the same year as the premiere of Kelly's play, Maurya Wickstrom explores the invasion of everyday lives by consumerist culture and the practices through which repetition becomes performance in its own right.[33] She uses case studies of megabrands and products, whether physical spaces such as stores or actual items, such as clothing, in a way that enables us to trace how the conceptual space that a brand occupies has the ability to colonize hearts and minds. This both promotes the ideal of consumption as noble goal and propagates the character of the faithful consumer. Wickstrom's discourse has a distinctly phenomenological slant, which serves well to capture the degree of embodied investment in this process on the part of the individual. As the text suggests, conglomerates prey on a consumerist urge spurred on by a lifestyle craving: '[the] corporeal desire to be like others, to take on shapes and forms unlike one's own'.[34] This is the rule, but there is also another side to the process of internalizing patterns of consumption and behaviour: more than becoming someone else, that mesmerizing figure of the wholesome mediatized Other that we aspire to attain for ourselves, there is also the projection of one's own ideal self. What becomes the aspiration is that idolized life not directly experienced, but haunting us with its plausibility. Ever so slightly out of reach, it taunts through its material availability and precipitates sacrifices for its attainment. They do not feel grave at first – but their consequences become obvious as the debt deepens. This is what we observe in *Love and Money*: particularly Jess, but also David, are keen to meld into their ideal selves, happier, wealthier, better put-together, whatever the fiscal or emotional cost.

The characters are more similar than they appear, as Kelly's text cleverly dismantles stereotypes of 'opposites attract' or the assumption that the pair of 'Jess/David' is a viable binary. The reverse chronological order serves to show how, in his end and her beginning – ironically signposting the beginning and end of performance respectively – David finds his materialist self whereas Jess falls in the allure of her romantic ideals. Kelly's text implies that these poles lie dangerously close within each person, leading to eventual implosions, experienced physically and mentally. Performing one's better self ideologically, or striving to escape individualism, can be as artificial a construct as acting out consumerism – and at the same time just as deeply rooted, carefully articulated into one's DNA.

Wickstrom suggests that individuals tacitly accept that the narrative that sustains the desirability of brands and simulated lifestyles is not realistic, but are willing to buy into the process anyway.[35] It is fair to suggest that there is a degree of complicity. Even if we do inhabit the era of the emancipated consumer, can we exclude the possibility that, at a certain level and considering that other grand narratives – politics, religion, the economy – have faced challenges or outright failed, brands emerge as the more enduring, safe and familiar narrative, bolstered by the ubiquitous rhetoric of advertising? In *Love and Money* we notice this when Jess channels all her longing for life into more possessions, or when David frames a higher state of being in the terms of owning the expensive car. Label names fall torrentially from the dialogue through-out the play: Eurostar, Disney, Xanax, Smirnoff, Audi, [Nissan] Micra, Terence Malone forks, Müller Fruit Corners, Nokia. The play exposes how companies have come to stand for emotions, states of minds, actions and, of course, social class or category, imposing their existence on our everyday lexicon in a now internalized way that we may fail to notice, and essentially branding it. As Wickstrom writes, this unabated exposure to brands aims at equating our identity to theirs; to devel-oping, I would add, a relationship of contingency between the two, where one relies on the other to survive, though certainly not in an equal or similarly rewarding way.[36]

The interspersion of brand names in the text, of these loaded words that seem to form the background of everyday communication though they are, in fact, its pivot, is as noteworthy as Kelly's choice to cite numbers in full words. A number may have limited signification; it may fail to establish contact – visually, aurally – in the way that a word does. Kelly's use of words to denote numbers may be more meaningful on the page, but it conditions the play on the stage as well, as the corpo-reality of the phrase qualifies utterances more fully: they take substance through delivery to slow down speech. They also add monumentality to what is said and the full extent of what it entails, especially when this is insurmountable debt. Words over numbers imprint a lingering affect on the spoken traces of meaning and create the ground for it to be communicated viscerally and intersubjectively, as for example, when David speaks of his wife's 'seventy thousand pounds worth of debt'.[37] Amounts do not come across as immaterial signifiers, displaced from their human cost and reduced to their numerical value, mere sums to be dealt with; they acquire the gravitas of physically experienced realities. Dramatically, this too contributes to how plays like *Love and Money* work to establish the state of inhabiting what Wickstrom calls 'a hybrid constitution of commodity, brand and human', of taking on different roles in an ongoing process of moral, emotional and material trade.[38]

Debts, dependencies and crises

The notion of debt persists not only in relation to proliferating cycles of material consumption, but also to emotional ties, while the family emerges as the ultimate problematic structure, its crises as confining as those of capitalism. Aleks Sierz accurately observes '[t]he depressing idea of the distressed family as metaphor for a nation torn apart by class', but it is important to remember the complicity in the process: the voluntary submission to the capitalist narrative.[39] In a number of contemporary plays capitalism and family are treated as closely interwoven narratives. We do not need to think of extended families either – close-knit circles in fact reveal how, more darkly, the failure to play up to one's class is the ultimate cause of dramatic implosion. *Orphans* (Traverse, Edinburgh, 2009), also by Kelly, or *Tusk Tusk* by Polly Stenham (Royal Court, 2009), are two such examples.[40] Intuitive in capturing a feeling of shared anxiety, the plays not only appeared in the same year but also very close to one another. Formally, they are not necessarily unconventional. Thematically, though, they are particularly intriguing since both their plots are as much plausible as hinting at the surreal. At a certain point in performance both plays abandon reality for a turn towards the nightmarish and even dystopian, before they reach their suspended endings. In very different ways, they both engage with frighteningly dysfunctional families in a world where adults have failed and 'growing up' proves to have been an empty promise.

In other cases, the feeling of awkwardness finds its way into plot and structure: in work such as that of Simon Stephens and particularly *Wastwater* (Royal Court, 2011) and *Morning* (Traverse, Edinburgh, 2012) the overwhelming feeling of inhabiting a strange new world that repeatedly cancels defence mechanisms is embedded in the characters' very makeup and even in that of the play.[41] Stephens's preoccupation with a malignant adolescence in the context of a failing or absent family, or both, is also recurring and it is followed by a constant need for consumption, whether emotional, materialist, physical or sexual. At the same time, in one of Martin Crimp's recent texts, *Play House* (Orange Tree Theatre, 2012), the sense of not reaching the promises of adulthood regardless of whether they have been theoretically achieved is dominant, from the title of the play to the characters' efforts to – literally – build a life around them through the objects that they own.[42] They deploy them as staples of their lives, as ways of punctuating their narrative, which eventually fails desperately.

The notion of stunted growth is, in such plays, removed from its financial context and returned to the everyday level of emotional experience, making it plain for us to see how the insipid play rules of capitalism have led to the trivialization of daily life, reducing it to a form of game, where the promise of success looms once a series of targets are achieved. In these plays we see characters longing for that next stage in their lives, but having to cope with ever changing conditions. They can never be entirely certain what is expected of them, therefore they surrender to spasmodic reactions in their present, to which they appear irretrievably confined. They cannot return to the womb, but they cannot break away from their beginnings either. What makes these plays groundbreaking is not simply that the womb – that semblance of family, or of an origin – that may have been there to begin with was flawed, but that through the metaphor of family ties they communicate the notion that habit, and the inherent characteristics that hold us back, are equally a matter of nature and nurture. The latter relies on our inherited environment, whose patterns we subconsciously reproduce. What we are witnessing in these radical crisis plays are the vivid after-effects of the previous generation's failure to sustain the malfeasances of capitalism. It is also the devotion to an institution which mimicked the protective features of a supportive system, only to be exposed as a vacuum. At an awkward time in theatrical representation, where even radical forms seem to have been overused and new stage languages – visual and verbal – have needed to be developed to capture the formerly unthinkable, these plays emulate the challenge through their form and content.

The pivot in *Orphans* and *Tusk Tusk* is the shared bond between or amongst siblings, who, in the absence of parents, allow their lives to be driven by their insistence to not be legally separated, at all costs. In both plays we observe the child role-play the parent: in *Tusk Tusk*, Maggie and Eliot, 14 and 15, make desperate and not altogether successful attempts to provide for their younger brother Finn, aged seven; in *Orphans* Helen is fiercely protective of her brother Danny, who even seems to take priority over her husband and child. Both plays capture the anxieties that originate in the failure of capitalism, albeit in different ways. For Stenham's characters, it is a quest for an alternative mode of survival – if adults are no longer part of the narrative, these children seek to discover how preservation instincts might guide them to a more primal state of being, where they fend for themselves, freed from institutions (whether we take these to be parenthood or a welfare state) whose authority has been discredited. The children's mother has disappeared, with a genuine sense of precariousness over her safety hovering over the entire play as a threat. Through extreme survival tactics the children manage to fend off adults for most of the play, until they are confronted by two family friends, the couple of Katie and Roland, in the finale. They decide to stay with one another rather than follow the adults into a world of reason and compromise. In one brief moment, they share an understanding and choose to make an entry into that primal, alternative world – their own, shaped only by the instinctive urge to remain together. While leaving these failed adults – an unhappily married couple maintaining the pretence – behind, the siblings seem tacitly aware that they are transitioning into a more honest state of being, an adulthood of their own that will potentially allow them to determine the rules. It would be an almost hopeful conclusion to the play if Stenham did not have her characters borrow the tools of the old world to break into the new one, but Eliot steals Roland's credit card to fund the escape. Ultimately the play does not allow us to feel satisfied that there can be a reinvention of the same saturated exchange system; if there is such a thing as a message, perhaps it is that idealism comes with its own set of limitations. The confines of middle-class existence seem ever pervasive.

The inability to break through and away from inherited norms as well as physical and mental predispositions in the context of the family to an extent mirrors our wider social conditioning – our place and part in the narrative of community and society and the invisible ties that bind. It is a sense that, through different formal and thematic means and to a different effect also emerges from Mike Bartlett's *My Child* (Royal Court, 2007) where the boy is a coldly mature character, in stark contrast to the emotional immaturity of adults, presented as entirely helpless at handling challenges with the familiar tools at their disposal.[43] Kelly's *Orphans* plays on this motif – the imperceptible difference and depressive bonds between childhood and adulthood in a society that seems to foster a kind of reverse growth, symbol of any rational narrative based on 'normal' order having been overturned. The young people, or children, seem to carry the seeds of hope for a different set of choices – but these are crushed in the realities of social or familial conditioning and the repetition of the cycle appears inevitable. In Bartlett's *Contractions* (stage version Royal Court, 2008), the title cleverly brings together both a financial and biological term to emphasize the physical impact of capitalism on family lives.[44] The point is painfully made when it is strongly suggested by the text that Emma kills her baby (from a relationship with a co-worker) once it is made clear by her Manager that having anything shared between the two will jeopardize their careers. Even Helen's pregnancy in *Orphans*, an element of promise and potential and a step further away from an injurious past, is in a precarious state at the end of the play – its very survival uncertain.

Orphans is a claustrophobic text, making us highly aware that there is an entire world outside 'the house', symbol of social status, as much as compromised safety. More importantly, all we need to know about this world is confined within the four walls of the house – the same feeling we derive from Stenham's play, but differently orchestrated. Danny has committed a racist crime, but Helen's instinct is to protect her brother by implicating her own husband in the cover-up. Until this point of no turning back, the couple had been doing everything the way they were supposed to so as to comfortably inhabit the middle-class ideal. Kelly's play hints at an innate predisposition spreading endemically though contemporary society – the seemingly spontaneous but really conditioned desire for upward mobility. Helen's instinct to protect Danny is equally fierce to that of protecting all she has achieved in the way of material possessions and social standing: her family is the emblem of that effort as well as the key bargaining tool in coercing her husband to cooperate. The two cannot be separated. What the play makes brutally obvious through its references to the violence that Danny's victim sustains, as well as through the visceral language throughout, which bleeds equally with desperation and loyalty, is that the sequence of choices we make in the social realm are as definitive and prone to chain reactions as one's DNA. We observe this in Helen's resolve to attack anything that threatens either, implications notwithstanding.

Though it touches upon some of, arguably, contemporary Britain's most persistent vices, intolerance, insularity and materialism, unabashedly attaching them to the aspirational middle classes, *Orphans*, like *Love and Money*, is not interventionist theatre per se. Its role is not to prevent, but to instigate a dialogue against the compliance of what is unfolding around us, not solely as spectators, but also as citizens. Such plays negotiate, like Stephens's *Wastwater*, *Morning* and even *Pornography* (Deutsches Schauspielhaus, Hamburg; Festival Theaterformen; Schauspielhannover 2007), the obsession with attaining something larger than the life already there, which has proved dissatisfactory, as it will not yield all that the characters had deemed to deserve.[45] In plays like Stephens's or Kelly's, the motive is never noble – self-preservation comes at a high cost. The emergent emphasis on childlike adults and the representations of young people or adolescents on stage, reflecting one of life's most awkward and at the same time promising stages, becomes the perfect metaphor for capturing that state of not quite inhabiting the life one wishes, but also being unable to disregard that it seems so attainable. Like Tantalus, these characters observe their bountiful surroundings within painfully close distance, but always slightly out of reach.

Conclusion

Moving away from the outwardly violent plays of the 1990s, a time when changing politics and the new millennium propagated the feeling of transitioning into a new state of more informed being, plays such as those discussed here capture the awkwardness in the anti-climax that followed in the 2000s and 2010s. This was rudely underlined by global events such as the financial crash.[46] There was no longer a 'big thing' to aspire to; no unifying narrative, or at least not an inspirational one. Representation became more subdued in what it actually showed, but increasingly frightening in what it expressed in the underlying tissues of the play. A bare, almost imperceptible quality entered the stage, haunting the empty spaces of discourse and causing a genuinely threatening sensation to materialize. Such plays, then, are, in reality, neither miscalculated nor naive, but texts that develop intuitive affinities to their space and time. These are plays that serve to trigger doubt within the audience, gently causing the metaphorical ground beneath our feet to shift a little, so as to gradually bring us to the point of realizing that what has been developing in our societies is a rather substantial crack. But playwrights such as those mentioned here rarely shock, or proclaim to hold the answer and, for this reason, they do not outright intervene. Their texts, in their own way, deal with the violence of now, a point in time when the individual is as much inundated by desires, whether materialist or not, as by the facts that prohibit him/her from attaining them – in most cases financial limitations. It is not a world devoid of emotion – but it is one where there is a kind of impotence at negotiating it. What these plays show is that with love and information does not always come understanding, and certainly not a shared narrative. It is a point that all these plays make in their own specific ways and that Caryl Churchill's recent full-length piece, playing with these very words (*Love and Information*, Royal Court 2012), clearly puts forward.[47] In its case, the sense of struggling to maintain clarity and maturity in thought and action is vivified through the shape of the play, which throws rational reasoning into disarray through its torrent of scenes – reflecting stunted thought and reaction in more ways than one. Plays such as those discussed here brazenly take on the violence in being confronted with more than one can process in societies where numbers and the old familiar system they functioned to uphold no longer add up. To sufficiently capture this violence of the present moment, which is manifest as much in private as in public episodes, many of today's cutting-edge playwrights appear to have arrived at the implicit understanding that explosions do need to inform the narrative, but there also needs to be a distinct turn towards the minimal and visceral on stage. At a time of emotional and fiscal austerity the theatre no longer relies on the extravagant spectacle, or even plot, to make its point.

In the past few years and especially since 9/11 and 7/7 the current generation of theatregoers has been identified not so much by means of shared attributes of age, gender or even class, but of social conditioning and a spiralling web of political developments that have made it increasingly difficult to retain a sense of cohesion. As Sierz notes, 'for a moment, at the turn of the millennium, the British middle classes seemed set to remake their world'.[48] In the years that followed, however, '[o]ptimistic Britain had turned fearful'.[49] We have seen many plays representing what may be described as directly political theatre, taking on the very real battles unfolding in actual time on government or military sets. Despite the specific remits of new writing powerhouses, what surfaced from many directions has been the need to return power to the audience, bringing them back to the theatre as a collective space of thought and action. The latter is not necessarily carried out in the public domain, but at the level of the spectator, as individual, in his/her private life, which forms part of the collective. We have seen an emergence of plays dealing with these private lives – not to placate, not to entertain, certainly not to assuage any concerns. The play confined within four walls became the new political forum, collecting the baton from where it had been left by playwrights such as Harold Pinter but with the tensions of today's world introduced into the mix. This kind of theatre recognized that to do politics, a term comprising the word 'polis' or city, one needed to look at precisely what the set of citizens of different origins, convictions, beliefs and incomes were being faced with in our time. A stronghold of the middle/upper classes – much of the time for practicalities alone, the cost of a ticket, no less – the theatre has all too often reassured or entertained them, but to activate the trigger of thought and response, to foster a higher level of perception and involvement, the theatre needed to challenge these audiences in different ways.[50] Political theatre acquired a form beyond verbatim, docudrama or tribunal and beyond direct reference or address, however affective such types of performance have the power to be. Representation became darker and more elliptical to take on the everyday shadows of a failing system: materialism, consumerism, debt or their offspring of inadequacy and dissatisfaction – and their persistent ghosting of lives. This, too, is politics.

Ambitious plays such as the ones discussed here and, more broadly, those that have in recent years been staged in theatres dedicated to new writing respond to and reflect the fear and hesitation at entering a world so systematically destroyed, whether by previous generations, capitalism, class systems or a seemingly unbreakable streak of misinformed choices. They achieve this by transposing the same overarching feeling to the audience through form and content, refocusing the gaze on them, so as to flesh out the necessary interrelationship between performer and spectator, play plot and our life narratives – albeit not in a predictable or patronizing way that might impose a false sense of distance. Plots deal with the violence in our contemporary moment, not just outwardly expressed in acts of aggression, but inwardly experienced in a private sense of frustration and disillusionment that spills onto the collective. The violence is not always immediately felt; it is more a persistent impression that lingers – the uncertainty in a world receding unto itself as resources, whether natural or economical, diminish; the indebtedness and liability to a system of exchange that has demanded everything and encouraged excesses but failed to show any accountability; the guilt that comes with subscribing to what has led to the emerging chaos and the ongoing, awkward attempt to make sense of it and assert some form of authority.

These concerns have been shared by playwrights and audiences alike, leading theatrical representation in our time to – however subconsciously – aspire to and reach new heights of resonance. In an entirely uncalculated way, these plays cohabit a concern with that state of, returning to Rancière's term, emancipation and at what cost it may be attained – not material, but ethical and emotional. Except, here, cost also implies the not always easy, or pleasant process to which we must surrender ourselves as bold spectators that rise up to the challenge of uncompromising theatre. Performing oneself as member of a problematic family unit becomes a reflection of the greater narrative – of the discontent within the broader social system of which we form part. In such plays the thread between the two is tangible: established institutions equally susceptible to their flaws within the capitalist context that has usurped them. The character, like the spectator, is an active participant in this process of attempting to attain emancipation – in the case of such texts, this is aptly staged as constantly trying to graduate into maturity. With all its flaws and uncertain outcomes, it remains a worthwhile pursuit, for dramatists and spectators alike.

Notes

1. The statement, in which all following references originate, was made by Featherstone as part of the Royal Court's press release, 'Royal Court Theatre Announces Vicky Featherstone as Next Artistic Director' (11 May 2012), http://www.royalcourttheatre.com/ (accessed 12 May 2012).
2. 'Royal Court Theatre Announces Vicky Featherstone as Next Artistic Director'.
3. 'Royal Court Theatre Announces Vicky Featherstone as Next Artistic Director'.
4. A. Smith, 'Cooke Unveils First Season at Royal Court', *The Stage*, 6 February 2007, http://www.thestage.co.uk/ (accessed 11 November 2007).
5. Smith, 'Cooke Unveils First Season at Royal Court'.
6. Cooke quoted in D. Maxwell, 'The Man Who Built Jerusalem', *The Times* Arts, 8 February 2012, p. 11.
7. Cooke quoted in Maxwell, 'The Man Who Built Jerusalem'.
8. Cooke quoted in Maxwell, 'The Man Who Built Jerusalem'.
9. See Smith, 'Cooke Unveils First Season at Royal Court'.
10. Quoted in M. Billington, '"You can sniff the best plays after half a page"', *The Guardian*, 7 November 2007, http://www.guardian.co.uk/ (accessed 13 May 2012).
11. J. Rancière, *The Emancipated Spectator*, trans. G. Elliott (London: Verso, 2009), p. 11.
12. Quoted in Billington, '"You can sniff the best plays after half a page"'.
13. D. Rebellato, 'Théâtre des boulevards' (2012), http://www.danrebellato.co. uk/ (accessed 7 May 2012).
14. For example, Nicolas Kent, whose tenure as artistic director of the Tricycle Theatre (where the repertoire has been a beacon of urgency and resonance in theatrical representation) was characterized by success as much as longevity, made the following statement as he was approaching the end of his time at the helm of the venue: '[i]f you ask me what the most important quality in life is, I'd say empathy. What theatre does best is to put people in other people's shoes. I suppose theatre is a quest for total empathy', quoted in

S. Jeffries, 'The Saturday Interview: Nicolas Kent', *The Guardian*, 18 February 2012, http://www.guardian.co.uk/ (accessed 15 March 2012). Statements such as this emphasize the need for new writing to instigate processes of perceptual engagement, recognition and understanding.

15. Rancière, *The Emancipated Spectator*, p. 19.
16. For a discussion of intersubjectivity in contemporary theatre within a phenomenological framework see V. Angelaki, *The Plays of Martin Crimp: Making Theatre Strange* (Basingstoke: Palgrave Macmillan, 2012).
17. Rebellato, 'Théâtre des boulevards'.
18. Rebellato, 'Théâtre des boulevards'.
19. Quoted in Anon., 'Dennis Kelly Opens the Stückemarkt', 10 May 2012, *Theatertreffen Blog*, http://www.theatertreffen-blog.de/ (accessed 1 June 2012).
20. Quoted in 'Dennis Kelly Opens the Stückemarkt'.
21. H. Freshwater, *Theatre & Audience* (Basingstoke: Palgrave Macmillan, 2009), pp. 9–10.
22. Quoted in 'Dennis Kelly Opens the Stückemarkt'.
23. Quoted in 'Dennis Kelly Opens the Stückemarkt'.
24. Quoted in 'Dennis Kelly Opens the Stückemarkt'.
25. H. Barker, *Arguments for a Theatre* (Manchester and New York: Manchester University Press, 1989, 1998). A representative example of Barker's position can be found in 'Honouring the Audience', pp. 45–7.
26. Quoted in 'Dennis Kelly Opens the Stückemarkt'.
27. D. Kelly, *Love and Money*, in *Dennis Kelly: Plays One* (London: Oberon Books, 2008), p. 222.
28. As Aleks Sierz observes, '[...] Dad is able to overcome his sense of loss for long enough to calculate the VAT on his daughter's gravestone', see A. Sierz, *Rewriting the Nation: British Theatre Today* (London: Methuen Drama, 2011), p. 109.
29. Kelly, *Love and Money*, p. 222.
30. Kelly, *Love and Money*, p. 222.
31. Kelly, *Love and Money*, p. 283.
32. Kelly, *Love and Money*, p. 286.
33. M. Wickstrom, *Performing Consumers: Global Capital and Its Theatrical Seductions* (London and New York: Routledge, 2006).
34. Wickstrom, *Performing Consumers*, p. 2.
35. Wickstrom, *Performing Consumers*, p. 2.
36. Wickstrom, *Performing Consumers*, p. 3.
37. Kelly, *Love and Money*, p. 216.
38. Wickstrom, *Performing Consumers*, p. 8.
39. Sierz, *Rewriting the Nation*, p. 167.
40. D. Kelly, *Orphans* (London: Oberon Books, 2009); P. Stenham, *Tusk Tusk* (London: Faber & Faber, 2009).
41. S. Stephens, *Wastwater and T5* (London: Methuen Drama, 2011); S. Stephens, *Morning* (London: Methuen Drama, 2012). For detailed references to Stephens's ways of subverting the norms of playwriting to convey the tensions in our exchanges and society see D. Rebellato, 'Wastwater' (2011), http://www.danrebellato.co.uk/ (accessed 7 May 2012). Rebellato writes, indicatively: 'I say he's exploring the complexity of sincerity. [...] At the risk of naivety, of being undramatic.'
42. M. Crimp, *Play House and Definitely the Bahamas* (London: Faber & Faber, 2012).

43. M. Bartlett, *My Child*, in *Mike Bartlett: Plays 1* (London: Methuen Drama, 2011).
44. M. Bartlett, *Contractions*, in *Mike Bartlett: Plays 1* (London: Methuen Drama, 2011).
45. S. Stephens, *Pornography* (London: Methuen Drama, 2008).
46. The 1990s and especially the influence of the period on emerging forms in British theatre are thoughtfully covered in R. D'Monté and G. Saunders (eds.), *Cool Britannia?: British Political Drama in the 1990s* (Basingstoke: Palgrave Macmillan, 2008), allowing the differences in the set of circumstances experienced by societies and of course audiences then and now to emerge.
47. C. Churchill, *Love and Information* (London: Nick Hern Books, 2012).
48. Sierz, *Rewriting the Nation*, p. 106.
49. Sierz, *Rewriting the Nation*, p. 107.
50. For a discussion of the reach and affordability of theatre, see L. Gardner, 'Theatre Tickets: Who Can Afford Them?', *The Guardian*, 25 September 2012, http://www.guardian.co.uk/ (accessed 26 September 2012).

4
Language Games and Literary Constraints: Playing with Tragedy in the Theatre of Caryl Churchill and Martin Crimp

Elisabeth Angel-Perez

Among the most innovative experimental dramaturgies of the turn of the millennium are those resorting to constrained writing: 'verbatim theatre', composed of a montage of straight-from-life declarations or political speeches (such as David Hare's *The Permanent Way*, examining the privatization of railways in the United Kingdom, or *Stuff Happens*, focusing on Tony Blair's decision to follow the United States of America in the war in Iraq), which certainly ranks as one of the major attempts at redynamizing political theatre. Plays based on language games, of Wittgensteinian inspiration, such as those initiated by Tom Stoppard in *Dogg's Hamlet, Cahoot's Macbeth*, and continued by the playfully tragic plays of Caryl Churchill or Martin Crimp, are particularly stimulating and inventive.

Constrained theatre is not a widespread practice. The best example of a constrained play can be found in the work of Georges Perec: his play *L'Augmentation*, first created in German as *Wucherungen*, then translated into French for Marcel Cuvelier's production in 1970, sets the rules of the game. The play explores and exhausts all the possible ways of asking for a rise in wages. As such, it provides a very stage-worthy version of the 'Exercises in Style' practised by Raymond Queneau. Although constrained theatre was a marginal practice, its influence was stimulating enough and led, across the Channel, to the creation in 1991 of the OuTraPo by Stanley Chapman, Queneau's translator, in London, after the model of the OuLiPo (Ouvroir de Littérature Potentielle). The OuTraPo (Ouvroir de Tragicomédie Potentielle) gathers such dramatists as Stoppard and, as I wish to argue here, may account for the dramatic strategies used by Churchill and Crimp in some of their most experimental plays.

To choose constrained writing reads as a way of acknowledging the crisis of language in our post-Adornian world. Theodor Adorno's essay 'Kulturkritik und Gesellschaft', published in *Prisms* (1955), explicitly condemns traditional forms of representation: Adorno's 'to write a poem after Auschwitz is barbaric', even though revised by the author himself in his *Negative Dialectics*, opens the way to postmodernist *aporia*. Maurice Blanchot's statement about the impossible linearity of all narratives as early as in *The Infinite Conversation* (1969) as well as his further exploration of the subject in the 1980s makes it clear that the codes and modes of writing that were valid 'before', have become obsolete and language can no longer be a vehicle for the humanist project that characterizes language by essence.[1] 'We come *after*', George Steiner strikingly asserts at the beginning of his seminal study *Language and Silence*.[2] Tragedy, such as it was being convincingly written before the philosophical *aporia* of the mid-twentieth century, can no longer express the complex tragic feeling of our time. If dramatists such as Edward Bond or Howard Barker endeavour to reconceptualize tragedy (see Barker's 'Theatre of Catastrophe' and later 'Art of Theatre') while remaining within the genre and drawing new contours for it, others hold that tragedy can no longer work and that one has to elaborate new modalities for expressing the tragic. In the wake of Samuel Beckett and Friedrich Dürrenmatt, dramatists prone to deriding the world export the tragic feeling towards theatrical modes which are not likely to welcome it, such as farce, or grotesque tragi-comedies, as well as explore the tragic potentiality of the inadequacy between form and content.

Constrained writing consists in situating the guiding principle of a text not within but outside of it.[3] It will be my contention here that abdicating the obsolete form of tragedy, which carries with it the great romantic project based on the 'natural' adequacy between form and content, and resorting to constrained theatre may well be a way of inventing a new tragic mode. Literary constraints make it clear that textual essentialism – the fact that one may think a text contains its own truth and the author is the undisputable master of it all – is no longer acceptable: what gives the text its *ontos* is the act of reading, and the act of reading is easily guessed to be not within the text but, rather, in its 'without'. The OuLiPo and, in theatre, the OuTraPo envisage literary constraints as a means of giving back some legitimacy to language and literature thanks to mathematics. When George Steiner affirms that we have entered a 'post-linguistic era', he foregrounds the illegitimacy of a language no longer able to speak and which one can no longer trust. Mathematics, and, in particular, types of mathematics that have to do with serialization, appear as a trustworthy alternative, a way of prompting logic back into a logos that seems to have gone mad. 'Procedurality', to use Marjorie Perloff's concept, consists here in subjecting verbal language to a mathematical rule alien to it so as somehow to rehabilitate language.[4] Using literary constraints, therefore, is simultaneously a way of exposing the necrosis and failure of verbal language and a means of overcoming this loss and bereavement. 'Procedurality', this playful over-fabrication of the text, may well be seen as the indispensable condition for addressing the question of tragedy in our postmodern age.[5]

Churchill and Crimp, very much in the wake of Stoppard at his most Wittgensteinian, resort to constrained literature so as to propose a playful yet irrevocably tragic sort of theatre, a kind of theatre playfully able to reveal the inhumanity of humanity and the linguistic and ethical disaster of modernity. An analysis of their most formally challenging plays shows us how literary constraints, by exiling the truth of the text into something exterior to the text, do not only confirm the incapacity of language to go on as before, but also, through the highly original reading compact they settle with the reader-spectator, delocalize the tragic to inscribe it in the sphere of playfulness. Therefore, playful literary constraints become the very locus of tragedy.

As well as writing plays abiding by the main rules of traditional dramaturgy, Crimp therefore writes theatre 'for a world in which theatre itself has died' and, consequently, needs to be reinvented. Crimp's theatre is polymorphous and amphibological. It displays an interest for all the ingredients of conventional dramaturgy while at the same time stepping out of the frame and repudiating such components as characters, plot, or even performed action ('drama' in Greek means 'action') in favour of narrated action. Crimp has commented on his development of two 'methods of dramatic writing' where '[o]ne is the making of scenes in which characters *enact* a story in the conventional way—for example my play *The Country*—the other is a form of narrated drama in which the act of story-telling *is itself dramatized*—as in *Attempts on Her Life*, or *Fewer Emergencies*'.[6] Crimp defines this kind of theatre as belonging to the category of the 'drama-in-the-head' and as taking place in a 'mental space, not a physical one'.[7]

In *Attempts on Her Life*, one of the critics comments on Anne's artistic installation:

It's theatre — that's right — for a world in which theatre itself has died. Instead of the outmoded conventions of dialogue and so-called characters lumbering towards the embarrassing dénouements of the *theatre*, Anne is offering us a pure dialogue of objects: of leather and glass, of Vaseline and steel; of blood, saliva and chocolate. She's offering us no less than the spectacle of her own existence, the radical *pornography* — if I may use that overused word — of her own broken and abused — almost Christ-like — body.[8]

Very playfully, in *Attempts on Her Life*, Crimp revisits several games played by Oulipian writers such as that of oralized literature. For example, as seen in the phrase '[w]ho listens quote expressionlessly unquote to the description of quote outrage unquote after quote outrage unquote after quote outrage unquote she has perpetrated'.[9] Crimp also plays the game that consists in matching a sentence with its immediate translation in an exotic language:

> *Each phrase is first spoken in an African or Eastern European language.*
> *An English translation immediately follows.*
> — [phrase]
> — The car twists along the Mediterranean road.
> — [phrase]
> — It hugs the bends between the picturesque hillside villages.[10]

These are isolated examples of the manner in which Crimp uses Oulipian devices in his own dramaturgy, thus contributing both to making the satire more pungent and to making the created theatrical object more unnaturalistic. However, the whole play can be read as an 'exercise in style' very much in the fashion of Queneau's *Exercices de style*. The play consists not of 99 retellings of the same story but of 17 scenarios that tend to exhaust all the possibilities of Anne: 'ALL THE THINGS THAT ANNE CAN BE'.[11] Yet these variations on the character of Anne, while constructing her as a protean world-character (as impossible to represent as Salome's dance) and bringing down ontological frontiers (Anne could be a car or a TV set), all abide by the same constraint: they never stage Anne. Anne remains the Mallarméan *'absente de tout bouquet'*, the ideal flower forever absent from the bouquet. In other words, Anne, the main character in this play, never truly appears. The enigmatic constraint – enigmatic since, of course, the reader-spectator is not straightaway made aware of the constraint – consists in writing a play whose main character remains unseen throughout the representational process: some sort of adaptation of the lipogram, in a way, as the 'void' here (to take up the title of Gilbert Adair's English translation of Perec's 1969 novel written without the letter 'e', *La Disparition*), refers not to the 'stolen letter' but to the main character.[12] Crimp's play comes very close indeed to the film Perec intended to shoot based on his novel. The film was to be called *Signe particulier: NÉANT* (*Distinguishing Features: NONE*). This film was conceived by Perec as an application of the same constraint as in the novel *A Void*. It was supposed to be an adaptation of it, or rather an equivalent, and Perec intended to show none of the faces of the actors involved: '*Distinguishing Features: NONE* was a film in which the spectator would have no access whatsoever to the actors' faces', Perec claimed.[13] Such a film would have become, in the words of Bernard Magné, a 'lipoprosopic film' (from the Greek *prosopon*, meaning face) highly appropriate for putting into images a kind of writing entirely devoted to conjuring up absence.[14]

Right at the heart of the playful lipoprosopic constraint are dystopia, absence, bereavement, and spectrality. Through its piling up of 17 vain attempts, *Attempts on Her Life* builds a theatre dedicated to the modalities of absence on the stage, in other words, 17 failures to represent. Theatre – a place of epiphany if any ('thea' in Greek means vision) – becomes a blind spot, a place where what is shown is not revelation but disappearance and void, the contrary of the expected spectacle, so to speak. Crimp traces the contours of a new post-Beckettian theatre of absence concerned with not-seeing, a new place where nothing takes place. To put it in Jean-Luc Nancy's words, the character 'only gives his/her truth in its withdrawn presence – a presence whose sense is *absense*' ('ne donne sa vérité que dans le retrait de sa présence — une présence dont le sens est un *absens*').[15] In this play that hinges on the dialectical opposition between construction and destruction – the word 'Attempts' in the title implies both trying hard and committing violence – the character is reduced to fragments and the pieces, in both senses of the term, have to be put back together by a puzzled spectator. Anne is both a character and a non-character – 'a *lack* of character, an *absence*, she calls it, of character' – and remains extant only in the form of traces, of vestiges to be remembered by others or in the deadly presence of the outgoing message on her answering machine.[16] Anne's only material *ontos* is one of words, as she is being 'remembered', in the Hamletian meaning of 're-limbed', by and through her acquaintances' or relatives' speaking about her. Nothing takes place onstage but language. Anne's absence is therefore metatheatrically replicated by an absence of 'drama' (action, in Greek) to the benefit of narrative. Crimp's play spectralizes the character and, in doing so, spectralizes the theatrical medium: *Attempts on Her Life* is a play of and for voices, in many respects anticipating the lyrical works written by Crimp for George Benjamin, *Into the Little Hill* and *Written on Skin*. A libretto-like quality pervades the text, and Crimp's theatre strikes me as one of the most accomplished examples of the vocal theatre that dominates the stage today, from Kane's 'solo symphonies' to debbie tucker green's polyphonic arias.[17]

Yet – and here is the paradox inherent in this type of literary constraint – 'void' breeds wholeness; the empty generates the full. Lipogrammatic or lipoprosopic writing calls on absence and vacuity, yet the play unfolds from this originating emptiness: language proliferates around and because of absence. Shortage entails abundance, and Crimp's play shows how vacuity or even viduity is a paradoxical matrix: in absence and bereavement, there is a resurrection – that of language which the practice of constrained writing stigmatized yet hoped to revive through mathematics.

The same amphibological discourse characterizes Stoppard's theatre and more recently, although it is ideologically different, Churchill's. Churchill loves systems, grids, figures and constraints: already in *Cloud Nine*, gender- and race-crossing appeared as techniques favoured by the playwright and demonstrated her taste for systematicity in poetics. Betty, the archetypal Victorian wife, is played by a male actor because Betty 'wants to be what men want her to be' and the black servant Joshua is played by a white actor because 'he wants to be what whites want him to be'.[18] As for Stoppard, he stands out as a pioneer in terms of linguistics-oriented theatre: he addresses Wittgenstein's seminal questions about the power of language and his stage becomes the site of his experimentation with words. With *Dogg's Hamlet, Cahoot's Macbeth* (1979), two plays which are seemingly separated by a comma yet cannot be performed separately, Stoppard takes as his starting point one of the 'language games' developed by Wittgenstein in his *Philosophical Investigations* and reads it in the light of Lewis Carroll's or Edward Lear's 'nonsensical' tradition:[19]

> 'When I use a word', Humpty-Dumpty said in rather a scornful tone, 'it means just what I choose it to mean—neither more nor less.'
>
>   'The question is', said Alice, whether you *can* make words mean so many different things.' 'The question is', said Humpty-Dumpty, 'which is to be master—that's all.'[20]

Before Stoppard, a number of French stage poets had inaugurated a kind of theatre that sought to turn the stage into a laboratory in linguistics.

Jacques Audiberti (*Quoat-Quoat*, 1946), Jean Vauthier (*Capitaine Bada*, 1952), Jean Tardieu, or René de Obaldia (*Du vent dans les branches de Sassafras*, 1965) open the stage to linguistic and poetic experimentation: the semantics of words is more often than not sacrificed to the benefit of their poetic and musical materiality.[21] In Britain, the nonsensical tradition that began with Lewis Carroll and Edward Lear offers fertile ground for carrying out linguistic investigations in the manner of Wittgenstein. The main question concerns the power of language, or, as a matter of fact, the limits of language. Easy, the English-speaking character of *Dogg's Hamlet, Cahoot's Macbeth* experiences precisely this incapacity of language to act upon the world. The play puts into practice one of Wittgenstein's most bewildering language games, which Stoppard quotes in his preface to the play. This is worth citing at length:

> A man is building a platform using pieces of wood of different shapes and sizes. These are thrown to him by a second man, one at a time, as they are called for. An observer notes that each time the first man shouts 'Plank!' he is thrown a long flat piece. Then he calls 'Slab!' and is thrown a piece of a different shape. This happens a few times. There is a call for 'Block!' and a third shape is thrown. Finally a call for 'Cube!' produces a fourth type of piece. An observer would probably conclude that the different words described different shapes and sizes of the material. But this is not the only possible interpretation. Suppose, for example, the thrower knows in advance which pieces the builder needs, and in what order. In such a case there would be no need for the builder to name the pieces he requires but only to indicate thus:
>
> > Plan = Ready   Block = Next
> > Slab = Okay   Cube = Thank you
>
> In such a case, the observer would have made a false assumption, but the fact that he on the one hand and the builders on the other are using two different languages need not be made apparent to either party.[22]

The literary procedure chosen here by Stoppard and implemented in the play closely resembles Jean Tardieu's game which consists in taking one word to mean another.[23] Such a game enables Stoppard to put Wittgenstein's language games to the test in the fashion of the OuLiPo. Easy, a native English speaker, is confronted with the necessity of understanding – and then speaking – Dogg language, a tongue shared by the native Dogg speakers around him, as he is supposed to deliver the planks for the construction of a stage on which *Hamlet* in

Dogg is to be performed. Dogg language is made up of English signi-fiers re-semanticized in a way which, more often then not, transforms them into the contrary of what they mean in English: as an example, the disrespectful word 'git' comes to mean 'sir' in Dogg. Moreover, all the words are used a-grammatically so that a noun can be used for a verb and vice versa. We therefore realize that even though it is a-syntactic and de-semanticized, Dogg language makes us hear a tongue that sounds like English and which, although it is deconstructed, can be forced back into a system (that of deliberate contraries).

The very same method is used by Churchill in one of her most disturbing plays: *Far Away* (2000). This piece, though politically and ideologically different from Stoppard's experimental dramaturgy, does, to some extent, resort to the same games. *Far Away* takes us straight into the post-Adornian world where all innocence is irretrievably obliterated. The play is made up of three scenes that can be read as so many successive lapses into nihilistic tragedy: an allegory of stifled innocence, the little girl Joan witnesses an implicitly barbaric scene during which her uncle locks people up in a van. Hushed and pre-vented from putting this half-seen reality into words, Joan is contami-nated by her aunt's negationist enterprise. Her aunt, Harper – whose meaningful name denotes her power of conviction – denies all the cruelty taking place that night and produces a tightly controlled and unfailing Newspeak. The words Harper matches to reality are totally alien to it. The characters start speaking a language that has abdicated its ambition to chart reality. Scene Two takes us forward some years: Joan, now an adult, has an artistic job in a workshop where she sews fantastical hats. These hats are meant to be presented during parodic and macabre fashion shows performed by prisoners on their way to the cremator: art can no longer fight horror; on the contrary, it gives shape to the deadly teleology of barbarous humanity. Art 'means' the inhuman. Scene Three stages characters in a world of hypertrophied threat: a general all-encompassing war has started. The universe 'stinks of corpses', to put it in the words of Beckett (*Endgame*). Yet, if people are killed far and wide, it is by coffee or pins, by 'heroin, petrol, chainsaws, hairspray, bleach, foxgloves'.[24] War has contaminated all the spheres of our universe: wasps and butterflies are uncommonly aggressive and 'the cats have come in on the side of the French' in this world affected by the war of all against all:[25]

> TODD: But we're not exactly on the other side from the French.
>   It's not as if they're the Moroccans and the ants.

HARPER: It's not as if they're the Canadians, the Venezuelans and the mosquitoes.
TODD: It's not as if they're the engineers, the chefs, the children under five, the musicians.
HARPER: The car salesmen.
TODD: Portuguese car salesmen.
HARPER: Russian swimmers.
TODD: Thai butchers.
HARPER: Latvian dentists. [...] Mallards are not a good waterbird. They commit rape, and they're on the side of the elephants, and the Koreans. But crocodiles are always in the wrong.[26]

This radical Hobbesian state of nature may well raise political questions and a Brechtian reading of the play is, of course, possible. However, in this universe that is so 'far away' yet so close, the mode of playful tragedy can be regarded as the only solution for conveying the sense of barbarity at hand.

The treatment of language here entails dismay for the spectator: are we in the presence of a language we know – English as a matter of fact? And is this world as mad as it sounds? Or are we being presented with an altogether different linguistic system, whose proximity to English would be misleading and whose inner rules would remain to be deciphered? Is one to cling to the conventional meaning of the signifiers one can recognize or has one to pierce the mystery of a literary constraint, a language game whose rules would have to be discovered in the process? Churchill does not say. She retains both options, and the text organically oscillates between its tragic account of the world in a state of global war and its playful (yet perhaps even more tragic) rendition of a language that seems to have gone mad. Thanks to the unusually extreme situation described, the first hypothesis invites the reader-spectator to imagine a grotesque world, whose deformity finds a physical manifestation in the presence of unhierarchically threatening mutants in the all-engulfing system considered here ('[...] because the deer are with us. They have been for three weeks').[27] However, the second hypothesis foreshadows a reality that may be even worse: Churchill may well be summoning signifiers that once upon a time made sense in a linguistic system now grown obsolete and whose new significations (and referents) still remain to be identified and elucidated. Threat is vocalized but its exact contours remain blurred for the imagination, as language no longer obeys the Saussurean triangle or respects the necessity of referentiality. Verbalized in a language bereft of its referents, the threat remains unrepresented; it obliterates any hermeneutical or imaginary attempts and leaves the spectator in a state of maximal anguish because of indeterminacy. For the spectator, language is no longer an instrument that helps them map the word and therefore control it, if to symbolize the world is to dominate it: it retaliates and confronts them with their own powerlessness.

Churchill's text also proposes to answer Wittgenstein's seminal question about the power of language by following one of the paths opened up by Wittgenstein himself: this new language, in a similar way to Stoppard's Dogg language, dispenses with 'surface grammar' and formalized language and opts for a language game ('a symbolic linguistic system artificially fabricated yet envisaged as a mode of communication complete in itself') so as to elucidate the way natural language works. However, although with Stoppard and his character Easy we are capable of teaching ourselves the meaning of this Newspeak, therefore confirming Wittgenstein's injunction '[l]et the words teach you their meaning', with Churchill the linguistic system thus created does not allow words to teach us their meaning.[28]

Stoppard, like Tardieu in *Un mot pour un autre*, offers a de-semanticized – re-semanticized – language which does not result in incommunicability, but in a recomposed meaning likely to be discovered and mastered again – even if most of the time this meaning is trivial and detached from the real issues. As Robert Abirached suggests, once the ambition to mean is forsaken – 'Mean something! You and I, mean something! (*Brief laugh.*) Ah that's a good one!', as Hamm and Clov put it in *Endgame*, language becomes 'an artefact to be exhibited'.[29] *Dogg's Hamlet, Cahoot's Macbeth* might well be studied in this light if the play were not, in the first place, a response – on the part of a dramatist whose Czech origins are well known – to the gagging of the population, and artists in particular, in post-Prague Spring Czechoslovakia. With Churchill, what is at stake is no longer the exhibition of language as artefact but language being thrown into a crisis: there is no situation, no clue to allow us to make sense of what is being said.

This distress as to what speaking means is explored further in one of Churchill's most puzzling plays: the Magrittean *This Is a Chair* (1999).

The Northern Ireland Peace Process
FATHER, MOTHER and MURIEL at dinner.

FATHER: Is Muriel going to eat her dinner?
MOTHER: Yes, eat up, Muriel.
FATHER: Have a special bite of daddy's.[30]

The unusual divide between the situation announced and the one actually shown onstage can be interpreted in two different ways: if we consider ourselves to be in a functional linguistic universe, we can understand the play as a realist rendition of the failure of ideologies and as an example of the radical divorce between the global situation (macro) and the individual situation (micro) in which, indeed, the representation of major political events does not alter the fundamentals of our everyday life (children do continue being fed during the peace negotiations in Northern Ireland). If, on the other hand, one considers that the play has tipped over into a post-linguistic universe, as may be the case in *Far Away*, the above-mentioned discrepancy between what is shown and what is announced corroborates the irreversible failure of language. Language becomes the site of menace, and the debunked metaphor of fratricidal war between Ireland and Britain finds an echo in the potentially incestuous situation which makes its way into the spectator's mind through such apparently harmless phrases as 'have a special bite of daddy's'. Taken at face value, the debunked metaphor reintroduces horror at the heart of everyday childhood routine.

With the extremely radical diptych *Blue Heart*, Churchill invites a double reading once more before showing us, 'live', the death throes of language. The first play of the diptych, entitled *Heart's Desire*, compels language into a given pattern: that of an unflinching, infallible repetition of the same (*'le ressassement éternel'* or 'eternal return' as Blanchot would put it) whereas *Blue Kettle* sentences language to death by autophagy. *Blue Heart* can be read as turning Freud's post-traumatic stress disorder and repetition compulsion into a poetic system close to that of screen-printing. The play radicalizes what was already contained in germ in the early radio play *Not Not Not Not Not Enough Oxygen* (1971). In the recent diptych, Churchill explores repetition and serigraphy on two different levels: *Heart's Desire* proposes a reflection on linearity and repetition at the level of the macrostructure, that is, at the level of the overall architecture of the play; *Blue Kettle*, in contrast, addresses the problematics of textual stammering at the microstructural level of the sentence or even the word. The play comes very close to Perec's *L'Augmentation* and, with this diptych, Churchill poeticizes serial reproduction, a dimension she later develops thematically in her play about cloning, *A Number*.

Heart's Desire shows a family (father, mother, brother and aunt) gathered at home while expecting the imminent arrival of the Daughter from Australia. Similarly to a broken record, the play develops to a point when it is compulsively sent back to its beginning:

> *ALICE and MAISIE. ALICE setting knives and forks on table, MAISIE fidgets about the room. BRIAN enters putting on a red sweater.*
> BRIAN: She's taking her time.
> ALICE: Not really.
> *They all stop. BRIAN goes out. Others resort to beginning and do exactly what they did before as BRIAN enters putting on a tweed jacket.*
> BRIAN: She's taking her time.
> ALICE: Not really.
> *They all stop. BRIAN goes out. Others resort to beginning and do exactly what they did before as BRIAN enters putting on an old cardigan.*

This is the incipit of the play, whose excipit reads:

> *ALICE and MAISIE. ALICE setting knives and forks on table, MAISIE fidgets about the room. BRIAN enters putting on a red sweater.*
> BRIAN: She's taking her time.
> ALICE: Not really.
> *They all stop. BRIAN goes out. Others resort to beginning and do exactly what they did before as BRIAN enters putting on a tweed jacket.*
> [...]
> SUSY: Here I am.
> BRIAN: Here you are.
> ALICE: Here she is.
> SUSY: Hello aunty.
> BRIAN: You are my heart's —
> *Reset to top. BRIAN enters putting on old cardigan.*
> BRIAN: She's taking her time.
> End.[31]

The play reads as the textual equivalent of Andy Warhol serigraphic portraits. It spectacularizes what Walter Benjamin would consider as the double *aporia* of art, which consists in defying its reification by proposing, unlike Warhol's mythified faces – those of Chairman Mao or of Liz Taylor, for instance – types of characters gaining all the more in empathy as they remain stalled in their situation. This aporetic aesthetics of fragmentation is the very clear marl of a 'post-' literature according to

Adorno. *Heart's Desire* reads as a stage version of Adorno's formula: '[a]rt is the ever broken promise of happiness', and as such comes very close to the ideology of serigraphic art as practised by Warhol.[32]

Churchill, not unlike Warhol, summons the series both to make clear the exhaustion of language and show how language cannot be dispensed with. The word, the image, with Churchill or Warhol, peters out because of too many repetitions, it becomes banal, it renounces its uniqueness or singularity – 'that which withers in the age of mechanical reproduction is the aura of the work of art' – yet it never gives up, it is insistently, hauntingly present.[33] The image, although made banal, is there, endlessly: it persists. The quality of Churchill's demonstration here strikes us as powerfully oxymoronic: it speaks out the failing-yet-triumphant nature of language in a way that comes very close to Jacques Derrida's concept of 'demeure' as explored in his eponymous book: 'demeure' as in 'to remain' and 'abode' or 'dwelling', but also as in the negation of what dies ('demeurt' as 'to un-die', somehow).[34] The image stays, both a sign of bereavement and a confirmation of immortality.

Thanks to serialization, Churchill comes to terms with the Faustian dilemma of mankind that she addresses anew in *A Number*: how to suspend time and reconcile death and life. The stammering of the play, while proposing a text always in the making and therefore alive, also carries the presence of death, as if engraved upon the play, in a mode not unlike photography and the 'this-was' ('*ça a été*') explored by Roland Barthes in his *Camera Lucida* (1980).[35] Serigraphy conjures up the ghost: language, both alive and obsolete no sooner uttered, continuously returns and becomes a witness of its own spectralization.

It is at the microstructural level of the word that Churchill addresses the issue in the second play of the diptych, *Blue Kettle*, in which the death of language is shown to us, 'live'. The Oulipian constraint of a word for a word finds a radicalized echo in this extreme linguistic farce. The play focuses on a character called Derek who visits old ladies and pretends he is the son they abandoned at birth. Yet the true main actors of *Blue Kettle* are words as they play out the death of language. Independently from their grammatical category, the words are progressively replaced by two entities: 'blue' and 'kettle', soon reduced to maimed vestiges of the latter (bl, kt), to eventually fade out and down to their initials, coughing their way into the spectators' ears: B.K. As the play develops, decomposition is well on its way: first we find ourselves in the presence of what could almost pass for a typing error: 'you don't have to blue anything up', that is, in the presence of the odd anomaly.[36]

We then move on to a type of utterance in which the expected word has disappeared and been replaced by 'kettle' or 'blue', yet is still easy for us to correct because we are familiar with what Wittgenstein would call the 'forms of life' displayed here onstage. This is a characteristic collection of phrases from the play:

> MRS OLIVER: Exactly and that's not like having nothing is it, having kettle of seeing your son or not, it's not life like before.[37]
>
> DEREK: So blue didn't anyone let you know?[38]
>
> MRS VANE: You think you're kettle old?[39]
>
> DEREK: I'm not the only qualified kettle without gainful employment at the present time.[40]
>
> MRS OLIVER: I'm his mother.
>
> ENID: Blue do you blue.
>
> DEREK: Kettle, I'd like you to meet my mother.[41]

The play then proceeds to expose how language is progressively made hollow. The Beckettian project finds an almost explicit extension here as the two imperialistic words 'blue' and 'kettle' literally eat up all the other words: 'ENID: Blue blue blue blue blue today in the street, I begged.'[42] However, in the end these two tyrants are equally subject to the same thanatographic process: first chaotically fragmented and stuttering, they are eventually reduced *ad absurdum* until all that is left is their initial:

> MRS PLANT: How bl bl bl this was bl son? (...) Ket b tle die of?
>
> MRS PLANT: Tbkkkkl ?
>
> DEREK: B.K. (*End*).[43]

After working on exhaustion at the level of the global composition of the play in *Heart's Desire*, Churchill wittily deconstructs the smallest unit of meaning: that of the sentence and eventually of the word itself. The different experiments she carries out in plays such as *Blue Heart*, *Far Away* and *A Number* resolutely inscribe her work in what I would call a theatre of the impossible narrative: a theatre doomed to stuttering and to endless repetition, a theatre of 'the eternal return'. Churchill proposes to our ears words that are only summoned to vainly and imperfectly encode a world – a world doomed to disappear as soon as it is uttered.

Constrained writing aims at making us aware of the end of a system: the 'linguistic era', to put it in Steiner's words, has reached a conclusion and the pact with the spectator needs to be renegotiated. Language has failed and the position of the reader-spectator can no longer be that of a gaping and respectful admirer in front of a sacred object: the text no longer contains its own truth, it becomes somehow contingent and therefore prone to being manipulated. However, by an ultimate ironical twist, constrained theatre (or literature, in fact) never reveals the nature of the constraint in the first place. The constraint remains enigmatic and the spectator is busy trying to work it out throughout the play. French poet Jacques Roubaud states the first principle of constrained writing: 'a text written with a constraint tells us about this constraint' ('Un texte écrit selon une contrainte parle de cette contrainte'). What happens then is a displacement of suspense: the suspense is no longer that of the story told (if any) but of the progressive deciphering of the constraint itself. Hermeneutics becomes vertical or paradigmatic, so to speak.

Martin Crimp and Caryl Churchill's theatres of the 'eternal return', though intrinsically playful, find a way of speaking out about the ethical disaster of our time: stepping out of the traditional contract that presupposes an adequacy between form and content – abdicating the grand romantic project, as it were – stands out as a means of reinventing tragedy.

Notes

A short version of this essay appeared in E. Angel-Perez, 'La contrainte comme artifice sur la scène anglaise contemporaine: Tom Stoppard, Martin Crimp, et Caryl Churchill', *Sillages Critiques*, 10 (2009). Permission to use the material in this collection has been granted to the author by the editor of the journal.

1. M. Blanchot, *L'Écriture du Désastre* (Paris: Gallimard, 1980); M. Blanchot, *Après coup et Le Ressassement éternel* (Paris: Minuit, 1983).
2. G. Steiner, *Language and Silence: Essays on Language, Literature and the Inhuman* (New Haven and London: Yale University Press, 1970, 1998), p. 4. Steiner's full phrase is: '[w]e come *after*, and that is the nerve of our condition' (original emphasis).
3. C. Reggiani, 'La rhétorique de l'invention de Raymond Roussel à l'Oulipo'. Thèse de doctorat, dir. Georges Molinié, Université Paris IV-Sorbonne, 1997.
4. M. Perloff, *Radical Artifice: Writing Poetry in the Age of Media* (Chicago: University of Chicago Press, 1991), p. 139.
5. Perloff shows that any text is artificial, any text is fabricated, any text is 'a made thing'. Artifice, Perloff writes, is what makes the reader/spectator aware of 'how things happen', see Perloff, *Radical Artifice*, pp. 27–8.
6. Interview with M. Crimp by Anon., 'Into the Little Hill', *Ensemble Modern Newsletter* (2006), http://www.ensemble-modern.com/ (accessed October 2006).
7. Interview with M. Crimp by Anon., 'Into the Little Hill'.

8. M. Crimp, *Attempts on Her Life* (London: Faber & Faber, 1997), pp. 50–1.
9. Crimp, *Attempts on Her Life*, p. 40.
10. Crimp, *Attempts on Her Life*, p. 30.
11. Crimp, *Attempts on Her Life*, p. 19.
12. G. Perec, *La Disparition* (Paris: Gallimard, 1969, 1992); translated into English by G. Adair (Boston: Verba Mundi, 2005).
13. B. Magné (ed.), 'Georges Perec: Signe particulier: NEANT, Projet de long métrage de fiction, déclaration d'intention', *Vertigo*, 11/12 (1994), 61–6, (p. 61).
14. Magné (ed.), 'Georges Perec'. Magné stipulates that the film had been conceived of in the 1980s by Perec and quotes David Bellos in *Georges Perec, une vie sans les mots* (Paris: Seuil, 1994).
15. J.-L. Nancy, *Au fond des images* (Paris: Galilée, 2003), p. 67.
16. Crimp, *Attempts on Her Life*, p. 25.
17. E. Angel-Perez, 'Je(ux) de voix: le théâtre de Martin Crimp', *Tropismes*, 17 (2011), 65–76.
18. C. Churchill, 'Preface' to *Cloud Nine*, in *Caryl Churchill: Plays One* (London: Methuen Drama, 1985), p. 245.
19. T. Stoppard, *Dogg's Hamlet, Cahoot's Macbeth* (London: Faber & Faber, 1979); J.-J. Lecercle, *Philosophy of Nonsense: The Intuitions of Victorian Nonsense Literature* (London and New York: Routledge, 1994).
20. The reference is to L. Carroll's (1872) *Through the Looking-Glass* and specifically to Chapter Six, 'Humpty-Dumpty'.
21. The play is entirely made of well-known distorted proverbs, such as 'Œuf d'autruche fait pas le printemps / – Et l'Printemps fait pas le moine' reading as distortions of 'Une hirondelle ne fait pas le printemps' and of 'L'habit ne fait pas le moine'. R. Abirached, *La Crise du personnage dans le théâtre moderne*, rev. edn. (Paris: Gallimard, 1994), p. 399 et seq.
22. T. Stoppard, 'Preface' to *Dogg's Hamlet, Cahoot's Macbeth*, p. 7.
23. 'Mme de Perleminouze (*à Irma qui vient de lui apporter le courrier*). ... Eh bien ma quille ! Pourquoi serpez-vous là ? (*Geste de congédiement*.) Vous pouvez vidanger!' J. Tardieu, *Un mot pour un autre. Le Professeur Frœppel* (Paris: Gallimard, 1954, 2003), pp. 51–2.
24. C. Churchill, *Far Away* (London: Nick Hern Books, 2000), p. 43.
25. Churchill, *Far Away*, p. 35. C. Dymkovski, '*Far Away* ... but close to home', *European Journal of English Studies*, 7.1 (2003), 55–68.
26. Churchill, *Far Away*, pp. 36–9.
27. Churchill, *Far Away*, p. 41.
28. L. Wittgenstein, *Philosophical Investigations*, trans. G. E. M. Anscombe (Oxford: Blackwell, 1953), p. 220.
29. Abirached, *La Crise du personnage dans le théâtre moderne*, p. 405.
30. C. Churchill, *This Is a Chair* (London: Nick Hern Books, 1999), pp. 7, 28.
31. C. Churchill, *Heart's Desire* and *Blue Kettle*, in *Blue Heart* (New York: Theatre Communication Groups, 1998), pp. 6, 36.
32. Adorno quoted by C. Bernard, 'L'art de l'aporie: penser l'impensable avec Adorno et Benjamin', *Études Anglaises*, 58.1 (2005), 31–41 (p. 32).
33. W. Benjamin, 'The Work of Art in the Age of Mechanical Reproduction', in W. Benjamin and H. Arendt (eds.), *Illuminations* (New York: Harcourt, Brace and World, 1936, 1968), pp. 219–53 (p. 223).

34. J. Derrida, *Demeure, Maurice Blanchot* (Paris: Galilée, 1998).
35. R. Barthes, *Camera Lucida: Reflections on Photography*, trans. R. Howard (New York: Hill & Wang, 1981).
36. Churchill, *Blue Heart*, p. 43.
37. Churchill, *Blue Heart*, p. 44.
38. Churchill, *Blue Heart*, p. 45.
39. Churchill, *Blue Heart*, p. 49.
40. Churchill, *Blue Heart*, p. 52.
41. Churchill, *Blue Heart*, p. 53.
42. Churchill, *Blue Heart*, p. 62.
43. Churchill, *Blue Heart*, p. 69.

5
Racial Violence, Witnessing and Emancipated Spectatorship in *The Colour of Justice, Fallout* and *random*

Mireia Aragay and Enric Monforte

Richard Norton-Taylor's *The Colour of Justice* (1999), Roy Williams's *Fallout* (2003) and debbie tucker green's *random* (2008) share a concern with the phenomenon of inner-city racial violence in contemporary Britain. As is well known, Norton-Taylor's piece, one of the Tricycle Theatre's tribunal plays, was written and produced in the wake of the racist murder of Stephen Lawrence in Eltham (south-east London) in April 1993 and the ensuing Macpherson Inquiry set up in March 1998. *Fallout* explores black-on-black street violence in the light of the killing of Damilola Taylor, a ten-year-old boy murdered in Peckham (south London) in November 2000. Finally, tucker green's play responds to the spate of youth killings in London in 2007 and 2008, where 90 per cent of the victims were black or Asian.[1] The three plays, however, take very different aesthetic approaches to their subject matter – documentary hyperrealism in *The Colour of Justice*, naturalistic social realism in *Fallout* and formal experimentation in *random* – with each mode representing an important strand within post-1989 British theatre. This chapter re-examines the three plays with reference to Jacques Rancière's concepts of the 'emancipated spectator' and the 'distribution of the sensible', as well as to Jenny Spencer's notion of the 'racialized spectator' formulated on the basis of Rancière's work.[2] This involves a problematization of an extended critical and historiographic view that sees documentary, social realist and formally innovative theatre as distinct trends and argues that only the latter – an experimental departure from realism – enables spectators to challenge established discourses and ways of seeing.

Institutional racism and the distribution of the sensible

The murder of Lawrence and the Macpherson Inquiry set up to investigate the mishandling of the case on the part of the Metropolitan Police are generally seen as 'a watershed' in the history of race relations in Britain.[3] In his study of the case, Brian Cathcart concludes that the debate on race in Britain has been thoroughly 'transformed' as a consequence.[4] Like Ambalavaner Sivanandan, Director of the Institute of Race Relations (IRR), Simon Cottle and Janelle Reinelt among others, Cathcart sees the Macpherson Report, made public on 25 February 1999, as instrumental in bringing about such a transformation.[5] Crucially, the Report introduced 'a significant new codification of racism' by identifying and naming 'institutional racism' 'for the first time within public legislative discourse', where it had 'never before been acknowledged by government or by official inquiry'.[6] In the terms of the Report, institutional racism does not imply that every individual member of an organization is racist; rather, it refers to:

> The collective failure of an organisation to provide an appropriate and professional service to people because of their colour, culture or ethnic origin. It can be seen or detected in processes, attitudes and behaviour which amount to discrimination through unwitting prejudice, ignorance, thoughtlessness and racist stereotyping which disadvantage minority ethnic people.[7]

In other words, it is a routine, taken-for-granted, barely perceptible kind of racism, all the more difficult to pin down and dismantle because of its 'institutional embeddedness'.[8] In Rancière's terms, we might say that institutional racism intangibly and therefore all the more powerfully forms part of a general, implicit law or order of things (*la police*) that determines the distribution of the sensible (*le partage du sensible*) – the boundaries, that is, between the visible and the invisible, the audible and the inaudible, the sayable and the unsayable: a 'system of *a priori* forms determining what presents itself to sense experience'.[9] From this perspective, the Macpherson Report made a decisive contribution to making institutional racism visible, thus reconfiguring the distribution of the sensible in this fraught area of contemporary British culture.

The Report concluded unequivocally that institutional racism existed not only within the Metropolitan Police, but also in other institutions across the country, such as the criminal justice system and various public service areas. With an initially reluctant or indifferent media – particularly the print press – becoming increasingly active players and 'making full use of all the communicative architecture and expressive means at their disposal [to] progressively envelop the case with emotional and moral intensity', the Stephen Lawrence case and the Macpherson Report became a turning-point.[10] '[A] learning process for the country at large', a 'critical benchmark in ongoing antiracist struggles' and 'a transformative moment in British society', 'whose repercussions would be felt for years to come' are indicative descriptions of how these events were seen.[11]

However, they did not ultimately trigger a decline in potentially violent racist attitudes: March 2001 saw the IRR report a substantial increase in racial violence in the United Kingdom since the Macpherson Report, including '19 deaths involving a racial motivation [...], of which 9 [...] in the London area'.[12] Its 2010 Briefing Paper *Racial Violence: The Buried Issue* estimates 'an average of five lethal attacks with a racial element [...] in the UK each year' since the death of Lawrence, the exceptions being 1999, 2000 and 2006, when numbers doubled.[13] A later IRR report documents 71 'murders with a suspected or known racial element' across the country from January 2000 to December 2011, while on 5 January 2012 the IRR webpage listed 96 racial murders since the death of Lawrence.[14] The murder of Taylor in 2000 and the 2007–8 series of racially motivated youth killings, which *Fallout* and *random* respectively respond to, are part of this wider picture.

Where the Lawrence case and the Macpherson Report did generate significant changes were the interconnected levels of discourse, representation and, to some extent, cultural and political institutional policies; the Rancièrian level of the distribution of the sensible. Thus, for Cathcart and the IRR, the concept of institutional racism became 'fixed in the national consciousness' and part of 'the national agenda' respectively.[15] Crucially, however, Cottle demonstrates that 'in its mediatisation, [the case] entered into a *contested field* of public discourse and representation' that went on to encompass racial relations at large and, in particular, the issue of racial violence.[16] Thus, while Cathcart was able to conclude, in 2000, that the media had become 'certainly more alert to the issue of race', in 2007 Chris Greer found that '[t]he under-representation of young people as victims of street crime [was] even more pronounced for those who are non-white [...] The everyday experiences of Black people as victims of crime and racial prejudice seldom make the headlines.'[17] Interruptions in the distribution of the sensible are, according to Rancière, momentary and discontinuous, yet no less essential for that.[18]

Contemporary British theatre, race and representation

Lynette Goddard has drawn attention to the institutional position of British theatre within the contested arena of discourse and representation around issues of race; she emphasizes the publication, in April 2002 – the wake of the Macpherson Report and in context with New Labour's drive for 'cultural diversity' – of the Arts Council's report *Eclipse: Developing Strategies to Combat Racism in the Theatre*, which identified institutional racism within 'all levels of theatre production' in Britain.[19] Since identities, as Stuart Hall argues, are produced and circulated within representation,[20] British theatre's institutional racism, certainly up to the *Eclipse* report and to some extent beyond, has meant that 'most of the images of Black identity that reach British stages are not far different from those found in popular media and television' – namely, deeply essentialist, stereotyped and limiting.[21]

Goddard suggests that the *Eclipse* report may well have contributed to the emergence of a new group of British-born black playwrights – Dona Daley, Kwame Kwei-Armah, Mark Norfolk, tucker green and Williams among others[22] – whose work began to be staged in a range of venues beyond 'community or non-mainstream theatre contexts', such as the Hamspstead, National, Royal Court, Tricycle or Soho Theatres that were responding to the report's recommendation of programming culturally diverse plays.[23] Following the successful run of Williams's *Sing Yer Heart Out for the Lads* during the 2002 National Theatre's Transformation Season, 2003 was a key year.[24] Indicatively, two of tucker green's plays, *dirty butterfly* and *born bad*, were staged at the Soho and Hampstead in February and April respectively; Kwei-Armah's *Elmina's Kitchen* opened at the National (Cottesloe) in May; Williams's *Fallout* had an extended run at the Royal Court Downstairs from June. Finally, tucker green's *random*, staged at the Royal Court Downstairs in March 2008, followed in the wake of that effervescence.

As Jetinder Verma, founder of the Asian theatre company Tara Arts, suggests, British theatre in the 1950s and 1960s largely ignored the transformations resulting from the post-war influx of non-white immigrants into the country.[25] In the 1970s and 1980s, with the rise of the second generation, the main aim became 'to *achieve presence*'[26] at different levels, mainly through the establishment of theatre companies, such as Temba (1972), Tara Arts (1976), Black Theatre

Cooperative (1979) or Talawa (1985), 'whose policy was to produce new plays by black writers on subjects of interest to black audiences, and to employ black actors and black technicians'.[27] The achievement of presence through the representation of black British identities and experiences was linked to a concern about the construction of a specific 'black aesthetic', with some, such as Kwesi Owusu, arguing that it was essential to resist 'the cultural domination of Western theatrical traditions' by blending together various forms – drama, music, dance – into one artistic whole, a defining feature of black artistic expression.[28] However, as Keith Peacock suggests, this was problematic for the second generation, both because of their distance from their source culture and because they had been brought up within a British context they were inevitably influenced by.[29] To this was added a perceived need of representing black experience in such a way that it would reach the white, middle-class audiences traditionally forming the bulk of the theatre-going public in Britain.[30] The result was the predominance of social realist aesthetics in plays written by black writers – such as Hanif Kureishi, Mustapha Matura or Winsome Pinnock – in the 1970s and 1980s and in the work of black companies – with the exception perhaps of Tara Arts.[31]

In her more recent revision of contemporary plays by black British women, Goddard acknowledges that the increased presence and representation of black British identities and experiences in the 1970s and 1980s was in itself a major achievement. However, she sees formal experimentation as 'vital to creating counter-aesthetics that present alternative messages that challenge dominant ideological representations', which realism, with its emphasis on structural unity, the production of an illusion of wholeness, the teleological drive towards closure and the fashioning of coherent subjectivities, is allegedly unable to offer.[32] Goddard's argument is part of a wider critical stance on the ethico-political potential of contemporary theatre at large that sees it as dependent on aesthetic experimentation or transgression. This encompasses not only feminist theatre theorists such as Sue-Ellen Case or Jeanie Forte, but also more recent articulations.[33] Thus, for Hans-Thies Lehmann, '[i]t is not through the direct thematization of the political that theatre becomes political but through [...] its *mode of representation*'.[34] The view is echoed in Nicholas Ridout's observation that '[t]heatre's greatest ethical potential may be found precisely at the moment when theatre abandons ethics'.[35] That is, only formally experimental theatre that is not explicitly about ethics has the potential to effect a redistribution of the sensible, in Rancière's terms, enabling spectators to access alternative ways of seeing and empowering them as ethico-political subjects. Similarly, Dan Rebellato argues that realist forms seem no longer adequate to represent the profoundly complex effects of globalization and that 'aesthetic experiment may be the right means to achieve an effective political response to the challenges of a consumer culture and a marketized world'.[36]

Seductive as they are, such views also need to be problematized. In the context of this chapter, they would lead to the conclusion that only tucker green's *random* has the potential to involve spectators in a process of active rethinking of dominant discourses on race leading to a reconfiguration of the distribution of the sensible.[37] The ethico-political import of *The Colour of Justice* and *Fallout*, conversely, would be severely limited. Yet empirical evidence, to start with, troubles this conclusion. As has been noted, the impact of documentary plays is 'both indisputable and extraordinary' and they 'continue to interest the bulk of the theatre-going [...] public'.[38] *The Colour of Justice* was particularly successful in terms of audience and critical reception, eventually televised on the BBC in February 1999 after an initial rejection. It also transferred from the Tricycle to the Theatre Royal Stratford East, subsequently to the West End (Victoria Palace Theatre) and the National Theatre, and went on national tour. In its wake, ITV produced and broadcast the four-part documentary *The Murder of Stephen Lawrence*.[39]

Academic views of documentary plays are far from homogeneous. For some, their verbatim hyper-realism, generally devoid of 'a self-conscious emphasis on the vicissitudes of textuality and discourse', provides a false promise of presence, authenticity and transparent representation.[40] In contrast with such postmodern scepticism, Reinelt, drawing on work on documentary film by Stella Bruzzi, argues that 'the tension between objective shards or fragments of reality and subjective treatments of it forms a structuring fault-line of all [documentary] representations', and crucially, spectators bring an awareness of such epistemological ambivalence – they do not necessarily 'expect unmediated access to the truth in question, but that the documents have something significant to offer [...] simple facticity [...] the corroboration that something happened, that events took place'.[41] Spectators become co-producers of plays' meanings, projecting own cultural itineraries and experiences onto the performance. The interaction between 'what is objectively there [and] what is creatively produced and ultimately received', Reinelt argues, may unlock the epistemological impasse of documentary – as well as, we might add, bring us one step closer to the Rancièrian emancipated spectator.[42]

The box-office success of *Fallout* resulting in an extended run and its adaptation into a Channel 4 feature film (2008), is as remarkable as the fact that, together with Williams's later play *Little Sweet Thing* (2005), it was instrumental 'in changing the racial constituency of the London theatre audience'.[43] *Fallout* contributed to establishing Williams as a key figure in post-millennial British theatre. His work as a whole is key to the perception that 'the first decade of the twenty-first century may soon become recognised as the period when Black drama in Britain emerged as a dominant mainstream force'.[44] Deirdre Osborne suggests that reviewers of *Fallout* were split along racial lines, with black commentator Darcus Howe voicing his disgust at both the play's 'images of stupid, self-destructive Blacks paddling through a cesspool of low-life behaviour' and the way '[t]he whites in the audience lapped it up'.[45] However, while it is true that white reviewers generally praised the play for exposing 'the divisions that exist within what we patronisingly term "the Black community"', and employing 'street slang [...] that's getting heard, at last, in the British theatre', opinions were divided here too.[46] Nicholas de Jongh dismissed it as 'thin socio-drama' and Rhoda Koenig argued that it did not bring any 'more insight or beauty [to the world of black, marginalized youth] than television can'.[47] Such division is to some extent replicated in academic criticism. On the basis of an unproblematically mimetic model of representation, Osborne objects that 'Williams offers a limited and bleak representation of his Black characters', reinforced, in her view, by the Royal Court's in-the-round staging of the play, where the audience was positioned to look down on the action from above, 'a familiar "viewing" position in relation to Black experience' for white spectators.[48] For Harry Derbyshire, in contrast, *Fallout* 'urges audiences to be repelled not by the characters [it] depicts but by the conditions in which they are shown to have developed'.[49]

Emancipated and racialized spectatorship

Taken together, the variegated responses to *The Colour of Justice* and *Fallout* may be seen as evidence of what Rancière is at pains to highlight through his concept of the 'emancipated spectator': the rejection of any view of audiences as passive voyeurs that need to be activated and the refusal to homogenize them. In relation to the traditional idea that 'being a spectator is a bad thing [because] viewing is the opposite of knowing' and 'the opposite of acting', Rancière challenges the implied equivalence between viewing and listening on the one hand and ignorance and passivity on the other on the basis of the 'equality of intelligence' of all individuals.[50] He argues that the spectator is always-already active, as

> [s]he observes, selects, compares, interprets. She links what she sees to a host of other things that she has seen on other stages, in other kinds of plays. She composes her own poem with the elements of the poem before her. She participates in the performance by refashioning it in her own way – by drawing back, for example, from the vital energy that it is supposed to transmit in order to make it a pure image and associate this image with a story which she has read or dreamt, experienced or invented. They are thus both distant spectators and active interpreters of the spectacle offered to them.[51]

And there are as many ways of being active as there are spectators:

> The collective power shared by spectators does not stem from the fact that they are members of a collective body [...] It is the power each of them has to translate what she perceives in her own way, to link it to the unique intellectual adventure that makes her similar to all the rest in as much as this adventure is not like any other.[52]

As Spencer notes, the unpredictability of both spectators and the effects of aesthetic work in general is central to Rancière's understanding of an ethico-political efficacy 'that cannot be measured directly nor determined in advance'.[53]

Rancière's insistence on the spectator's always-already active participation and the impossibility – and undesirability – of predicting their responses not only troubles the traditionally unidirectional, semiotic understanding of the relationship between stage and audience, but forms part of a wider exploration of the relationship between politics and aesthetics, articulated through the aforementioned concept of the distribution of the sensible. In effect, the ethico-political potential of aesthetic practices revolves around 'interrupting the distribution of the sensible' in a way that will bring about acts of resubjectivization on the part of their receivers – spectators – which are, for Rancière, sporadic and discontinuous, yet essential to reconfiguring 'the sensible delimitation of what is common to the community, the forms of its visibility and of its organization'.[54] In this respect, Rancière negates any 'hierarchies of representation', that is, 'any relationship of necessity between a determined form and a determined content'.[55]

Spencer's recent re-reading of Adrienne Kennedy's plays combines the concept of the 'racialized spectator' with Rancière's emancipated spectator.[56] Kennedy's plays, Spencer suggests, make spectators intensely aware of their own racial identities so that 'a racialization of perception' is brought about that may result in interruptions of the distribution of the sensible; at the same time, they model spectatorial experience 'by placing reading, writing, watching, and responding centre stage' not in order to proffer a ready-made 'message', but so as to self-consciously prompt 'the gaze of "an emancipated spectator"' who will access the play on its own terms.[57] The dynamic relationship between these two positions, Spencer argues, 'release[s] [...] spectators to their own imaginations' to produce diverse, unpredictable responses.[58] A textual and performance analysis of *The Colour of Justice*, *Fallout* and *random* will hopefully reveal how each of them enables – without predetermining – acts of ethico-political resubjectivization on the part of spectators by positioning them as simultaneously racialized and emancipated.

The Colour of Justice

Reviews of the Tricycle's production of *The Colour of Justice* confirm Reinelt's aforementioned argument as to the active role played by spectators of documentary theatre. A number of critics pointed out that rather than deliver ready-made judgements the play posed questions for spectators to ponder on as they left the theatre and required them 'to face facts and think for themselves'; the play 'ha[d] not been shaped into a traditional courtroom drama – there [was], after all, no conclusion'; it did not 'have a real ending' nor did it 'answer the questions you cannot help asking' – as much as it 'speculate[d] about the personalities of the lawyers and witnesses'.[59] Audience members, in other words, were modelled as emancipated spectators, encouraged to find their own answers. This was combined with an intense racialization of spectatorial perception, as becomes apparent through the *kind* of questions posed by the play. Benedict Nightingale usefully lists the major ones:

Why was Stephen's bleeding not stemmed as he lay dying in Eltham back in 1993? Did the police really think this decent young man was a burglar who had been in a fight? Why was the initial hunt for his killers a desultory matter of roaming the local streets with torches that didn't work? Did one of the suspects' fathers, a drug baron, nobble the police inquiry? Why was officer XXX, who stands accused of conniving with this gentleman, asked to look after a key Black witness when the Lawrences launched their abortive prosecution of the alleged killers? Is there institutionalised racism in the Met?[60]

In other words, through its very title, open-endedness and laying before spectators, in a series of fragments of interrogations extracted from the Macpherson Report, of a range of 'differing accounts of events and complex and often contradictory evidence', *The Colour of Justice* positions spectators as both emancipated and racialized.[61] It invites them to consider much broader, fundamental issues about the racial divisions in contemporary British society and its assumed multiculturalism and eventually perform ethico-political acts of resubjectivization.

Although *The Colour of Justice* was first staged in areas largely popu-lated by ethnic minorities such as Kilburn (Tricycle), and the East End (Theatre Royal Stratford East) – its subsequent production history enabled it 'to gain a national profile and wider audience' – specifically, we would add, a larger *white* audience.[62] Indeed, with its emphasis on the Metropolitan Police or the judiciary and the predominance of white, mostly middle-class characters as both interrogators and wit-nesses – black characters such as Stephen's parents Doreen and Neville Lawrence, or his friend Duwayne Brooks, have a minor presence – *The Colour of Justice* seems to speak particularly to white spectators.[63] It is they above all who are made intensely aware of their racialized identity positions and impelled to reflect on the questions raised by the play as emancipated audience members. It is they above all who may – or may not – decide to carry out (momentary) acts of resubjectivization that may contribute to bringing about a redistribution of the sensible regarding the (in)visibility of both overt and unconscious racism in contemporary Britain.

The testimony given by Conor Taaffe plays a major role in that connection, since he is a white man honestly admitting that racial prejudices made him suspect initially that Stephen and Duwayne had perhaps 'been involved in a violent fight' or that Stephen's falling to the ground might be 'a ploy' to try and mug whoever approached them.[64] Yet, he did approach them, along with his wife, who cradled Stephen's head and muttered 'You are loved. You are loved' into his ear as he lay dying.[65] The Taaffes' act of resubjectivization and redistribution of the sensible on the scene of Stephen Lawrence's murder stands in the play as a moment that models spectatorial activity, particularly for white audience members. While they first saw, through the prism of covert racism, possible danger to themselves, they instantly reconfigured the sensible so as to perceive, and be able to feel compassion for, two suffering fellow human beings. This moment is followed by Taaffe's unsentimental account of the mourning ritual he performed when he got home:

> [I] washed the blood off my hands with some water in a container, and there is a rose bush in our back garden, a very, very old, huge rose bush – rose tree is I suppose more appropriate – and I poured the water with his blood in it into the bottom of that rose tree. So in a way I suppose he is kind of living on a bit.[66]

Certainly, the response of a number of reviewers seems to have been modelled by Taaffe's testimony. Susannah Clapp describes him as a 'thoughtful witness [who] was also one of the most truthful'; Paul Taylor states that Taaffe was 'the witness who moved [him] the most'; Nightingale calls the moment 'intensely moving'; but what seems particularly significant is that all agree that it is Taaffe's admission of his unconscious racism – and what we may call his and his wife's acts of resubjectivization – that struck them the most.[67]

Taaffe's testimony is strategically placed near the start of the play, underlining its modelling function as regards spectatorial activity. His is actually the second evidence heard, its relevance further enhanced as it is bracketed by the two sharply contrasting testimonies given by Police Constables Bethel and Gleason, who were the first to reach the crime scene. Both Bethel and Gleason vehemently deny the existence of racism within the Metropolitan Police and in their own handling of the situation. Still, when pressed with questions it becomes apparent that they failed to administer first aid to Lawrence, take his pulse or establish the source of the bleeding. Lawyer Stephen Kamlish, acting for the Lawrence family, pointedly links Bethel's 'failure to touch Stephen' to questions about her awareness of the presence of racism in the Met.[68] Equally, it becomes apparent that they treated Brooks more as suspect than victim, not radioing his description of the attackers, and that Gleason is simply lying when he insists that, as family liaison officer, he went into the resuscitation room at the hospital with Neville Lawrence for the identification of Stephen's body.[69] It is in this way, by aseptically letting the racist undertow emerge through the evidence given by police officers and the accused James Acourt, that the play positions spectators, in their dual role as racialized and emancipated, to potentially engage in acts of resubjectivization. These may, in turn, lead to interruptions in the distribution of the sensible as regards racial relations in contemporary Britain.[70] Like the Macpherson Report, *The Colour of Justice* exposes institutional racism, particularly within the Metropolitan Police. However, as the Taaffe episode highlights, the play's focus crucially extends to tracing a potentially all-pervasive presence of unconscious racism across British society, leading to violence which, as Neville Lawrence's description, read by one of the lawyers, states, 'is much worse nowadays'.[71]

Fallout

The racialization of spectatorial perception engendered by *Fallout* troubles any simple dichotomy between white and non-white audience members. Already in 1999, in an article reflecting on the transformations in the history of race relations that took place in Britain between the 1981 Scarman Report and the 1999 Macpherson Report, Hall pointed out that the 'fundamentally binary terms in which British race relations have been mapped have essentially collapsed' through the growing differentiation between and within the various ethnic minority groups.[72] A major focus in *Fallout* is precisely on intra-racial divisions between black characters. The play opens with the murder of a young black student, Kwame, by a gang of four young boys who live on the same estate. Thus, the identity of the actual perpetrator of the murder is not at stake; rather, following the opening scene, the play dissects a range of tensions within the 'black community'.

There is, to start with, the animosity between the murderers – Dwayne, the leader of the group; Emile, who performs the actual killing prompted by the rest; Clinton, who is studying for his BTEC; and Perry. Then there is hard-working Kwame, aspiring to become an architect. Shanice, Emile's girlfriend, accounts for this animosity by claiming that 'Kwame loved to show how smart he was, like deh is two kinds of black, and he come from the better one, he was havin a laugh. People weren't gonna tek dat.'[73] The boys' group also displays its own internal loyalties and rivalries – in particular, Emile and Dwayne are engaged in increasing sexual competition for Shanice's attentions, which involves Dwayne's taunting the far more insecure Emile, who feels he needs to prove himself before the group by inflicting the fatal injuries on Kwame and subsequently stating, 'I want respect, I want it now, bredren.'[74] At the same time, the gang is contrasted with the two young black girls, Shanice and Ronnie. Both have been recently excluded from school, yet, again, important distinctions are made between them – it was the more difficult, confrontational, foul-mouthed Ronnie who caused their expulsion by stealing a wallet, while the brighter Shanice, apparently led by some kind of race, class and gender solidarity, was caught 'red-handed [...] puttin it back'.[75] According to their white teacher, Miss Douglas, whom the two girls assault on her way back home, Shanice has potential while Ronnie is an irresponsible good-for-nothing who is leading a 'scared' Shanice astray; Shanice herself denies this, stating 'I am people like [Ronnie].'[76] There is also the tension between an older embodiment of black masculinity, represented by Manny, Dwayne's absent father, and Dwayne himself, deeply ashamed and aggravated by Manny who, in his drunken stupor, is unable to tell his children by different women apart from each other, as Dwayne reveals. 'Yer so drunk, yu don't even know which yout of yours yer chattin to. Wass my name? Say my name before I buss yer claart all over dis street.'[77]

The most intricate subject position among the black characters is that of Joe, a police constable in his mid-thirties who is sent back to the area he grew up in to investigate the murder of Kwame and confront both the kind of background he himself has escaped from and, equally importantly, the situation in the Metropolitan Police in the wake of the Macpherson Report. As Derbyshire notes, 'Joe is a complex character; it is intentionally left unclear how an audience is meant to respond to him.'[78] On the one hand, in contrast with his white sergeant Matt, Joe is highly critical of the consequences of the Macpherson Report on the day-to-day work of the police force. While Matt insists '[t]he Met needs to change. We can't keep making mistakes', Joe accuses him of being 'a cool liberal', is impatient about what he calls 'all this PC shit', shows his awareness of why he has been brought into the case – '[w]e both know [... i]t's bring out the poster boy. [...] Macpherson report. [... B]ut you had better step back, boy, and let me do my job' – and, in his frustration, ends up wishing 'the old school of police' was back.[79] As Joe becomes increasingly obsessed about convicting the boys for the murder and attempts to cut corners by feeding Ronnie information about Kwame's trainers so she will use it in her statement, the cautious Matt tries to stop him making a serious mistake and identifies the grounds for Joe's anger – 'You were Kwame. Weren't you?'[80] Eventually, Joe loses control of the situation. After the unnamed white female inspector realizes that Ronnie's statement has been primed and that there is no evidence for prosecuting the gang, Joe steps out of limits in order to find

Emile and interrogate him on his own, ultimately unleashing his rage on the young boy:

> Kwame had a life. He was a decent kid. But you, you! (*Slaps him repeatedly.*) You want a life, bwoi, get your own. Why you have to tek his? You know what, it's fuckers like you, [...] why I had to leave. Now it's fuckers like you that bring me back to where I started. You had to drag me down, innit? You had to drag Kwame down. [...] (*Slaps him.*)[81]

Nor do the white characters in the play – Matt, the inspector and teacher Miss Douglas – form a homogeneous group. Matt, as has been mentioned, clearly embodies a post-Macpherson attitude within the police force. Miss Douglas and the inspector, to be played by the same actor according to the author's specifications, are both authority figures.[82] However, as a victim of Shanice and Ronnie's aggression and also someone who has tried to reach out to Shanice, Miss Douglas differs from the more one-dimensional inspector, who bluntly exercises her power to blame and demean Ronnie – '[y]ou will love anything that will stop you from being reminded of what you really are, a sad, lonely little girl, with no friends', she tells her.[83] In sum, by foregrounding not only the racial but also the class, gender, educational and age identity positions of the various characters, most particularly the black ones, *Fallout* invites a racialized mode of spectatorship that stretches far beyond any homogeneous perception of the black or white communities. It interpellates both black and white audience members, making them vividly aware of their own particular, multifarious identities without anticipating a specific response – spectators remain, in this sense, emancipated and unpredictable. They are invited to bring to bear on the play their culturally located itineraries and eventually proceed to acts of ethico-political resubjectivization, without a specific outcome being either predicted or determined.

random

In *random* one single black actress – Nadine Marshall in the Royal Court premiere production – plays all the characters, standing practically still on a bare stage, switching between the voices of the four members of a West Indian family, Sister, Brother, Mum and Dad, as well as those of a few other minor characters, including Brother's teacher, three police officers, Sister's work colleagues or Brother's friends. Sister, the main narrative voice, recounts the events of an ordinary day, starting from the family's early morning routines, which becomes extraordinary when she is urgently summoned back home from the office by a text from Mum – '[c]ome home. Now'[84] – to learn her school-age Brother has been stabbed to death in a street incident. Unlike *Fallout*, as Goddard notes, *random* does not show the murder itself and the focus is on the family's reaction rather than the police investigation.[85]

It can be argued that the primary way in which *random* makes spectators acutely aware of their racialized identity positions is through its use of a vivid black urban vernacular, mixed Caribbean and British. This emerges from several white reviewers' reactions at the Royal Court production, expressing difficulty in following Marshall's monologue. De Jongh found it 'too often unintelligible', Quentin Letts stated the urban patois was 'hard for a middle-class, white ear to follow', Charles Spencer pointed out that the 'strongly-accented delivery' was a challenge to spectators 'more familiar with RP English' and John Nathan mentioned the play's 'colloquial language, which is sometimes hard to understand'.[86] In contrast, reviewers noted how the young black audience members who were present on opening night instantly recognized and identified with the language spoken on stage – for them, 'it was clearly a blast to hear the language of home and street legitimised on the Royal Court stage'.[87] At the same time, the play makes white spectators aware of their racialized identity by 'bringing [them] up against their prejudices', as Taylor's review acknowledged in connection with his own assumption that the presence of the police in the family home meant that 'the brother had got into trouble'.[88] In another instance, assumptions seeped through with the reviewer seemingly being totally unaware – 'it is almost a shame the play has to stray into an Issue [*sic*]: Black-on-Black violence', Christopher Hart asserted, when in fact the text makes no reference whatsoever to the racial identity of the assailants.[89] However, *random* refuses to endorse monolithic racial identities, on stage or in terms of spectatorial identification. It makes spectators racially self-conscious and asks them to step out of any rigidly defined identity category, enabling them to become emancipated and perform (sporadic) acts of resubjectivization through an intense imaginative and emotional engagement.

Sister's polyphonic monologue itself, as Marissia Fragkou argues, turns '[t]he performer's body [into] a fluid representation of identity cutting across gender, race and age'.[90] Indeed, she seamlessly glides between genders – female (herself, Mum, teacher, Brother's female friends, Sister's work colleagues Jane and Sally, Victim Support Officer), male (Brother, Dad, Brother's male friends, Sister's work colleagues Deepak and John) and unmarked (the three police officers), ages – the younger generation (Sister, Brother, Brother's friends, Sister's colleagues) as opposed to the older characters (Mum, Dad, teacher, possibly the police officers), as well as races – black (herself, Mum, Dad, Brother, Brother's male and female friends), white (teacher, Jane, John and Sally), Indian (Deepak) and unmarked (police officers and Victim Support Officer). Importantly, differences are highlighted within those groups through variations in accent, rhythm, pace of delivery and tone as well as minimal bodily gestures, exemplified by one reviewer suggesting that '[o]ne moment [Marshall was] Mum – slight stoop, concerned brow, sentences scattered with "raas" and "smoddy"; then Sister, all street-stroppy attitude [...] with a belligerent back-tilt of the head and slashing hand movements; the Brother, with twisted smile, gangly limbs, sleepiness'.[91] This dissolves any semblance of homogeneity within the various identity positions, foregrounding instead a diversity that provides spectators with a range of points of imaginative and emotional access to the play which do not cancel each other out, but rather coexist in a dynamic, ongoing relationship. Thus, as in *Fallout*, the absence of homogeneous identity positions on stage 'complicates viewers' traditional modes of identification and thwarts [...] any unified audience response'.[92] Instead, *random* invites the gaze of emancipated spectators who, released to their emotions and imaginations, will listen to and engage with Sister's monologue in terms which may lead to (momentary) acts of resubjectivization and redistribution of the sensible in relation to issues of race and violence in contemporary Britain.

Such ethico-political acts of spectatorial resubjectivization are enabled, in the first part of the play – up to the moment Mum sees 'the shadow of some somebodies', the police, through her front door and sends her ominous text message to Sister – by an emphasis on the family's shared daily routines presented through a humorous prism.[93] In a play where action, as Fragkou notes, 'is confined in the imaginary and the discursive', spectators are invited to engage emotionally and imaginatively in ways that go far beyond race, class, age, gender and other self-contained, rigidly defined categories in order to recognize the human ordinariness of the lives of others.[94] As one reviewer states, 'you can mentally see the children unwillingly waking up, coming down to breakfast, being fussed over by Mum'.[95] In the second part of the play, where the focus is on a range of reactions to the murder of Brother, spectators are impelled to 'share the feelings of grief inflicted upon the family irrespective of fixed racial, class, age or gender identity positions'.[96] Fragkou's reading of such emphasis on grief and vulnerability from the perspective of Judith Butler's work on our shared human precariousness and mutual dependence seems pertinent in that connection. Moreover, as Osborne notes, the decision to have *random* performed at the Royal Court Downstairs, on a stage 'stripped of its illusion-making apparatus (no props, set, lighting special effects, or other actors) [...] accentuated actor Nadine Marshall's vulnerability'.[97] According to the record of first-night spectatorial reactions provided by reviewers, while the first part of the play was indeed greeted with 'laughter of recognition', the second part was shrouded by 'a pin-drop silence as tragedy erupt[ed]'.[98]

At the same time, the family's, particularly Mum's, muted expressions of grief interestingly evoke and yet unsettle, once again, spectators' racialized identities by both 'being so English'[99] – unexpectedly so perhaps in a first-generation migrant – and yet making no concessions to the white, liberal, post-Stephen Lawrence conscience which, Hall argues, was touched and moved by the Lawrence parents being 'so exceptional in their dignified forbearance throughout, so manifestly a serious, responsible and respectable couple'.[100] Mum explicitly refuses to visit her son's 'street shrine' precisely to avoid being described as 'dignified' and 'strong', the adjectives that were recurrently used to qualify the Lawrences – 'I don't got nuthin nice to say. / Nu'un polite / nu'un / broadcastable / nu'un / righteous / nu'un forgivin / juss pure ...'[101] Ultimately, spectators – simultaneously racialized and emancipated – are prompted to engage in a reconfiguration of the sensible that involves the play's title itself. While a number of commentators have taken it as a statement of fact – that is, that the murder of Brother is a purely random act of violence – a questioning of the randomness of the assault is embedded in Sister's monologue at two crucial points.[102] Firstly, when she forensically describes the wounds on Brother's body, which she goes to identify with Dad – the fatal wound was 'the smallest / The cleanest [...] Not no random'.[103] And then, near the close of the play, when she poses an unanswered question – '[r]andom don't happen to everybody [...] / How come / "random" haveta happen to him?' – that reads as an invitation to spectators to rethink the alleged randomness of such incidents.[104] That is particularly so perhaps when Sister's question is placed alongside mediatised accounts such as Hugh Muir's significantly titled 'Random Violence Leaves Five Dead and Locals in Fear', published in *The Guardian* at the start of the 2007–8 spate of street crime in Britain.[105] Muir avoids any explicit reference to race and insists that 'the violence [is] random. The only common strands are the proliferation of guns and the fact that the shooters and their victims are getting younger';

however, some of those quoted in his article, such as Uanu Shesmi, director of a Peckham-based charity that works with local youths, draw attention to the deep-running social causes of the crimes, whose victims, as noted in the IRR *Youth Deaths* report referenced at the start of this chapter, were 90 per cent non-white.[106]

Spectators as witnesses

Spectatorial activity in relation to *The Colour of Justice, Fallout* and *random* is not only jointly racialized and emancipated but, crucially, it is also modelled by the centrality of witnessing in the three plays. As a 'tribunal' documentary play, both the staging and the understated acting of *The Colour of Justice* at the Tricycle Theatre meticulously evoked a courtroom where a range of individuals involved in one way or another in the Stephen Lawrence case were called in to account for their actions. As noted earlier, the play does not pass any judgement on the different testimonies but rather allows each of them individually and collectively to speak for themselves and interpellate spectators as witnesses of the entire proceedings. It seems significant, in this connection, that spectators at the Tricycle very much felt as if they were attending the proceedings themselves.[107] In the case of *Fallout*, the Damilola Taylor case false witness code-named 'Bromley' is significantly mirrored in the character of Ronnie, whose unreliable testimony, partly fed by black police constable Joe, is foregrounded towards the end of the play. At the same time, the Royal Court in-the-round production of the play, designed by Ultz, arguably placed spectators themselves in the position of rather self-conscious witnesses, looking down from the circle on the characters, who were caged in by wire meshing – a stage picture that evoked the grim landscape of council estates and placed spectators in a particular, unusual perspective.[108] In *random*, witnessing defines what Sister does – she becomes the main narrator of the day's events, the voice that channels all other voices and bears testimony to the family's suffering and their grief. At the same time, witnessing is thematized within Sister's narrative itself, in particular when she refers to the range of responses to the crime scene, from people turning it into a 'street shrine' by leaving testimonies of their grief, to others passing by without even looking, to Brother's schoolmates 'witnessin somethin they shouldn't', the mainstream white press's stereotypical, sensationalistic approach, or people who saw the assault refusing to bear witness.[109] Finally, the intimacy generated between the solo performer and the audience clearly casts spectators as witnesses to Sister's narrative.

The witness, Shoshana Felman and Dori Laub claim, is entrusted with a double task – they are witness both to the testimony that is presented to them and a witness to themselves.[110] Since the act of giving testimony/bearing witness does not simply involve the reproduction/absorption of a 'factual given', but is rather 'an event in its own right', a 'situation of discovery of knowledge', the modelling of spectators as witnesses in *The Colour of Justice, Fallout* and *random* enhances their emancipation – rather than anticipate a specific ethico-political response, it engages them in a path of discovery that is also, crucially, an activity of self-discovery.[111] That its end result may be (temporary) acts of spectatorial resubjectivization and reconfiguration of the distribution of the sensible is strongly inscribed in the plays themselves and their contexts of production, but is not a foregone conclusion. What does seem certain is that, to the extent that the plays achieved that dual aim, they did not do so in isolation, but as part of a much wider canvas of political, social and cultural developments, all of them contributing to effecting significant interruptions in the distribution of the sensible regarding race relations in contemporary United Kingdom.[112]

Notes

1. R. Wood, *Youth Deaths: The Reality behind the 'Knife Crime' Debate* (London: Institute of Race Relations, 2010), p. 4. For further details about the Stephen Lawrence case, see B. Cathcart, *The Case of Stephen Lawrence*, 2nd edn. (Harmondsworth: Penguin, 2000); S. Cottle, *The Racist Murder of Stephen Lawrence: Media Performance and Public Transformation* (Westport, CT and London: Praeger, 2004); and S. Laville, 'Stephen Lawrence Case: Timeline', *The Guardian*, 3 January 2012, http://www.guardian.co.uk/ (accessed 23 March 2012). More information on the Damilola Taylor case is available at 'Damilola Taylor: Timeline' (2006), BBC News, http://news.bbc.co.uk/ (accessed 4 June 2012). Wood, *Youth Deaths*, and K. Barling (2007), 'Teen Deaths on London's Streets', BBC News, http://www.bbc.co.uk/london/ (accessed 4 June 2012), discuss the 2007–8 surge of street crime.
2. See J. Rancière, *The Politics of Aesthetics: The Distribution of the Sensible* (London and New York: Continuum, 2004) and J. Rancière, *The Emancipated Spectator* (London and New York: Verso, 2009); J. Spencer, 'Emancipated Spectatorship in Adrienne Kennedy's Plays', *Modern Drama*, 55.1 (2012), 19–39.
3. Institute of Race Relations, *Counting the Cost: Racial Violence since Macpherson* (London: Institute of Race Relations, 2001), p. 5.
4. Cathcart, *The Case of Stephen Lawrence*, p. 416.
5. The full report, W. Macpherson, *The Stephen Lawrence Inquiry: Report of an Inquiry* (Norwich: The Stationery Office (House of Commons), 1999), is available at http://www.archive.official-documents.co.uk/document/cm42/4262/4262.htm. A summation, 'The Macpherson Report: Summary',

was published in *The Guardian* on 24 February 1999 and is available at http://
www.guardian.co.uk/lawrence/Story/0,,208693,00.html. See A. Sivanandan,
Macpherson and After (London: Institute of Race Relations, 2000), http://
www.irr.org.uk/2000/february/ak000001.html (accessed 20 December 2011);
Cottle, *The Racist Murder of Stephen Lawrence*, pp. 189, 192–3 and passim; and
J. Reinelt, 'Toward a Poetics of Theatre and Public Events: In the Case of Stephen
Lawrence', *TDR: The Drama Review*, 50.3 (2006), 69–87 (pp. 73 and 76).

6. Sivanandan, *Macpherson and After*; Cottle, *The Racist Murder of Stephen
Lawrence*, p. 193. It is relevant to note that in the wake of the April 1981
Brixton race riots, Lord Scarman was appointed by Margaret Thatcher's government to conduct an official inquiry into their causes. While the Scarman
Report, published on 25 November 1981, concluded that institutional racism in Britain did not exist, Stuart Hall has argued that it was distinctive in
that it made strong case for a social and historical explanation of the riots
(S. Hall, 'From Scarman to Stephen Lawrence', *History Workshop Journal*, 48
(1999), 187–97 (p. 189)).

7. Quoted in Cathcart, *The Case of Stephen Lawrence*, p. 409.

8. Hall, 'From Scarman to Stephen Lawrence', p. 195.

9. Rancière, *Politics of Aesthetics*, p. 13.

10. Cottle, *The Racist Murder of Stephen Lawrence*, p. 191.

11. Sivanandan, *Macpherson and After*; Cottle, *The Racist Murder of Stephen
Lawrence*, pp. 188 and 194; Cathcart, *The Case of Stephen Lawrence*, p. 402.

12. Institute of Race Relations, *Counting the Cost*, pp. 5–6.

13. H. Athwal, J. Bourne and R. Wood, *Racial Violence: The Buried Issue* (London:
Institute of Race Relations, 2010), pp. 5–6.

14. H. Athwal, *Deaths with a (Known or Suspected) Racial Element 2000 Onwards*
(London: Institute of Race Relations, 2011), http://www.irr.org.uk/2002/
november/ak000008.html (accessed 3 May 2012).

15. Cathcart, *The Case of Stephen Lawrence*, p. 419; Institute of Race Relations,
Counting the Cost, p. 5.

16. Cottle, *The Racist Murder of Stephen Lawrence*, p. 20 (emphasis added).

17. Cathcart, *The Case of Stephen Lawrence*, p. 419; C. Greer, 'News Media,
Victims and Crime', in C. Greer, P. Davies and P. Francis (eds.), *Victims, Crime
and Society* (London and New Delhi: Sage, 2007), p. 36.

18. Rancière, *Politics of Aesthetics*, p. 18.

19. L. Goddard, *Staging Black Feminisms: Identity, Politics, Performance* (Basingstoke:
Palgrave Macmillan, 2007), p. 10.

20. S. Hall, 'Cultural Identity and Diaspora', in P. Williams and L. Chisman (eds.),
Colonial Discourse and Post-Colonial Theory: A Reader (New York: Columbia
University Press, 1994), pp. 392–403

21. Goddard, *Staging Black Feminisms*, p. 10.

22. Goddard, *Staging Black Feminisms*, p. 36.

23. D. Osborne, 'The State of the Nation: Contemporary Black British Theatre
and the Staging of the UK', in C. Houswitschka and A. Müller (eds.), *Staging
Displacement, Exile and Diaspora* (Trier: Wissenschaftlicher Verlag Trier, 2005),
p. 130.

24. Osborne, 'State of the Nation', p. 129.

25. J. Verma, 'Cultural Transformations', in T. Shank (ed.), *Contemporary British
Theatre*, 2nd edn. (Basingstoke: Macmillan, 1996), p. 55.

26. Verma, 'Cultural Transformations', p. 55.
27. K. Peacock, *Thatcher's Theatre: British Theatre and Drama in the Eighties* (Westport, CT and London: Greenwood Press, 1999), p. 180.
28. Quoted in Peacock, *Thatcher's Theatre*, p. 175.
29. Peacock, *Thatcher's Theatre*, p. 175.
30. Peacock, *Thatcher's Theatre*, p. 184.
31. According to Verma, Tara Arts has developed a style of '"total theatre" that pose[s] a challenge to the largely realistic conventions of the majority of British theatre' ('Cultural Transformations', p. 56).
32. Goddard, *Staging Black Feminisms*, pp. 50–1.
33. Goddard, *Staging Black Feminisms*, p. 51.
34. H.-T. Lehmann, *Postdramatic Theatre* (London and New York: Routledge, 2006), p. 178 (original emphasis).
35. N. Ridout, *Theatre & Ethics* (Basingstoke: Palgrave Macmillan, 2009), p. 70.
36. D. Rebellato, 'From the State of the Nation to Globalization: Shifting Political Agendas in Contemporary British Playwriting', in N. Holdsworth and M. Luckhurst (eds.), *A Concise Companion to Contemporary British and Irish Drama* (Oxford: Blackwell, 2008), p. 259. See also Rebellato, *Theatre & Globalization* (Basingstoke: Palgrave Macmillan, 2009), p. 29.
37. Such is the view put forward by L. Goddard, '"Death never used to be for the young": Grieving Teenage Murder in debbie tucker green's *random*', *Women: A Cultural Review*, 20.3 (2009), 299–309 (p. 306).
38. C. Megson, '"This is All Theatre": Iraq Centre Stage', *Contemporary Theatre Review*, 15.3 (2005), 369–71 (p. 371); D. Paget, '"Verbatim Theatre": Oral History and Documentary Techniques', *New Theatre Quarterly*, 3.12 (1987), 317–36 (p. 325), respectively. The success of *The Riots*, a new documentary play by Gillian Slovo on the trouble that first erupted in Tottenham in the summer of 2011 and then spread to other parts of London, confirms the continuing popularity of the genre. Like *Guantanamo* (2004), co-authored by Slovo and V. Brittain, *The Riots* opened at the Tricycle Theatre (17 November 2011), where it had a sell-out run and received critical acclaim.
39. For further details on the production history of *The Colour of Justice*, see V. K. Lucas, '"There's No Justice – Just Us": Black Britons, British Asians, and the Criminal Justice System in Verbatim Drama', in R. V. Arana (ed.), *'Black' British Aesthetics Today* (Newcastle: Cambridge Scholars Publishing, 2007), pp. 263–4.
40. S. Bottoms, 'Putting the Document into Documentary: An Unwelcome Corrective?', *TDR: The Drama Review*, 50.3 (2006), 56–68 (p. 57).
41. J. Reinelt, 'The Promise of Documentary', in A. Forsyth and C. Megson (eds.), *Get Real: Documentary Theatre Past and Present* (Basingstoke: Palgrave Macmillan, 2009), pp. 8–10. Reinelt draws on S. Bruzzi, *New Documentary*, 2nd edn. (London and New York: Routledge, 2006).
42. Reinelt, 'The Promise of Documentary', p. 11.
43. E. Barry and W. Boles, 'Beyond Victimhood: Agency and Identity in the Theatre of Roy Williams', in D. Godiwala (ed.), *Alternatives within the Mainstream: British Black and Asian Theatres* (Newcastle: Cambridge Scholars Publishing, 2006), p. 311. Regarding *Little Sweet Thing* in particular, Barry and Boles note that it marked 'a turning-point in terms of social theatre history, having achieved in a mainstream London theatre [Hampstead Theatre] an audience that was over sixty per cent non-white' (p. 310). Channel 4's *Fallout*

was part of their 'Disarming Britain' season, which ran for three months from
May to August 2008 as a response to the 2007–8 surge of street crime.

44. Barry and Boles, 'Beyond Victimhood', p. 312.
45. D. Osborne, 'Roy Williams', in M. Middeke, P. P. Schnierer and A. Sierz
(eds.), *The Methuen Drama Guide to Contemporary British Playwrights* (London:
Methuen Drama, 2011), pp. 499–500; D. Howe, 'Review of *Fallout*', *Theatre
Record*, 23.11–12 (2003), 760.
46. G. Brown, 'Review of *Fallout*', *Theatre Record*, 23.11–12 (2003), 757; J. Peter,
'Review of *Fallout*', *Theatre Record*, 23.11–12 (2003), 758; M. Billington, 'Review
of *Fallout*', *Theatre Record*, 23.11–12 (2003), 759; K. Bassett, 'Review of *Fallout*',
Theatre Record, 23.11–12 (2003), 756.
47. N. de Jongh, 'Review of *Fallout*', *Theatre Record*, 23.11–12 (2003), 756;
R. Koening, 'Review of *Fallout*', *Theatre Record*, 23.11–12 (2003), 756.
48. Osborne, 'State of the Nation', p. 137.
49. H. Derbyshire, 'Roy Williams: Representing Multicultural Britain in *Fallout*',
Modern Drama, 50.3 (2007), 414–34 (p. 430).
50. Rancière, *Emancipated Spectator*, pp. 2, 17.
51. Rancière, *Emancipated Spectator*, p. 13.
52. Rancière, *Emancipated Spectator*, pp. 16–17.
53. Spencer, 'Emancipated Spectatorship in Adrienne Kennedy's Plays', p. 22.
Joe Kelleher also underlines the unpredictability of spectators' responses.
J. Kelleher, *Theatre & Politics* (Basingstoke: Palgrave Macmillan, 2009), pp. 22
and 24.
54. G. Rockhill, 'Translator's Introduction: Jacques Rancière's Politics of Perception',
in Rancière, *Politics of Aesthetics*, p. 3; Rancière, *Politics of Aesthetics*, p. 18.
55. Rancière, *Politics of Aesthetics*, p. 14.
56. Spencer, 'Emancipated Spectatorship in Adrienne Kennedy's Plays', p. 23.
57. Spencer, 'Emancipated Spectatorship in Adrienne Kennedy's Plays', pp. 25, 27.
58. Spencer, 'Emancipated Spectatorship in Adrienne Kennedy's Plays', p. 30.
59. J. Peter, 'Review of *The Colour of Justice*', *Theatre Record*, 19.1–2 (1999), 44;
S. Clapp, 'Review of *The Colour of Justice*', *Theatre Record*, 19.1–2 (1999), 41;
A. Macaulay, 'Review of *The Colour of Justice*', *Theatre Record*, 19.1–2 (1999),
41–2; and J. Gross, 'Review of *The Colour of Justice*', *Theatre Record*, 19.1–2
(1999), 42.
60. B. Nightingale, 'Review of *The Colour of Justice*', *Theatre Record*, 19.1–2 (1999),
42–3.
61. Lucas, '"There's No Justice – Just Us"', p. 265, and C. Spencer, 'Review of
The Colour of Justice', *Theatre Record*, 19.1–2 (1999), 43.
62. Lucas, '"There's No Justice – Just Us"', p. 263.
63. Lucas, '"There's No Justice – Just Us"', p. 271.
64. R. Norton-Taylor, *The Colour of Justice* (London: Oberon Books, 1999),
p. 37. Duwayne Brooks's statement, which is read out later in the play, confirms that the Taaffes seemed suspicious when they first saw himself and
Stephen, p. 91.
65. Norton-Taylor, *The Colour of Justice*, p. 36.
66. Norton-Taylor, *The Colour of Justice*, p. 36.
67. Clapp, 'Review of *The Colour of Justice*', p. 41; P. Taylor, 'Review of
The Colour of Justice', *Theatre Record*, 19.1–2 (1999), 42; Nightingale, 'Review
of *The Colour of Justice*', 42–3.

68. Norton-Taylor, *The Colour of Justice*, pp. 29–30.
69. Norton-Taylor, *The Colour of Justice*, pp. 42–4.
70. The exception among the police officers is Mr William Mellish, formerly Detective Superintendent, who was in charge of the second investigation into the Stephen Lawrence murder set up in May 1994 (Norton-Taylor, *The Colour of Justice*, pp. 116–22).
71. Norton-Taylor, *The Colour of Justice*, p. 61. Comparison is made to when Lawrence first moved to Britain, in the 1960s.
72. Hall, 'From Scarman to Stephen Lawrence', p. 191.
73. R. Williams, *Plays: 3* (London: Methuen Drama, 2008), p. 36. It is worth noting, in connection with Kwame, that Stephen Lawrence was planning to study architecture at university (Hall, 'From Scarman to Stephen Lawrence', p. 196). As Derbyshire ('Roy Williams: Representing Multicultural Britain in *Fallout*', p. 418) points out, *Fallout* was not only a response to the Damilola Taylor case, but was also written in the long shadow of the Lawrence case.
74. Williams, *Plays: 3*, p. 65.
75. Williams, *Plays: 3*, p. 59.
76. Williams, *Plays: 3*, p. 61.
77. Williams, *Plays: 3*, pp. 90–1.
78. Derbyshire, 'Roy Williams: Representing Multicultural Britain in *Fallout*', p. 422.
79. Williams, *Plays: 3*, pp. 50–1, 97.
80. Williams, *Plays: 3*, p. 96.
81. Williams, *Plays: 3*, p. 112.
82. Williams, *Plays: 3*, p. 4; Derbyshire, 'Roy Williams: Representing Multicultural Britain in *Fallout*', p. 429.
83. Williams, *Plays: 3*, p. 109.
84. d. tucker green, *random* (London: Nick Hern Books, 2008), p. 23.
85. Goddard, 'Grieving Teenage Murder', p. 300.
86. N. de Jongh, 'Review of *random*', *Theatre Record*, 28.6 (2008), 284; Q. Letts, 'Review of *random*', *Theatre Record*, 28.6 (2008), 284; C. Spencer, 'Review of *random*', *Theatre Record*, 28.6 (2008), 285; and J. Nathan, 'Review of *random*', *Theatre Record*, 28.6 (2008), 287.
87. S. Edge, 'Review of *random*', *Theatre Record*, 28.6 (2008), 285. There is no agreement as to the racial composition of audiences for the premiere production of *random* at the Royal Court. Most reviewers point out that the first-night audience was largely formed by young black people; Kelleher notes that on the night in March 2008 when he attended the performance, 'a large proportion of the audience [were] Black people' (*Theatre & Politics*, p. 20); M. Fragkou adds that throughout its run, 'the play attracted large numbers of young audience members, especially black youths, who literally flooded the predominantly white, middle-class Royal Court auditorium' (M. Fragkou, 'Intercultural Encounters in debbie tucker green's *random*', in W. Huber, M. Rubik and J. Novak (eds.), *Staging Interculturality* (Trier: Wissenschaftlicher Verlag Trier, 2010), p. 79). However, in the context of a discussion of *Fallout*, Osborne points out that 'the Royal Court are unable to confirm demographics of its theatre-goers' (Osborne, 'State of the Nation', p. 137).
88. P. Taylor, 'Review of *random*', *Theatre Record*, 28.6 (2008), 284–5.

89. C. Hart, 'Review of *random*', *Theatre Record*, 28.6 (2008), 286; see also C. Allfree, 'Review of *random*', *Theatre Record*, 28.6 (2008), 284. Sister reports that the police think the murderer is 'a "yout – another yout"' (tucker green, *random*, p. 28) – no race is specified.

90. Fragkou, 'Intercultural Encounters in debbie tucker green's *random*', p. 83.

91. Hart, 'Review of *random*', p. 286; see also M. Shenton, 'Review of *random*', *Theatre Record*, 28.6 (2008), 286. Goddard draws attention to the importance of the front room in West Indian households ('Grieving Teenage Murder', pp. 301–2); in that respect, it might be inferred that the police officers who walk into the family's front room in *random* without even taking off their '[d]ark boots an' heavy shoes' (tucker green, *random*, p. 26) are possibly white, without that being an inevitable inference. On the other hand, the Victim Support Officer does take off her shoes (tucker green, *random*, p. 43).

92. Spencer, 'Emancipated Spectatorship in Adrienne Kennedy's Plays', p. 26.

93. tucker green, *random*, p. 22.

94. Fragkou, 'Intercultural Encounters in debbie tucker green's *random*', p. 78.

95. B. Nightingale, 'Review of *random*', *Theatre Record*, 28.6 (2008), 285.

96. Fragkou, 'Intercultural Encounters in debbie tucker green's *random*', p. 83.

97. D. Osborne, 'How Do We Get the Whole Story? Contra-dictions and Counter-narratives in debbie tucker green's Dramatic-Poetics', in M. Tönnies and C. Flotmann (eds.), *Narrative in Drama* (Trier: Wissenschaftlicher Verlag Trier, 2011), p. 199. Some reviewers, in contrast, felt the play would have worked better in the smaller Upstairs space (Allfree, 'Review of *random*', p. 284; G. Brown, 'Review of *random*', *Theatre Record*, 28.6 (2008), 286; de Jongh, 'Review of *random*', p. 284), or even as a radio play (de Jongh, 'Review of *random*', p. 284).

98. M. Billington, 'Review of *random*', *Theatre Record*, 28.6 (2008), 284; see also A. Sierz, 'Review of *random*', *Theatre Record*, 28.6 (2008), 287.

99. Sierz, 'Review of *random*', p. 287.

100. Hall, 'From Scarman to Stephen Lawrence', p. 196.

101. tucker green, *random*, pp. 40, 42.

102. See, for instance, Goddard, 'Grieving Teenage Murder', p. 301; Fragkou, 'Intercultural Encounters in debbie tucker green's *random*', p. 81; Kelleher, *Theatre & Politics*, pp. 18, 21; and Sierz, 'Review of *random*', p. 287.

103. tucker green, *random*, p. 37.

104. tucker green, *random*, p. 49.

105. H. Muir, 'Random Violence Leaves Five Dead and Locals in Fear', *The Guardian*, 16 February 2007, http://www.guardian.co.uk/ (accessed 15 December 2011).

106. Muir, 'Random Violence Leaves Five Dead and Locals in Fear'.

107. See, for example, M. Billington, 'Review of *The Colour of Justice*', *Theatre Record*, 19.1–2 (1999), 40–1; Clapp, 'Review of *The Colour of Justice*', p. 41; R. Foss, 'Review of *The Colour of Justice*', *Theatre Record*, 19.1–2 (1999), 43; Macaulay, 'Review of *The Colour of Justice*', pp. 41–2; Peter, 'Review of *The Colour of Justice*', p. 44; and Spencer, 'Review of *The Colour of Justice*', p. 43.

108. Osborne, as already noted, finds that spectators were positioned as voyeurs and encouraged to objectify the characters and the action ('State of the Nation', p. 137).

109. tucker green, *random*, pp. 40–1, 45. Some reviewers objected to Sister's dismissive reference to 'blue-eyed reporters' as expressing black-on-white racial prejudice (Hart, 'Review of *random*', p. 286; Letts, 'Review of *random*', p. 284), one more indication, perhaps, of the intense racial self-consciousness generated by the play.

110. S. Felman and D. Laub, *Testimony: Crises of Witnessing in Literature, Psychoanalysis, and History* (New York and London: Routledge, 1992), p. 58.

111. Felman and Laub, *Testimony*, p. 62.

112. Research towards this chapter was supported by the Spanish Ministry of Science and Innovation (research project FFI2009-07598/FILO) as well as, in the case of Mireia Aragay, by the research group GRAE-Grup de Recerca en Arts Escèniques, funded by AGAUR-Generalitat de Catalunya (2009SGR1034).

6
Old Wine in a New Bottle or Vice Versa? Winsome Pinnock's Interstitial Poetics

Elizabeth Sakellaridou

In her critical anthology on black and Asian British theatre *Alternatives Within the Mainstream: British Black and Asian Theatres* (2006), Dimple Godiwala makes a dynamic and impressive claim about the central position of black and Asian dramatists and theatre practitioners in contemporary British culture.[1] Drawing on Bourdieu's sociological theory, Godiwala creates a strong locus for diasporic/interstitial writers and artists as the best qualified to tackle the heterogeneity of contemporary British culture. In this upgrading process, she rejects the 'postcolonial' as a 'now tired term', which, being relational to colonialism, perpetuates a subordinate understanding of all other cultures by the Eurocentric 'doxa'.[2] In highly hierarchical countries, like Britain, this has led to the institutionalization of racism and a peculiar 'tokenization' of the black artist.[3] It is precisely the role of the diasporic/interstitial subject to fill in what exist as lacunae in the indigenous British subject's 'doxic field'.[4]

Firmly grounded in contemporary theory, Godiwala's position is convincingly assertive by comparison to some earlier postcolonial views, for instance, Gabrielle Griffin's wishful thinking in her article 'Constitutive Subjectivities: Contemporary Black and Asian Women Playwrights in Britain' (2003).[5] Godiwala's is a fresh and original voice speaking for a holistic understanding of New Britishness, a notion which also compels a redefinition of indigenous, not only migrant identities.[6] This is an advanced, post-millennial view about the functioning role of black (and Asian) creativity in the theatrical field and its contribution to the construction of a multi-faceted cultural image of contemporary Britain. What is more, it is also pragmatic enough to take into account the difficulties of doing black theatre in Britain because of the different audience expectations, which, as has been observed elsewhere, are dictated by 'a racialized regime of representation'.[7]

A synthesis of such post-millennial views theorizing the cultural condition of contemporary Britain can form a very useful frame, together with earlier and/or more specific critical works on dramatists and theatre practitioners, for a post-millennial reassessment of Winsome Pinnock. She is one of the most distinguished black women playwrights in Britain today, recipient of a number of theatre awards and the first one to have had work staged at the National Theatre. Despite the recent appearance of new black female voices, Pinnock remains a major figure: active, resourceful and innovative both in her thematic concerns and expressive tools. It is this incessant mobility and renewal of her art – I wish to contest – that secures her a central position in the contemporary British theatrical scene.

Post-millennial criticism of black British culture, especially in the domain of the theatre, has moved away from the binarism of earlier critical terms such as post-/imperial or post-/colonial and embraced more positive terms originating in the maturing cultural theory of the late 1980s and 1990s. This new criticism focuses mainly on such key terms as 'diasporization' and 'interstitiality', notions introduced into cultural studies by Stuart Hall and Homi Bhabha respectively. The advantage of these neologisms is that they have geared cultural theory to more conciliatory, syncretic perspectives, not only speaking for the broadening scope of theory itself but also reflecting the feelings and tendencies of the majority of black artists and theatre practitioners.

Specifically regarding black women's theatre, Meenakshi Ponnuswami, in the seminal 'Small Island People: Black Women Playwrights' (2000), modifies this newly articulated black aesthetic to the work of contemporary women dramatists (with specific reference to the work of Pinnock), defining it as a politicized, diasporic postmodernism and putting forward a new, explicit (albeit prescriptive) black feminist poetics.[8] This renewed perspective changed substantially the critical map charted by earlier critics of the 1990s like Mary Karen Dahl and Elaine Savory.[9] Ponnuswami's millennial essay became a key source for most subsequent studies in the field, such as Griffin's or Elaine Aston's, which carried Ponnuswami's modified diasporic aesthetic onto the analysis of specific writers and texts.[10] In both cases Pinnock figures as a model black artist vindicating the theoretical presuppositions set. More recently (2006), DeLinda Marzette conducted a more systematic analysis of Pinnock's work, though focusing on her earlier plays only. What is remarkable in her study is the application of a fresh cultural discourse, which combines Bhabha's notion of 'interstitiality' with that of Cixous's 'entre-deux' and highlights this British-Caribbean writer's 'diasporic stylistics'.[11]

What remains problematic in these studies of Pinnock's work is that the critics' invariable reference to this writer's 'poetics', 'aesthetics' or 'stylistics' is vague and what often starts as general praise of her innovative tactics soon narrows down to a thematic renewal alone, while the formal aspect is silenced or at best treated with caution or an admission of a basically traditional realistic form. In *Staging Black Feminisms: Identity, Politics, Performance* (2007), Lynette Goddard is the only critic to observe Pinnock's diasporic politics as a double shift, thematic and formal alike, introducing examples from the plays to substantiate her view. A number of other critics with an exclusive or partial focus on Pinnock's work seem to limit themselves to the playwright's more obvious thematic shifts or broadening of ideas, thus succumbing to an earlier 'black' canon which – no doubt – reflects the indigenous 'doxa' about the work of diasporic writing in Britain today rather than illustrating the full dimensions of the multicultural face, psyche and aesthetic of the New Britain. My purpose is to demonstrate how Pinnock's challenge to the Eurocentric tradition has led her from a diasporic to a post-diasporic discourse and aesthetic, which affects both her thematic preoccupations and theatrical form. Her new syncretic inclusions reflect a full awareness of her interstitial position as hybrid artistic subject negotiating with a dual history and facing the limitations imposed by the racialized (even if benign) expectations of critics and audiences in a socially and cultur-ally heterogeneous but institutionally unequal British society. Through her amplified thematic and eclectic form Pinnock both avoids the 'tokenism' of black art as 'Other' to essential 'Englishness' and brings to the mainstream the richness and critical acuteness of her dual cultural belonging.

The five plays I have chosen from her dramatic oeuvre (a totality of 13 so far) from the 1990s and the new millennium, *Talking in Tongues* (1991), *Mules* (1996), *Can You Keep a Secret?* (1999), *Water* (2000) and *One Under* (2005), all mark distinct stages in the dramatist's development; her passage from a prescribed black migrant narrative and aesthetic to the interstitial poetics of a hybridized British culture and society.[12] Through her specific treatment of subject matter and amalgamated style Pinnock has managed to become a 'constitutive subjectivity' of the contemporary British stage as Griffin had hoped for, even if her acceptance by the mainstream can be seen as a double-edged victory.[13] What elevates her above such critical ambiguities is the fact – as will be shown in the analysis of her play *Water* – that she is fully aware of the moral agonies and the dilemmas that living in the interstices of culture entails for a creative and ambitious artist, who strives to acknowledge and simultaneously transcend the barriers of gender and race in her vision of the world.

Black performative dynamics: exploding Eurocentric realism

Pinnock first appeared on the theatre scene in the late 1980s (1987), at a time when the migration narratives of the first generation of Caribbean immigrants in Britain were still vividly ringing in the ears of their British-born children. As a child of Caribbean migrant parenthood, Pinnock was brought up in this aural tradition of deterritorialization and nostalgia for a lost country of origin.[14] As noted in relevant cultural histories, among the main features of black British literature in the 1980s was its preoccupation with the trauma of migration, including geographical dislocation, racial discrimination, social degradation and the quest for an identity. Naturally, Pinnock's work was not exempt of such anxieties. All her major plays of that period, the award winning *Leave Taking* (1987/88), *A Rock in Water* and *A Hero's Welcome* (both 1989) reveal a persistent attachment to a tormented past, which had to be revisited several times through such contradictory feelings as nostalgia, hurt pride, anger and revenge before the present and future in the new host country, Britain, could be faced with more positive and constructive visions of belonging.[15] This long pilgrimage into ethnic and racial history – a mixture also of psychological journeys, mythical travels and imaginary constructions – is best illustrated in *Talking in Tongues* (1991), which actually concludes this early cycle of Pinnock's works, treating the same material with much more containment, maturity and control.

The opening of the play at the Royal Court Theatre was accompanied by an interview with *The Guardian*, in which the writer appeared fairly outspoken about her gender and race politics. The interview sounded more like a black feminist manifesto, expressing a bitterness for the black woman being still 'the mule of the world' and giving out a polemical note in its conclusion that although 'committed to integration [...] it's going to be an uphill struggle'.[16] In an Afterword written for the first published version of the play three years later, Pinnock appears more appeased and affirmative about the message of her work. Although still showing understanding for the angry, vengeful separatism represented by one of her black female characters (Claudette), she stresses more her intention to explore 'other ways to heal the wounds', to quest for ways of proximity rather than separation.[17] Certainly the ending of the play, where the earlier hostile but later enlightened Leela (Pinnock's protagonist) at last strikes a friendly conversation with Kate (a white expatriate British girl she met in Jamaica and made the random victim of her gender and race vengefulness), agrees with the writer's own optimistic view. The closing scene runs as follows:

KATE: I know some good walks. [...] I could show you. Let me put my shoes on.
LEELA: Actually ...
KATE: You don't want to?
LEELA: Not right now. Next time.
KATE: It's a deal, next time you're here I'll show you.
LEELA: Sounds like my kind of walk. I've got used to walking here. I'm not so frightened of the pitfalls now. It's the way you displace the weight of your body, isn't it? You've got to be in touch with your body. It soon gets used to sudden challenges. That sounds like my kind of walk.
KATE: The next time you're here then.
LEELA: It's a deal.[18]

From the stylistic point of view the quasi-Beckettian or Pinteresque circularity and repetitiveness in this short dialogue give the play a sense of openness and uncertainty. However, from the perspective of narrative line and despite stylistic ambiguity, an approximation has been achieved on both sides. Leela has reclaimed her black body through her visit to her homeland, Jamaica, and, unexpectedly, she finds a similar feeling of physical territorial belonging to the Caribbean landscape in a white British woman, who has decided to 'exile' herself there permanently, by contrast to Leela, who feels committed to her British reterritorialization. Thus, the play concludes in potential reconciliation, having destroyed gendered national barriers and stereotypes from and for black and white race, culture and ethnicity alike. The basic pattern of the story – the visit to Jamaica by a second-generation British Caribbean immigrant, as a journey back to the roots and a primal black identity, the frustration of not finding the cultural and national purity dreamt of, the confusion of a neocolonial reality in the Caribbean with the same Western capitalist hierarchies as in Europe – are all predictable themes from much similar postcolonial writing in this period. It is an almost inevitable psychic process for a migrant subject, which will lead – in psychoanalytic terms – to forgetting, forgiveness and an affirmative nod to a culturally relocated present and future.

In this sense, *Talking in Tongues* has nothing very new to offer since it reiterates recognizable issues from an already typified literary subgenre, that of the black narration of migration. However, what distinguishes this play from other attempts in the same thematic area and emotional vein is its specific representational politics that marks it out for its originality. Voice and body are the two powerful channels of personal expression that early feminist theory had set out to reclaim for women. In that direction Hélène Cixous's seminal essay 'Aller à la mer' is a pertinent theoretical reference.[19] For black women, whose tradition relies much more on bodily expression than Western codes of communication, the organic connection of the two is also much more natural. Pinnock makes these two the target of her protagonist, who agonizes in their double lack. Leela confesses at a point:

> LEELA: Words are sometimes like lumps of cold porridge sticking in my mouth. [...] It's because this isn't my first language, you see. Not that I do have any real first language, but sometimes I imagine that there must have been, at some time. [...] If you don't feel you belong to a language then you're only half alive aren't you, because you haven't the words to bring you into existence. You might as well be invisible.[20]

She also seems unable to master her body. At a party she is invited to with her (black) husband she is expected, as a black girl, to set the tone for dancing. Leela admits: 'Honestly. I'm not very good. I bump into people. It takes all my effort to keep myself upright.'[21] A few lines later she explains further: 'I never forget my body. That's the trouble.'[22]

Preoccupation with the 'oppressor's language', English, and the double colonization of the black female body have been prominent on the agenda of American women of colour from the 1970s onwards. Ntozake Shange invented the form of the 'choreopoem', beautifully exemplified in her widely performed – now almost emblematized – piece *For colored girls who have considered suicide when the rainbow is enuf* (1975).[23] Chicana women responded with a similar form, the 'teatropoesia'. In both artistic forms body language is equally important to the articulation of words, with solo performance emerging as an important means of self-expression. As Dominic Hingorani asserts, Asian languages are closely related to performance, where words are not mere text but mediated through actors' bodies and voice.[24] Hence their phenomenological, incarnated dynamic. In Britain the prevailing model of social-realist theatre has worked repressively for the free development of a similar stage language aesthetic. The white, male, mainstream canon still dictates the criteria of acceptable/ successful playwriting, repertory choices and staging methods, setting the tone of reviews and the direction of audience expectations. Pinnock is aware of this industry's rigidity and the additional difficulties for the black artistic minority in the theatrical establishment, where racism is also, arguably, institutionalized.[25] Despite this adverse climate, she has found a personal way for drawing on both cultural traditions she was raised in and addressing mixed audiences without betraying one or the other, or indeed herself.

Talking in Tongues offered itself as suitable ground for a bold experiment in a mixed style that departed from the linearity and discursive clarity of the social-realist model through temporal and spatial ruptures and an affective physicality, which implicated the audience emotionally without cancelling its rational function. Ritual male wrestling between a Briton and an indigenous Jamaican, limbo dancing and a scene of physical violence against an innocent white female victim (Kate) by the two hate-ridden British Caribbean girls – Claudette and Leela – are the most obvious examples where race and gender antagonisms are performed spectacularly to the audience, though never reaching (in the third case especially) the intensity of an 'in-yer-face' aesthetic. Pinnock prefers subtler modes of stimulating the audience into recognition and sharing of the protagonist's plight concerning the psychological and social positioning of the black self in a multicultural, yet still unequal British society.

The play is classically divided into two acts, the first located in London and the second in Jamaica, thus offering a balanced representation of Leela's split self. However, this classical structure is not the usual one for a realist play, punctuated by a prelude and interlude, which inject illogical sequences that disrupt temporal and spatial unity. The play opens with a short scene where a young Jamaican woman, Sugar, delivers, in Creole, a monologue on her fleeting memory of old female rituals, as she massages a young black British female tourist, whom we later identify as Leela. This is a flash-forward scene actually belonging to the setting of the second act, since Act One soon relocates us to a party scene in metropolitan London. It takes us, in a series of climactic scenes, through Leela's complete disintegration after her husband's betrayal with a white female guest. It is precisely here that Pinnock once again surprises her audience with the insertion of an interlude scene, which, like the prelude discussed above, follows a different logic of spatiotemporal existence. Pinnock marks this rupture with the brief note '[l]ights change' and the rest unravels in the directorial and dialogical texts as if normal.[26] The surprise lies in the sudden appearance of a bizarre party guest, Irma, a hermaphrodite (to be played either by a male or female actor), who literally falls from the sky to a stupefied, inconsolable Leela, in order to appease her with her own traumatic story of interstitial sexuality and then vanish from the play as unaccountably as she entered it.

The stylistic arbitrariness of this scene is a notable intervention in the pre-established order of the Eurocentric dramatic tradition, which Pinnock became familiar with through her British schooling and which she generally practises in her work. However, its use is more than a teasing surprise for her audience's expectations since the figure of Irma, who talks about the wound of her ambiguous sexuality, illustrates Leela's own trauma of a split and undecided cultural identity. The colourful, 'freak-like' appearance of Irma is a vivid visual representation of Leela's understanding of herself as a cultural 'freak'.

Taken together, Sugar's monologue and Irma's bodily 'freakishness' foreground in vivid stage language Leela's estrangement from linguistic and body language in a different representational style that breaks down the rigid codes of social realism. Their surrealistic effect culminates in Leela's quasi-epileptic seizure in the penultimate scene of the play. The stage direction is clear and precise:

> Leela's speech becomes a garble as she struggles to get the words out, her body trembling out of her control. She's breathing very quickly. She starts to mutter under her breath. [...] Leela's muttering becomes louder as she starts to talk in tongues. Sugar is bewildered at first, then frightened as Leela releases all her rage and anger that she has repressed for so long.[27]

In the Western discursive frame Leela's seizure would be analysed in medical, essentially psychoanalytic terms. Pinnock, however, has already created a trance-like, mythical atmosphere of a black tradition of old which is evoked through the dislocated narratives of Sugar and Irma respectively. Pinnock's strategy is to give these characters a double status within and outside the fictional world of the play. On the one hand they operate as ordinary characters belonging to the plot (Irma to a lesser degree), while on the other they function as gurus of an alternative, more remote, ritualistic culture, from which they themselves have been alienated. Sugar calls her own memory of her tribal women's kinetic and vocal ecstasies 'madness' while Irma sceptically dismisses her mother's – and other black women's – therapeutic application of religion.[28] To this, Leela adds her own Westernized verdict: 'mass hysteria'.[29] However, it is to this inexplicable state of ecstasy that Leela is made to resort: a state of epiphany, before she reconstitutes her split self and accepts her hybrid subjectivity. Through the double narrative representation of black experience as distant memory Pinnock paves the way for the staging of Leela's re-membering of the self in an extreme physical way, as a relived experience of suffering that goes beyond any voyeuristic expectations of white audiences from the spectacular enactment of black ritual.

The strength and effectiveness of Pinnock's weaving two theatrical traditions into her personal aesthetic can be more fully appreciated if one compares, for example, her play to Tanika Gupta's *Sugar Mummies* (2006), which, in its treatment of female sex tourism in a similar neocolonial Jamaican setting, does not ultimately surpass the predictable, limited scope of the traditional sardonic English comedy.[30] Although mildly critical in a materialist post-feminist way, this play does not reach beneath the glib surface of a rather journalistic topical theme. By contrast, Pinnock constructs a fresh, deep and complex politics of representation for the race, gender and class inequalities in today's multicultural, though still first world, or Western-dominated societies and global economy.

Filtering black culture into the post-Brechtian aesthetic

The innovation of *Talking in Tongues* became a steady feature in Pinnock's work, as her subsequent play *Mules* proves (1996). Unlike its predecessor though, it abandons the intimate and confessional tone of a traumatic journey into the black diasporic self and chooses a more detached collective survey of young women, whom a certain combination of gender, race and national belonging has placed at the bottom of the social scale, turning them into victims of global capitalist practices. Pinnock focuses on the exploitation of unqualified, unemployed girls from countries such as the West Indies and Africa as couriers, or 'mules', in the international drug trade.[31] The despairing poverty in which these countries are kept through the neocolonial policies of transnational capitalism becomes in this case as important as the gender and race of the protagonists, indicating the author's broader materialist critique. The adoption of a post-Brechtian style with its fast-moving episodic structure gives the play critical agility as it rapidly alternates the setting from London to Kingston (Jamaica), internal to external scenes and realistic to surrealistic images, treating the temporal dimension accordingly. This structural fluidity helps the writer develop a bird's-eye view of the global situation, extending beyond a narrow ideological entrapment in race and gender politics as in her previous work.

There was a strong critical debate around the centrality of blackness in the play, as its Royal Court production employed three black actresses for all twelve female roles, although the play was initially written for a mixed cast. Pinnock was categorical that her play 'isn't about race', repeatedly using the generic and gender/race-neutral word 'people' when referring to her poverty-stricken characters, who resort to illegal activities in order to escape the bottom-line of economic and social oppression and their absolute lack of power.[32] Although the play was a commission by the Clean Break Theatre Company, whose social mission is to create theatre by and for women prisoners and as such had to comply with unbendable prerequisites regarding topic, cast and audience, Pinnock found a way to deviate and create her space as an outside observer, 'a commentator'.[33] In the interviews where she describes at length the research stage for the writing of *Mules* she emerges as an independent artist 'negotiating her own role' to meet the specific requirements of her commission.[34]

The result was laudable; Pinnock mentions her fascination with the double-edged attitude of many female inmates in Holloway Prison, where she conducted most of her research, to criminality. Probing into existential, ideological and psychological motives, the 'greyer areas of identity', her scope developed from the narrowness of docudrama to a broader sociological treatment which peered beyond black female victimization.[35] Her bold initiative involved treating the theme of female criminality at the edge of condemnation and heroism, as a dubious form of empowerment.[36] With genuine incisive vision, Pinnock observed 'the irony in the way that people were rebellious and in another sense conformist and unaware of that conformity'.[37] Carefully weaving this paradox in her representation of criminality throughout the play, she leaves the audience with an ambiguous ending, which also baffled the critics concerning the idealized or ironized state of the two main characters, the Jamaican sisters Lyla and Lou back in Kingston after the fiasco of their 'mule' mission: is it an utter and final defeat or a blessing in disguise – a new, figurative kind of empowerment? This openness helps the text escape from the moralistic and didactic pitfalls lying behind the normative rules of both the Western socialist play and the black play and marks the writer's independent and original line of thought.

What adds to Pinnock's originality is her play with style, which here possesses more certainty and authorial *jouissance* than in *Talking in Tongues*. There is a teasing attitude in *Mules* which blends with empathy for the characters and a sharp social criticism, thereby turning the play towards ambiguity and an alternative, darker vision of reality. There are stark realistic scenes which show precisely how the sites of power are constructed. However, this materialist mode of representation is continuously injected with an irrational one, which introduces a peculiar mixture of transcendental elements of evil as magic, invoking fear and fascination and challenging the audience's expectations for solid moral messages. It is hard to decide where these elements come from. Bernhard Reitz, who questions more the aesthetic codes of the play, locates the influence in Shakespeare.[38] To these Western classical influences we should add the impact of seminal socialist writing of the 1970s and 1980s, namely Caryl Churchill's *Top Girls* (1982) and *Serious Money* (1987), as well as Howard Brenton and David Hare's *Pravda* (1985).[39] We sense an awareness of Churchill's theatre, especially, at various points in the play. Bridie is another 'top girl', in the image of Churchill's protagonist Marlene and her London-based agency, who rehearses the tough work patterns and cynical ethics of that play. But beyond such possible, more conventional ideological loans, an inspiration from Churchill's conceptual and visual tactics in her later play *The Skriker*, where she grapples with old and new modes of representation of the invisible and the unreal, should be highlighted.[40] The transcendental way the evil 'spirit' is often represented in Pinnock's play certainly brings to mind the prank-style representation of the elusive figure of the 'skriker' in Churchill's text, with more overt Brechtian overtones for both plays when a gestic transaction of money enters the pranksters' game, that is, the skriker's and Bridie's respectively.

However, the intertextual investigation for a black diasporic writer like Pinnock cannot possibly stop at the limits of the Western theatrical tradition. Her own black Caribbean legacy with its emphasis on spiritual rituals of high performativity should not be forgotten as they can be put to excellent theatrical use. Through narrative references and occasional enactment, the likes of which we have seen in *Talking in Tongues*, this legacy has always been present in her previous work. It is this that imbues the post-Brechtian perspective of the play with an alternative world vision, a 'flight' into the often intractable, mute and invisible fears, desires and ambitions of all destitute humans for some position of power.[41]

The most culturally hybrid moment in the play, the same one that the writer leaves in complete spatiotemporal vacuum, is Scene 9, which thus functions like an interlude to the overall realistic plot. Bridie performs death in a highly melodramatic style as she is recalling a children's murder game. Although the ludic pattern itself can place the game in the Western tradition, the fact that Bridie comes from the West Indian ghetto certainly invests her bodily performance with the different aura accompanying the expressive codes of her Jamaican origin. In this 'other' ritual role Bridie is transformed into a guru figure from elsewhere, who predicts in words and motion one of her 'mule' victims', Olu's, onstage death, proceeding to cover up her dead body with the gnomic remark '[l]ive like a mule, die like a mule'.[42]

This double representation, seen through the contrastive filters of Western rational thought and the different cultural discourse of Caribbean spiritualism, points to a more complex critique of the condition of contemporary multicultural societies where the paradigms of race, gender and class blend in multiple ways and create new configurations in the struggle for equal material and social recognition and constitutive subjectivity.[43] In this sense, Aston is right in her claim that Pinnock's play 'is not about being black and female, but about the way in which "mules" as stateless citizens figuratively come to stand for the way in which women, across nations, face a variety of exclusions on account of their material, gender, racialized and sexualized states'.[44]

Carrying on her bitter statement from the time she was working on *Talking in Tongues* that the black woman is still the mule of the world, Pinnock makes this deprecating image the title of her new play while also amplifying the term to include all 'people' whom poverty, lack of education and employment opportunities deprive of their basic human right to dignified citizenship. For Pinnock this is a spectacular step forward, which breaks her earlier insularity of thematic preoccupations. In this she is remarkably aided by an occasional recourse to the alternative dynamics of her Caribbean legacy which gives her strong materialist critique a momentary, inexplicable – by Western standards – flight into imaginary thinking and empowerment in an otherwise desperate material reality.

Beyond colour and gender: exploring youth culture in contemporary multicultural Britain

Pinnock's move away from the confines of race and the effort to address wider issues of national and transnational interest in *Mules* are confirmed in the writing of her next play, the one-hander *Can You Keep a Secret?* (1999), which was commissioned by the National Theatre for its youth theatre project 'Connections'. At approximately the same time Pinnock wrote the essay 'Breaking Down the Door', which clearly reflects her positive response to Labour's political agenda of promoting 'New Britain' (or 'Cool Britannia') – and London in particular – 'as a successfully multicultural society led by the desires and ideas of the young'.[45] It also defined the focus of her new play on the development of a British youth culture whose pop character was greatly shaped through the inscription of distinctive features of black culture – mainly linguistic and behavioural codes. Writing about this new hybrid youth culture soon became a trend and many writers, both black and white, responded to the call. Rebecca Prichard's *Yard Gal* (1998) is a case in point.[46]

Pinnock's thematic choice was not a novelty in itself, given also that it was dictated by her commission for the 'Connections' project. What was novel, however, was that the writer did not limit herself to a superficial presentation of the crude school and street life semiotics characterizing the metropolitan youth as happens, for example, in Gupta's *White Boy* (2007).[47] On the contrary, Pinnock created a systematic frame of critical discourse which combined a mixed sociological and psychological approach to her characters and institutionalized social life. Although the plot is linear and the scenes follow a basically realistic pattern of development, the author's perspective brings to mind the precise operation of a control-room with a plan of action that guides the spectatorial gaze and ear to various aspects of contemporary British life, cutting across not only the usual triad of gender, race and class but also age, profession, education and social institutions such as family, church, police and justice. In a marked shift from the second- to third-generation black population in Britain she underlines their gradual normalization as middle-class citizens with all the rights of 'redistribution' and 'recognition' fulfilled. The opening scene of the play between two young girls, one black and one white, striking up a friendly chat as they are waiting for their dates to go to the movies, gives precisely this image of black normalization into the contemporary British social system. In her note accompanying the script the writer explains that she saw the girls as 'ordinary young Londoner[s]'.[48] In later scenes, she enlarges the possibility of social, material and educational upgrading of her black characters in contrast with images of personal, professional and social degradation in the correspondent familial milieux of her white characters.

However, the dramatist is sceptical about such reverse social inequalities. She keeps her distance from the triumphant boasting of her young black protagonist, Derek, who exclaims provocatively 'New world order: The Niggers Rule OK and you, my dear Nancy Boy, are the new victim.'[49] The development of the story soon brings back the issue of racism for further negotiation when the bright, ambitious but also boastful black boy becomes the fatal victim of a racist street fight. One is reminded of debbie tucker green's *random* (2008) and its sensitive poetic vision of bereavement, which, however, chooses to obscure a materialist critique of street youth violence.[50]

Not so with Pinnock, who prefers an alternation of materialist and psychological incision. The essentially naturalistic setting of the play secures its firm socialist enquiry but at the same time a journey into existential and moral issues gears the play elsewhere. One can feel in some scenes the affliction of the victim's family when the cold wind of death blows through their door. More centrally for the plot, the guilt of withholding the truth about the murder afflicts Kate, the white girlfriend of the similarly white young perpetrator. In her plight, the police inspector is an eager assistant, transgressing the role of the stern institutional functionary and becoming – in a strange manner – her spiritual guide towards the confession of truth. Two more surrealistic presences help the guilt-ridden Kate out of her agony. Pinnock introduces amidst the list of her realistic characters an unidentified figure labelled simply 'Weirdboy'. This mysterious figure remains an outsider to the plot and functions as an external observer, a mute eyewitness and kind of scapegoat to the atrocity performed. His persistent though marginal presence on the stage is a constant reminder to all – characters and audience alike – of the moral pressure for a catharsis of the committed crime and, especially for Kate, it is a personal call for proper action: disclosure and absolution. This moral pressure of a guilty conscience is further enhanced by the constant appearance of Derek, the black victim, as a ghost to Kate alone.

These two rather supernatural presences could be likened to the function of the *Eryinies* in classical Greek drama, as Shakespeare's love for ghosts might be mentioned as a possible influence from within the British canon. The Eurocentric reservoir of the ghost convention can also comprise the modernist example of T. S. Eliot's dramatic oeuvre – an apt comparison if one considers the unnatural benignity with which Pinnock invests the police inspector, turning him into a kind of Eliotian guardian angel figure. Such associations with the long European cultural legacy are certainly legitimate, but, again, one cannot rule out the rich cultural baggage the writer carries from her Caribbean origin. Although her Europeanized self may have alienated her from her black immigrant background, the memory of transcendental life practices and divinations of a spiritualist nature, alien to the rationalism of the Western lifestyle, persists. Echoes of such spiritualist practices can be considered as an immediate source of inspiration for Pinnock's diasporic imagination, leading her, quite naturally, to a regular interruption of the European realist tradition via the injection of a Caribbean ontology and codes of behaviour.

Considered in all its thematic and staging potential, this short cross-gender and cross-race play proves Pinnock's development to a mature contemplation of all the complexities, conflicts and ambiguities of the image of a New Britain, especially in the depiction of its pop youth culture.[51] This new dramatic endeavour shows her continuously striving to appeal with equal vigour both to the variously institutionalized expectations of the contemporary British stage and to her 'other' cultural heritage and experience so as to bring the two into a creative dialogue. Its double benefit is that of broadening Pinnock's thematic enquiry and fashioning the right idiom for a full expression of her interstitial artistic personality.

The black artist as nationwide success

Of all Pinnock's plays *Water* (2000) is the most freed from the clichéd themes expected of black British writers, as it is also freer in form. It deals with the compromises and strategies an artist (who is also black and female) must go through in order to confront the systems determining the art forms and market. Just as *Talking in Tongues* can be said to be semi-autobiographical since it traces the black female subject's quest for a post-migration identity, *Water* can be similarly categorized since the writer shares with her protagonist (JS) the same dilemmas for artistic survival and wider national recognition. It is a 50-minute one-hander, commissioned by the Tricycle Theatre for a double bill with another, earlier black play of the 1950s, *Wine in the Wilderness*, by the African American playwright Alice Childress, to which it would act as a contemporary response.[52] The double production was part of the 'Black History Month' at the Tricycle, signalling a steady cooperation between Pinnock and the specific organization, whose policy since the early 2000s has been to promote black and Asian writing for the stage and create new inter-racial audiences.[53]

Although Pinnock had repeatedly set herself against labels and forcefully rejected the limitations of racial interests, this is the first time that the racial identity of her dramatis personae remains so concealed that it is only disclosed in the dialogue between the two characters when the play has almost run half its performance length. That the dramatic diction stays race neutral for a large part of it proves Pinnock's widening perspective of the contemporary human condition and also her artistic skill to thrust race identity in as a surprise technique of thwarting the audience expectations she had created. Of course, in the stage production the choice of black actors for the two roles in the play makes their racial belonging visible from the start. For the reader, however, the characters' definition in minimal gender terms as Ed, a man, and SJ, a woman, gives no further identity clues. In its radio production the play is equally elusive because it holds its race neutrality until a key reference in the characters' speech throws light on their racial identity and refocuses the concerns of the play.[54]

The black, male, middle-class journalist Ed is granted an interview by SJ, a rising female black painter, who has become famous for her raw depiction of low street life. Ed, who is in a steady relationship with Julie, has casual sex with SJ on the day of his interview visit. After this encounter, the apparent intra-racial class and gender tensions between the two protagonists deepen into an open confrontation, which rubs salt on the old racial wound that they both seemed to have healed through their social and professional advancement in the white British establishment – SJ through admission to the competitive world of art and Ed to the stern world of the mass media. In other words, they have both, apparently, been admitted as equally valued contributors to mainstream British culture. Surprisingly, their skin colour suddenly emerges as a weapon in the hands of both to insult each other for an unspoken, at first, betrayal. SJ addresses Ed with the cuttingly ironic 'Mr speaky spoky Black journalist' and Ed retaliates with the heavier insult 'Ms Hard as nails, straight from the street, picky haired on the black fringes of the brit art pack, artist'.[55]

Thus the racial trauma of the black diaspora Briton, displaced to the periphery of the host culture, which had been at the core of Pinnock's earlier work for the theatre, resurfaces: only this time it is located differently. This racial revisioning certainly contextualizes the characters' hybrid identity, but as a theme it is left in the margins of the dramatic structure. Here, the two black characters seem to have fully attained both the material 'redistribution' and social 'recognition' that Griffin had discerned as the basic political agenda for the complete equalization of contemporary black and Asian British citizens. Class, race and gender differences seem to have been smoothed over (as also dubiously suggested in *Can You Keep a Secret?*). What takes precedence for her more developed millennial characters is individual ambition, again a theme already partly tackled in *Mules* and *Can You Keep a Secret?*, now relocated to the centre of a highly competitive and fast-moving global capitalist system of ethics and economy. One can draw a parallel with Pinnock's own ambitious agenda as a British female playwright of the black diaspora, moving into the mainstream with ambivalent feelings she has repeatedly voiced in interviews and prose texts. Goddard asserts that this play envisions a time of liberation for the black female artist: Pinnock herself.[56]

In a sense *Water* is a triple combination of major themes brought to the English stage during the Thatcherite era: more specifically, the capitalist politics and ethics critically depicted in aforementioned plays by Churchill, Brenton and Hare and – more pertinently to this play – the strategies and manoeuvres of the art industry explored in Timberlake Wertenbaker's *Three Birds Alighting on a Field* (1992)[57] now seem to be transferred to the socially upgraded black British milieu some 20 years later. Of course the ruthless road to middle-class success at the time of late- and turbo-capitalism had already been foreshadowed by Pinnock herself in *Talking in Tongues* and *Mules*, in an inter- and intra-racial setting respectively.

As Ed and SJ hurl injurious language to each other, they gradually disclose the real nature of their dishonesty: hypocrisy and collusion to the hegemonic system. Ed admits to the suppression of his humble, working-class origin (especially the rejection of his brother) for the promotion of his own social and professional status. One cannot fail to remember Bridie's fabrication of a sham cultural origin to build her social and professional image of success in *Mules*. Ed has used a similar strategy of pretence in constructing the myth of his identity. As for SJ, she confesses to the concealment of her standard middle-class provenance and the appropriation of another girl's rough life to make her art more appealing to the pre-set tastes of the white art dealers and buyers. She has actually borrowed somebody else's story to create her artistic image, her own mythical identity. For each of them there is a disgraced black shadow character looming behind.

Enlarging the issue of art as commodity, SJ's situation may be said to reflect the Tracey Emin trend of art '"authenticity"'.[58] In this respect, *Water* enters the art debate in more general terms, transcending the gender and race enquiry and is, therefore, a remarkable stage in the development of Pinnock beyond her labelling as a black female writer with prescribed politics and patterns of form. Her two characters handle the situation with pragmatic dexterity and, rather than playing the losers, they make a pact to their mutual interest, even if they back-step on the level of moral integrity. Pinnock had already shown the double coin of ethical behaviour and criminality in her handling of this delicate subject in *Mules*, where, again, avoiding victimization legitimized the characters' decision to challenge the laws of an unjust hegemonic system. It is in this context that the right of every individual to ambition is highlighted. Beyond their polar stories of social origin, the characters' one common identity feature, ambition, will make them consent to keeping up the mythology of constructed identity for the professional benefit of both.

Pinnock has woven a story which critiques the narrowness and pre-dictability of a marginalized black art as well as the naive generalities about it produced by the white hegemonic centre. In addition to the particularized black experience of social integration and cultural sophis-tication, the play observes the gloss of global economy, which has corroded the contemporary arts and media network. The categories of good and evil, as also prefigured in *Mules* and *Can You Keep a Secret?*, whether in their traditional binary form or as postmodern deconstructed mélange, now apply to all, irrespective of race, class and gender divisions.

What is also remarkable in this short play is the innovative form that the writer has adopted to match her multiply border-crossing thematic. This is the first time that Pinnock has been so successful in breaking through the naturalistic style which often burdened her writing with tediousness, overwriting and unnecessary complication. In this play, reducing the characters to two and keeping all others offstage is the first step to selective minimalism and greater thematic concentration, signalled also by the contracted form of characters' names. Similarly, linear spatiotemporal realism is abandoned for a more flexible, freer scheme where voice-off, recorded speech and review text blend with onstage dialogue, monologue and regular stage enactment, creating a Beckettian effect of dislocation in place and time, while also foregrounding the play's concern about how stories are woven and narratives become continuously revised and reconstructed. The use of mediated speech through telephone, playback and journalistic report is a new representational strategy for Pinnock, which helps her stage effectively the artificiality and instability of identity formation through layers of narratives and discursive mythologies. Pinnock has indeed invented a form which at last can be said to justify the 'hybrid-ized, postmodern aesthetic' and 'diasporic stylistic' that ambitious postcolonial critics such as Ponnuswami and Marzette had predicted – perhaps slightly prematurely – for her dramatic writing.

Responding to Beckettian and Pinteresque humanism

Gupta's often quoted protest that 'nobody goes round describing Harold Pinter as a Jewish white playwright, so why does everyone go round call-ing me an Asian woman playwright? If you get labelled you get boxed in' can well be seen as expressing the collective indignation of contemporary black and Asian women writers of Britain.[59] It certainly fits Pinnock, who has repeatedly protested against her own labelling, but in more general terms. What is of special interest in Gupta's more particularized statement

is that Pinter becomes the yardstick for kindling the ambition and meas-
uring the artistic achievement of women dramatists. Of course Pinter is
an undeniable cornerstone in the contemporary British theatre canon,
whatever the antagonistic race and gender resentment of black or Asian
women playwrights may be. For Pinnock in particular, Pinteresque overtones can be easily traced, for instance, in *Mules*, in the rather unnecessary
long digression in Scene 2 on renting a room and seeing it as potential
refuge from outside invaders. Strong echoes from Pinter's later mood and
style (especially in *Moonlight* and *Ashes to Ashes*) reappear in her darker
play *One Under* (2005).[60] The epigraph attached to the published text
already sets its brooding and mournful tone:

> Bereavement can overshadow life:
> The dead can destroy the living[61]

The play traces the spiritual journey of a London tube driver, Cyrus,
after he becomes the inadvertent aid to one of the frequent suicide incidents recorded in the London Underground. Although essentially inner
and underground, this journey brings the suffering protagonist into
real contact with other people's similar ordeals. Thus, a common thread
of human suffering is woven that extends beyond race, gender and
age barriers as an entire list of perennial human afflictions is formed,
centring round the general theme of loss and dispossession where
parents abandon or lose children and vice versa. The general mood of
mournfulness for a meaningless and enigmatic existence could well be
relegated to Beckett's inscrutable, philosophical universe, while more
concrete patterns of loss, quest and recognition between parents and
children, or between siblings, may be of Shakespearean provenance.
More central and conscious seems to be the writer's response to Pinter's
aesthetic of clashing stories and unstable, insecure or contradictory
characters in realistic settings, which are simultaneously enveloped in
inexplicable mystery.

By insisting on an extreme realism of setting (Underground platforms,
dry-cleaner's counter, a Russell Square hotel room and other more conventional venues such as a flat or house interior, a back garden, etc.),
Pinnock invents her own formal idiom to make more striking the
aimed antithesis between a glib external reality and her actual focus on
interiority, darkness, the invisible. Seen retrospectively, the title itself,
One Under, becomes the bearer of a double, overt and hidden meaning: a
real suicide on the rail track and a surrealistic voyage in the underworld –
perhaps the realm of death, or the human psyche. This underground

effect is further assisted by the insertion of two nocturnal scenes in Act Two – a rather rare inclusion in the practice of realistic theatre – which enhance a different perception of reality, an opaque and shadowy one which relates more to imaginary or psychic sensations. They are both associated with the most transcendental character of all, the suicidal Sonny. In Sonny's nocturnal, culture-specific meditation in the first of these scenes (Scene 2) London figures like 'a different animal at night', evoking ancestral memories from the Caribbean. 'Close your eyes', Sonny exhorts, 'you'd think you was in the Caribbean'.[62] The same atmospheric change into unreality takes place in Scene 5 of the same act, where Sonny makes a sepulchral appearance in his foster mother's garden in the darkness of night. Contrasting with the locational clarity of all the scenes, the temporal fluidity creates ambiguity on whether Sonny's visit comes before or after his suicide. Pinnock, having dealt with eerie characters before, handles Sonny's transcendental qualities with much dexterity. Even before his death, he is invested with a spectral touch and when his physical presence is truly erased by death 'he's left his shadow behind'.[63] As Sonny has been the one to evoke Caribbean memories into the play, his whole conception as a figure of liminal existence and therefore his representation as a ghost/character can be justifiably associated with the transcendental Caribbean experience of spiritualism, encountered many times before in Pinnock's plays.

Having exhausted her specific political agenda of race and gender enquiry in her earlier works, to which she subsequently added a penchant for psychological probing into the characters, Pinnock made a clear move to a more philosophical contemplation of humanity and the world, where the compartmentalization of individuals according to material possessions or power hierarchies as well as class, gender and race divisions are of secondary importance. *One Under*, although an imperfect play in terms of dramatic economy, is Pinnock's most ambitious attempt in that, for the first time in her career, she shifts focus on the male gender (Sonny and Cyrus) and has her black middle-class protagonist Cyrus stand for the painful ordeal and visionary journey of a contemporary Everyman.

Conclusion

Liberated in a triple sense, the mature Pinnock emerges as a post-feminist and post-diasporic post-millennial writer and establishes herself as a representative voice of the New Britain who dares new amplified inscriptions of the nation and global humanity, arriving to Beckettian and Pinteresque humanist world-views of fragmentation, diffusion and ambiguity through different channels of cultural experience. Her idiolect is a true mosaic of sources, which she brings into new configurations of thought and modes of theatrical representation. In all this her black female identity figures – to borrow the words of Heidi Safia Mirza – 'only as a useful strategy but no more. As a form of strategic essentialism [...] not to be confused with substantive essentialism'.[64]

Although one is bound to acknowledge that the radical breaking away of black British writing from conformity to existing or hypothetical canons has been finally achieved by such forceful but also poetic, cynical and yet lyrical voices of the younger generation of black British artists as debbie tucker green, this fact does not at all diminish the importance of the slightly earlier Winsome Pinnock for her very personal trajectory. It is the process of a dramatist from particular individual to collective ethnic and then ampler universal quests, who has kept the balance between a caring proximity to her characters and a detached critical spirit, and an ability to address mixed audiences in an artfully mixed stage code accessible to all: an interstitial poetics indeed.

Notes

1. D. Godiwala (ed.), *Alternatives Within the Mainstream: British Black and Asian Theatres* (Newcastle: Cambridge Scholars Publishing, 2006).
2. Godiwala (ed.), *Alternatives Within the Mainstream*, pp. 3–4.
3. Godiwala (ed.), *Alternatives Within the Mainstream*, p. 5.
4. Godiwala (ed.), *Alternatives Within the Mainstream*, pp. 4, 6.
5. G. Griffin, 'Constitutive Subjectivities: Contemporary Black and Asian Women Playwrights in Britain', *European Journal of Women's Studies*, 10.4 (2003), 377–94.
6. It must be noted that this sensitization to a revisioning of the British identity is recently becoming visible in white British cultural expressions as well: for instance in the theatre domain the title and front cover of Aleks Sierz's 2011 survey of the contemporary British stage *Rewriting the Nation: British Theatre Today* (London: Methuen Drama) and in a wider, more global expression, in Danny Boyle's highly cinematic Olympic Games opening spectacle. However, these are rather superficial, emblematic indications of a 'politically correct' awareness rather than a forceful desire, an experiential will for a change as in the case of cultural representations by the black and Asian British communities.
7. S. Malik, *Black and Asian Images on Television* (London: Sage, 2002), p. ix.
8. M. Ponnuswami, 'Small Island People: Black British Women Playwrights', in E. Aston and J. Reinelt (eds.), *The Cambridge Companion to Modern British Playwrights* (Cambridge: Cambridge University Press, 2000), pp. 217–34.
9. See M. K. Dahl, 'Postcolonial British Theatre: Black Voices at the Center', in J. Ellen Gainor (ed.), *Imperialism and Theatre* (London and New York: Routledge, 1995), pp. 38–55; E. Savory, 'Strategies for Survival: Anti-Imperialist Theatrical

Forms in the Anglophone Caribbean', in Gainor (ed.), *Imperialism and Theatre*, pp. 243–56.

10. See E. Aston, 'Feminist Connections to a Multicultural "Scene"', in *Feminist Views on the English Stage* (Cambridge: Cambridge University Press, 2003), pp. 125–48; G. Griffin, *Contemporary Black and Asian Women Playwrights* (Cambridge: Cambridge University Press, 2003); Griffin, 'Constitutive Subjectivities: Contemporary Black and Asian Women Playwrights in Britain'; G. Griffin, 'The Remains of the British Empire: The Plays of Winsome Pinnock', in M. Luckhurst (ed.), *A Companion to Modern British and Irish Drama: 1880–2005* (Oxford: Blackwell, 2006), pp. 198–209; G. Griffin, 'Theatres of Difference: The Politics of "Redistribution" and "Recognition" in the Plays of Contemporary Black and Asian Women Playwrights in Britain', *Feminist Review*, 84.1 (2006), 10–28.

11. D. Marzette, 'Coming to Voice: Navigating the Interstices in Plays by Winsome Pinnock', in E. Brown-Guillory (ed.), *Middle Passages and the Healing Place of History: Migration and Identity in Black Women's Literature* (Columbus: Ohio State University Press, 2006), pp. 32–51 (p. 33). For a concise but comprehensive critical reception of the work of Winsome Pinnock see also E. Sakellaridou, 'Winsome Pinnock', in M. Middeke, P. P. Schnierer and A. Sierz (eds.), *The Methuen Drama Guide to Contemporary British Playwrights* (London: Methuen Drama, 2011), pp. 383–402.

12. W. Pinnock, *Talking in Tongues*, in Y. Brewster (ed.), *Black Plays: Three* (London: Methuen Drama, 1991, 1995), pp. 171–227; W. Pinnock, *Mules* (London: Faber & Faber, 1996); W. Pinnock, *Can You Keep a Secret?*, in S. Graham-Adriani (ed.), *New Connections 99: New Plays for Young People* (London: Faber, 1999), pp. 93–137; W. Pinnock, *Water* (unpublished typescript, 2000, British Library); W. Pinnock, *One Under* (London: Faber & Faber, 2005). Regarding the comment on the number of plays Pinnock has written, this chapter was completed in the summer of 2012.

13. Griffin, 'Constitutive Subjectivities: Contemporary Black and Asian Women Playwrights in Britain'.

14. Pinnock was born in Britain in 1961.

15. W. Pinnock, *Leave Taking*, in K. Harwood (ed.), *First Run: New Plays by New Writers* (London: Nick Hern Books, 1989), pp. 139–89; W. Pinnock, *A Rock in Water*, in Y. Brewster (ed.), *Black Plays: Two* (London: Methuen Drama, 1989), pp. 45–91; W. Pinnock, *A Hero's Welcome*, in K. George (ed.), *Black and Asian Women Writers* (London: Aurora Metro Press, 1993), pp. 21–55.

16. Interview published 27 August 1991.

17. In Brewster (ed.), *Black Plays: Two*, p. 226.

18. Brewster (ed.), *Black Plays: Two*, p. 225.

19. H. Cixous, 'Aller à la mer', in R. Drain (ed.), *Twentieth Century Theatre: A Sourcebook* (London and New York: Routledge, 1995), pp. 133–5. (Originally published in *Le Monde*, 28 April 1977, p. 19.)

20. Brewster (ed.), *Black Plays: Two*, p. 195.

21. Brewster (ed.), *Black Plays: Two*, p. 183.

22. Brewster (ed.), *Black Plays: Two*, p. 184.

23. N. Shange, *for colored girls who have considered suicide when the rainbow is enuf* (New York: Scribner Poetry, 1997).

24. D. Hingorani, *British Asian Theatre: Dramaturgy, Process and Performance* (Basingstoke: Palgrave Macmillan, 2010), p. 12.
25. See W. Pinnock, 'Breaking Down the Door', in V. Gottlieb and C. Chambers (eds.), *Theatre in a Cool Climate* (Oxford: Amber Lane Press, 1999), pp. 27–38.
26. Brewster (ed.), *Black Plays: Two*, p. 193.
27. Brewster (ed.), *Black Plays: Two*, p. 223
28. Brewster (ed.), *Black Plays: Two*, pp. 174, 194.
29. Brewster (ed.), *Black Plays: Two*, p. 194.
30. T. Gupta, *Sugar Mummies* (London: Oberon Books, 2006).
31. Griffin, *Contemporary Black and Asian Women Playwrights*, p. 213. Griffin uses the more precise neologism 'sexploitation'.
32. Quoted in H. Stephenson and N. Langridge, *Rage and Reason: Women Playwrights on Playwriting* (London: Methuen Drama, 1997), pp. 45–53 (p. 52).
33. Quoted in D. Edgar, *State of Play: Playwrights on Playwriting* (London: Faber & Faber, 1999), pp. 58–9 (p. 59).
34. Edgar, *State of Play*, p. 59.
35. Stephenson and Langridge, *Rage and Reason*, p. 48.
36. Stephenson and Langridge, *Rage and Reason*, p. 52.
37. Stephenson and Langridge, *Rage and Reason*, p. 52.
38. B. Reitz, '"Discovering an Identity Which Has Been Squashed": Intercultural and Intracultural Confrontations in the Plays of Winsome Pinnock and Ayub Khan-Din', *European Journal of English Studies*, 7.1 (2003), 39–54 (p. 44).
39. C. Churchill, *Top Girls* (London and New York: Methuen, 1982); C. Churchill, *Serious Money* (London: Methuen, 1987); H. Brenton and D. Hare, *Pravda* (London: Methuen, 1985).
40. C. Churchill, *The Skriker* (London: Nick Hern Books, 1994).
41. Pinnock, *Mules*, p. 71.
42. Pinnock, *Mules*, p. 43.
43. I am borrowing the terms from Griffin's earlier mentioned articles 'Constitutive Subjectivities' and 'The Politics of "Redistribution" and "Recognition"'.
44. Aston, 'Feminist Connections to a Multicultural "Scene"', p. 136.
45. Pinnock, 'Breaking Down the Door', p. 27.
46. R. Prichard, *Yard Gal* (London and Boston: Faber & Faber, 1998).
47. T. Gupta, *White Boy* (London: Oberon Books, 2008).
48. Quoted in 'Something to Be Reclaimed', in Graham-Adriani (ed.), *New Connections 99: New Plays for Young People*, pp. 138–41 (p. 138).
49. Pinnock, *Can You Keep a Secret?*, p. 99.
50. d. tucker green, *random* (London: Nick Hern Books, 2008).
51. Another brief comparison here to Tanika Gupta's *White Boy*, which shows on the surface a similar ambition to cut across race and gender and explore the difficulties of forging a new white personality in the changing and conflicting multicultural reality of today's London society, can prove the much greater complexity and sophistication of Pinnock's thought as much as her innovative and effective representational tactics. In contrast, Gupta does not seem to surpass the limitations of a descriptive realism.
52. A. Childress, *Wine in the Wilderness* (New York: Dramatists Play Service, n.d.).
53. Tricycle Theatre has so far staged three of Pinnock's more recent plays: *Water* (2000), *One Under* (2005) and *IDP* (2006).

54. In a personal note to me the author underlined the radio production of *Water*, thus – to my mind – emphasizing the importance of its radio version for a more effective reception by the audience of its various ambiguities.
55. Pinnock, *Water*, p. 10.
56. L. Goddard, *Staging Black Feminisms: Identity, Politics, Performance* (Basingstoke: Palgrave Macmillan, 2007), p. 193.
57. T. Wertenbaker, *Three Birds Alighting on a Field* (London and Boston: Faber & Faber, 1992).
58. L. Booth quoted in Griffin, 'The Remains of the British Empire: The Plays of Winsome Pinnock', p. 46.
59. Gupta quoted in Hingorani, *British Asian Theatre*, p. 166.
60. H. Pinter, *Moonlight* (London: Faber & Faber, 1993); H. Pinter, *Ashes to Ashes* (London: Faber & Faber, 1996).
61. Pinnock, *One Under*, p. 1.
62. Pinnock, *One Under*, p. 62.
63. Pinnock, *One Under*, p. 40.
64. H. S. Mirza, *Black British Feminism: A Reader* (London and New York: Routledge, 1997), p. 182.

7
Acting In/Action: Staging Human Rights in debbie tucker green's Royal Court Plays

Marissia Fragkou and Lynette Goddard

Since her emergence on to London's new writing scene in 2003, debbie tucker green has become widely recognized as one of the most innovative (black) British (woman) playwrights of the early twenty-first century. Her first two plays were produced within weeks of each other at the Soho Theatre (*dirty butterfly* (2003)) and Hampstead Theatre (*born bad* (2003)), and subsequent productions have been shown in the Royal Shakespeare Company (RSC) New Works Festival in Stratford and at the Soho Theatre (*trade* (2005)), and at the Young Vic (*generations* (2007) and *dirty butterfly* revival (2008)). tucker green has also become established as a Royal Court writer (*stoning mary* (2005), *random* (2008) and *truth and reconciliation* (2011)), and she is the first black woman to have two plays premiere on the main stage downstairs.[1] International recognition, which is rare for black British playwrights, is further testament to her groundbreaking acclaim.[2]

tucker green's plays can be understood within the context of an era that saw renewed energy in political theatre in the wake of the terror crises in the new millennium. Her urgent responses to traumatic issues coincide with trends in contemporary British playwriting in an age of terror while also tapping into current feminist concerns and discourses. Each of her plays responds to specific local and global human rights concerns, including domestic and sexual abuse, incest, the AIDS crisis, child soldiers and public stoning in Africa, female sex tourism in the Caribbean, and the epidemic of fatal teenage stabbings in London. But she breaks away from the familiar traditions of social realism and documentary theatre by focusing on the emotional aftermath of these instances of violence, abuse and murder. Her plays also differ from the socially realist explorations of contemporary black British experience that were produced in London's main theatres during this period, many of which showed an overwhelming concern with portraying issues of black masculinity.[3] These early twenty-first century black British playwrights have started to expand the identity politics narratives that predominated during the 1980s and 1990s, broadening the terrain of black playwriting to address urgent topical concerns, often issues reported in news media – the rise in urban violence for example, or debates about institutional racism. In previous decades, plays by black playwrights were produced primarily for black audiences within the context of black (and women's) theatre companies, whereas this contemporary raft of plays by black British playwrights are produced in London's mainstream theatre venues, seemingly garnering a wider appeal for black *and* white audiences because they engage with high-profile concerns in contemporary Britain. tucker green's innovative, experimental, dramatic form breaks new ground by placing (black) women at the centre of poetically realist narratives that focus on the emotional impact of human rights injustices, while foregrounding 'universal' emotions of loss, grief and anger.

This chapter examines tucker green's plays within the context of contemporary British political new writing in the early twenty-first century and debates about human rights and theatre. Scholarship on her plays has either emphasized their aesthetic qualities or focused on the political and feminist imperatives in her portrayals of topical social issues.[4] Our approach examines the three plays that premiered at the Royal Court to explore how dramatic and production strategies are used to stage pertinent concerns about global human rights and vulnerability. We argue that her portrayal of these issues deploys a range of dramatic devices to address and often implicate the predominantly white middle-class Royal Court audiences in the consequences of inaction and complacency towards world problems. The dramatic form, casting and production aspects of tucker green's plays carefully position audiences as witnesses to the emotional impact of violent atrocities on her characters, which makes a statement about how inaction towards global crises amounts to complicity in human rights abuse. After laying out our chief theoretical frames in the following section we will focus on how the three Royal Court plays examine topics of human waste, grief, witnessing and reconciliation.

Human rights, affect, witnessing

According to Harry Derbyshire and Loveday Hodson 'human rights can be envisaged as a discursive space in which injustice and suffering are described and claims to redress imbalances of power are made'.[5]

The authors specifically locate the success of the cross-fertilization of human rights concerns and theatre in the fact that the latter allows 'those with an interest in human rights to understand them more imaginatively and more empathetically'.[6] Human rights concerns interlace with justice, action, power and responsibility; these issues have become more and more central in recent theatrical work that responds to local and global injustices and new-millennial uncertainties. A salient example is the resurgence of Weiss's 'theatre of actuality' in the guises of 'verbatim' and 'documentary theatre' since the 1990s, which offers a public platform for debating human rights and social justice through 'facts' and testimony and for making 'socio-political interventions by projecting voices and opinions which otherwise go unheard into a public arena'.[7] Examples of such plays can be found in the Tricycle Theatre's acclaimed verbatim and tribunal plays, which are powerful pieces that examine global and local human rights concerns.[8] Human rights and justice have also been the focus of much recent dramatic work written by women: Kay Adshead's *The Bogus Woman* (2001) and Caryl Churchill's *Iraq.Doc* (2003) (both based on verbatim testimonies) and *Seven Jewish Children* (2009) are examples of immediate responses to real events and social injustices that the authors wanted to urgently address.[9]

A common aspect of these plays is the intention to 'move' audiences towards 'action' by promoting affective engagement through 'experiential' vocabularies that depart from social realism. Elaine Aston situates post-1990s plays by women as part of an 'experiential genealogy of women's playwriting [...] concerned with how to *form* a social critique' on pressing societal issues.[10] In a similar vein, Janelle Reinelt draws attention to the role of affect in documentary theatre: '[p]roffering a range of affects, documentary theatre can catalyse public engagement and activism, although this is not a guaranteed outcome of its performances'.[11] A popular technique employed to achieve this level of engagement is situating spectators in the position of a witness. Witnessing is often discussed by theatre scholars as a device that promotes an affective response, particularly in the context of verbatim theatre.[12] For example, Chris Megson argues that witnessing in verbatim theatre aims to 'retrieve a sense of the complexity of issues that have been too easily turned into digestible headlines'.[13] It is necessary here to point out the two different meanings of the word 'to witness', which are pertinent to its usage in the context of the theatre. In *Witnessing: Beyond Recognition*, Kelly Oliver highlights that the word 'to witness' carries the connotation of 'eye-witnessing' but also 'bearing witness to something that cannot be seen'.[14] Witnessing therefore implies a complex ethical position, particularly with regards to trauma, torture and abuse; by being addressed as witnesses, spectators are asked to take responsibility for what they see and hear and are offered the space for a more enduring engagement and critical reflection on issues of social injustice and human rights abuse.

tucker green shares a number of the concerns delineated above; her plays offer a platform to sidelined voices and often expose human rights abuse. Although not explicitly focusing on the 'real' through the inclusion of testimony and facts, her plays reflect a strong political commitment to current affairs; in addition, she interrogates how reality is represented and constructed through the media leading to the desensitization of the viewer to images of horror. tucker green's work points to, but also seeks to overcome, the gap between perception and action through a range of dramaturgical choices and use of language; her oeuvre can be read through the lens of Hans Thies Lehmann's understanding of 'an aesthetic of *responsibility (or response-ability)*', that is, an affective engagement that 'makes visible the broken thread between personal experience and perception' and which, by extension, reconnects personal experience with the world.[15] What opens the space for eliciting affective responses is the lack of care and emotional attachment evidenced in the portrayal of brutal relationships among siblings, mothers and daughters, couples, and neighbours who exhibit selfish behaviours at the cost of recognizing others as human beings with rights. tucker green's 'aesthetics of responsibility' problematizes the nature and limitations of response and facilitates a politics of affect that could lead to a better world. As Aston summarizes, tucker green's aim is 'to dis-ease her spectators into viewing the dehumanizing effects of an inability to care for "others", locally and globally'.[16]

In *Theatre & Human Rights* Paul Rae argues that one of the motivating forces that often drives plays that revolve around human rights is the question 'who did what to whom' also evoked in official human rights discourse.[17] Rae warns however, that due to the complexity of '"the subject of human rights" [...] it is arguably better served in theatre that reflects the complexity than by one that seeks to resolve it'.[18] An implication of Rae's point here is the need to pay attention to the ethical complexities of human rights concerns before seeking to impose any definitive judgements. In her exploration of human rights abuse, tucker green does not rely on simple binary opposites such as victim/abuser but rather imbues her narratives with an ethical ambivalence that 'has the potential to stimulate ongoing reflection, engagement and participation with the ideas raised by a work'.[19] Examples of ethical ambivalence and an exploration of response-ability can be found in her earlier work: in *dirty butterfly* Amelia remains unperturbed by the signs of abuse carried by her abused neighbour's vulnerable body; instead of taking care of Jo who bleeds in Amelia's café she is rather more concerned with maintaining her pristine clean floor. In *born bad* a mother chooses Dawta to become the object of her husband's sexual abuse, while Dawta's sisters refuse to accept her testimony as authentic. Dawta's relationship with her father is symbolized when she is shown sitting between his legs at the end of the play.[20] tucker green's focus on human rights and 'what it means to be human' does not, however, advocate a 'new humanism' as she focuses on different axes of power and how these shape the contours of human life. In *trade* she poses a critique on frames that promote 'universal' models of identity and community; by foregrounding the power relations across three women's experiences of sex tourism in the Caribbean – Local, Regular and Novice – tucker green articulates different sites of ongoing oppression between 'First' and 'Third' world countries in the context of global capitalism.[21] In her work, victims do not seek to be recognized by their oppressors as, according to Kelly Oliver, this need for recognition suggests a perpetuation of a master–slave hierarchy; they rather primarily seek to elicit a response from their witnesses.[22] In this vein, tucker green's emphasis on witnessing, grief and vulnerability suggests an intention to implicate the audience in order to promote an ethical response in the outside world. In the following sections, we will be expanding on the triumvirate human rights, affect and witnessing with specific focus on *stoning mary, random* and *truth and reconciliation*.

Human waste: *stoning mary*

Human rights is a key focus for *stoning mary*, debbie tucker green's most performed play to date; since its opening at the Royal Court Theatre Downstairs in April 2005, the play has received further productions in Germany, Spain, Australia and Canada. The playwright's note to directors instructs that '*[t]he play is set in the country it is performed in. All characters are white*'[23] but the issues at the heart of the play – AIDS genocide, child soldiers and stoning – are most commonly associated with the African subcontinent. The play narrates three separate stories of suffering and abuse which gradually become strongly interconnected: a couple are fighting over an AIDS prescription, for they need two but can only afford one; another couple argue about their son who was taken away to become a child soldier; meanwhile, Mary, the daughter of the AIDS prescription couple, is condemned to stoning by her community for killing the child soldier who murdered her parents.

Perhaps more so than any of tucker green's other plays, *stoning mary* responds to the West's failure to connect with the world at large. Although she stipulates that 'the play isn't a documentary about Africa', it articulates an urgent response to material issues affecting Africa and the narratives of mediated reality by raising awareness about the practice of stoning, child soldiers and the AIDS crisis in sub-Saharan Africa.[24] According to the United Nations' general secretary Kofi Annan, AIDS is the cause of most deaths in sub-Saharan Africa, exceeding even the death toll attributed to conflict in 1999.[25] In Lyn Gardner's 2005 interview with tucker green it is mentioned that 'the charity Action Aid estimates that 90% of HIV positive people live in developing countries, 13.2 million children have been orphaned by Aids and by 2010 one in four adults of working age in 10 African nations will have died of the syndrome'.[26] Marianne Elliott, who directed the Royal Court production, describes *stoning mary* as a 'state-of-the-nation' play, in that it deals with our 'selfishness and inability to touch each other'.[27] She also comments on the reasons behind our lack of response towards problems in other continents: '[w]hen things happen in a different continent like Africa, we're not particularly bothered about [them] because we find it very difficult to imagine what their world is: it feels so far away from us that a lot of the time we're not very active in helping'.[28] *stoning mary* therefore serves a double function: it asks the audience to imagine what it would be like if things experienced in Africa were part of the West's social fabric but also draws attention to our inability to respond to crises which do not inhere directly in our quotidian lives. For tucker green, this inability is largely determined by how news circulates through mainstream media and its strategies of silencing and disempowering particular issues while paying attention to problems that preoccupy the West. In a conversation with the Royal Court's education officer Emily McLaughlin, tucker green points out that 'there are certain things that are happening in the world and I'm intrigued by what isn't being talked about, what falls out of the news'.[29]

Sociologist Zygmunt Bauman discusses the ways in which the representations of developing countries as 'a subhuman world beyond ethics and beyond salvation' through news media operate as alienating practices against which humanity is measured.[30] He specifically points out how certain lives are represented as 'a waste', as 'the unintended and unplanned "collateral casualties" of economic progress'.[31] Similarly, Lehmann observes the catastrophic implications of the proliferation of images of lives under peril: 'the continual presentation of bodies that are abused, injured, killed through isolated (real or fictive) catastrophes' collapses 'the bond between perception and action, receiving message and "answerability"'.[32] *stoning mary* aims to restore this bond by presenting 'human waste' in the context of a seemingly recognizable world of white characters which is rendered unrecognizable due to lack of empathy and cruelty to one another.

Human waste surfaces not only in the absence of the right to live under human conditions but also in the characters' acerbic comments. The two couples are afraid of proximity, reluctant to touch each other during their long exchanges of bickering. In 'The Prescription' Husband and Wife often avoid each other's 'face' by averting their gaze to the skies in the hope of divine intervention, which not only highlights the lack of care and affection but also the transformation of the human to 'human waste'. For Emmanuel Levinas our encounter with 'the face' of the Other is primarily ethical in that it asks us to acknowledge the Other's humanity; in this light, the refusal to look at or address the Other's face suggests a negation of the intelligibility of human life.[33] A poignant example of undermining human intelligibility can be found in the story entitled 'The Child Soldier'. Dad denigrates Mum as a waste by questioning her human qualities; he compares her perfume to contamination by a 'genetically modified contaminated fuck' and accuses her of being responsible for the fact that their son has turned into a soldier. [34] In Scenes 9 and 11, Mum questions her son's humanity by avoiding his gaze while her feeling of love expressed in Scene 4 has mutated to fear; 'I can't sleep with him in the house. I can't sleep with him back in the house. *Beat.* He scares me.'[35]

Bauman's notion of 'human waste' echoes Butler's writings on the differential distribution of vulnerability across the globe; for Butler '[c]ertain lives will be highly protected' while '[o]ther lives will not find such fast and furious support and will not even qualify as "grievable"'.[36] Mary's retaliation to her parents' violent murder is an act of grief for those lives that did not count as 'grievable'. In turn, she becomes another wasted life who fails to generate empathy from her sister and wider community. Older Sister contests the fact that Mary has rights; the fact that Mary's eyesight has improved because she was given a pair of glasses in prison, and that she has quit smoking, signals a healthier body that Older Sister resents: '[y]ou don't got the right – you lost the right – you lost that right when you started me startin – you lost the right before you lost your rights, right?'[37] In Kelly Oliver's terms, the refusal to respond to the Other's call 'destroys subjectivity and thereby humanity'.[38] Older Sister's refusal to witness the stoning signals the refusal to act in response to Mary's vulnerability. Moreover, Mary's body is dehumanized by her own community, who did not sign a petition that would stop the stoning from going ahead; she will not be grieved but rather stoned to death for disrupting the community's ethics. The play further troubles the notion of responsibility and action, as Mary's ethical response to the brutal murder of her parents contributes to a cycle of violence that 'wastes' human lives. Mary considers her killing of the child soldier to be an act of responsibility, an ethical response: 'I done somethin. Least I don somethin – I did. I did. I done something.'[39] The cycle of abjection, grief, responsibility and action is punctuated at the end of the play, when Mum (the child soldier's mother) 'picks up her first stone' as a response to her child's death.[40]

tucker green employs a number of stylistic strategies based on affect that open the possibility to push audiences towards action and responsibility by triggering our *ability to respond* in the face of calamity. For Marianne Elliott *stoning mary* is an 'angry' play[41] while Elaine Aston attributes the author's anger to her gender and racial identity.[42] At this stage it is worth locating tucker green's 'politics of anger' within feminist critiques of inequalities and abuse of human rights; 'anger' has served as a mobilizing force for 1970s feminism to speak against injustices towards women. Sara Ahmed particularly draws attention to the efficacy of the politics of anger within the context of black feminism, specifically alluding to the work of black lesbian feminist poet Audre Lorde whose 'anger' constituted the main emotive force that would break 'the tyrannies of silence'.[43] Ahmed goes on to make a case that anger opens up the possibility for creatively translating pain through language that is moving: '[a]nger is creative; it works to create a language with which to respond to that which one is against'.[44]

tucker green's angry 'dramatic poetics'[45] can be read in the light of Ahmed's and Lorde's understanding of anger as a language that interrupts silence and injustice. What is more, it functions as a creative strategy to deal with grief. Mary's furious outburst against the lack of solidarity amongst women who failed to rally for her cause allows her to articulate her grief but also works to resist the label of the vulnerable victim:

MARY: So what happened to the womanist bitches?
... the feminist bitches ...
the professional bitches?
What happened to them? [...]

The bitches that love to march?
The bitches that love to study
the music lovin bitches [...]
the bitches that love to fight
the bitches that love a debate [...]
Not one of them would march for me? [...]
Not a one a them would sign for me?[46]

Mary's enraged speech underscores her vulnerable position towards social injustices and the differential allocation of precariousness across the globe; at the same time, through replacing vulnerability with anger, the speech performs an act of resistance against expectations of 'genuine' performances of victimization as 'vulnerable, frightened and traumatized'.[47]

Another salient affective strategy employed in *stoning mary* is the shift of the perspective of Western audiences from a distant location (Africa) to their own home, rendering the unfamiliar problems that trouble the characters familiar. As explained earlier, this Brechtian *Verfremdungseffekt* draws attention to transnational concerns regarding the uneven distribution of wealth and unequal material conditions between Africa and the Western world. The use of projected scene titles accompanying each scene, evoking a type of Brechtian placard, functions as a device to signpost and foreground dramatic action and to also offer alternative 'news' headlines that capture the audience's attention. As Victoria Segal describes, the titles create an 'impact [that] is immediate and intimate, a headline you cannot look away from'.[48] D. Keith Peacock has argued that tucker green's 'intention is not to distance the audience but, by altering their perspective and thereby forcing them to read the situations portrayed in terms of their own environment, to generate empathy'.[49] Ruth Little, who chaired the performance post-show talk, departs from Peacock's point of view, pointing out that tucker green's plays require a new way of positioning oneself as an audience member that moves beyond conventional theatrical devices that elicit compassion and empathy.[50] What is more, in response to Little's questions, an audience member confessed that he 'found it hard to empathize'.[51] Scrutiny over the concept of empathy is therefore needed here, particularly taking into account the utilization of Brechtian devices. James Thompson signals that Epic theatre does not preclude emotion but rather seeks to promote 'an impression that must be felt'.[52] Thompson specifically borrows the term 'astonishment' from Walter Benjamin who argues that '[Epic theatre] consists in producing astonishment rather than empathy [...] instead of identifying with the characters, the audience should be educated to be astonished at the circumstances under which they function'.[53] In this vein, tucker green's portrayal of selfish characters who blatantly refuse to care about others or acknowledge them as human beings works towards 'astonishing' audiences and shaking them out of their complacency in order to invite them to care. In a British context, astonishment might be quite effective considering the cultural codes of politeness, which do not tolerate such behaviours of cruelty.[54] In addition, the device of witnessing as applied in the Royal Court production further works to promote the astonishment that Benjamin infers. Ultz's set design removed the seats from the stalls and replaced them with a 'blue, horse shoe-shaped arena', having some audience members stand around the front of the space where the action took place.[55] This particular mode of interpellating the audience as eyewitnesses to Mary's imminent stoning punctuates their complicit position and directly points to their responsibility towards Mary's body. Audiences also become the target of Mary's enraged speech, which invites them to consider their own ethical stance and responsibility. This participation as eyewitnesses is interrupted before the moments of death: spectators never witness the murder of Mary's parents or Mary's stoning because the play ends just as Mum 'picks up her first stone'.[56] Their position then shifts from eyewitnesses to *bearing witness to* the horror of death which lies beyond recognition and representation. In this light, tucker green's affective strategies do not encourage a simple empathetic response but rather a complex ethical positioning that points towards the body's failure to arouse empathy.

Teenage murder: *random*

Human rights victims are often the more vulnerable members of populations, particularly women, children and elderly people. In *random* (2008), which was first performed at the Royal Court Theatre Downstairs and launched the 2010 Theatre Local season at Elephant and Castle Shopping Centre, tucker green shifts her attention from global human rights to the topic of urban violence that has largely affected younger generations living in urban communities.[57] The play is a poignant response to the unprecedented epidemic of fatal teenage stabbings in London in 2007 and 2008. Still, tucker green does not focus on the reasons for the sudden rise in knife crime, instead portraying the grief of a family bereaved by the murder of its youngest member. *random* is not an issue-based play that explores events leading up to the death of a young black man. This differs from the predominantly realistic representations of 'urban' violence in black British playwriting, which have tended to emphasize the material and contextual factors that can manifest in youth crime, disenfranchisement and disaffection.[58] Rather, by placing the murder in the middle of the play, audiences experience its aftermath through the family's grief.

random departs from techniques employed in earlier work where attention to the body's vulnerability is paid through the representation of lack of empathy in the aftermath of cruelty and abuse. In contrast, tucker green highlights the vulnerability and human rights of young black men and women through the dramatic ploy of grief as the play's narrative focuses on a family's immediate emotions following the murder of Brother. The style of staging the play, in which *'[o]ne Black actress plays all characters'*, is a groundbreaking moment on the Royal Court theatre's main stage.[59] In the original production actress Nadine Marshall stands alone in a harsh white spotlight at the front of a completely bare stage. She is the main narrator of the story of an ordinary day in the life of an ordinary family that turns into tragedy when the police arrive on the doorstep with news that Brother was murdered in a random altercation in the street during his school lunch break. Her vulnerability as actress and storyteller is literally manifested in having to create the environment of the story entirely through her description and maintain the audience's attention without the usual theatrical accoutrements of set, lighting and sound effects. Audiences take on a more active role as they are asked to imagine the story unfolding in their mind's eye. The actress's vulnerability and loneliness on stage mirrors the feelings of isolation of each individual family member privately coming to terms with the news in the second part of the play. Sister feels alienated by her parents and is unwelcoming towards her workmates who stop by to offer their condolences, Dad takes the phone off the hook, and Mum sits with the Victim Support Officer in the family's front room, refusing to talk to the press, for she 'don't got nuthin nice to say. / Nu'un polite / nu'un / broadcastable / nu'un / righteous / nu'un forgivin'.[60]

Significantly, tucker green highlights the vulnerability of young black men who are often demonized within discourses on teenage murder and urban violence that determine whose lives count as 'grievable'. Most of the teenagers who were stabbed to death in 2007 and 2008 were black boys and young black men, leading then Prime Minister Tony Blair to declare '[w]e won't stop this by pretending it isn't young black kids doing it'.[61] Blair claimed that 'the spate of knife and gun murders in

London was not being caused by poverty, but a distinctive black culture
[...] the recent violence should not be treated as part of a general crime
wave, but as specific to black youth' and he urged the black community to get involved in trying to stop the problem.[62] Yet much of the
media attention around the epidemic of teenage knife crime focused
on the murdered white boys who were killed in random attacks and are
thus somewhat deemed more grievable than young black men whose
deaths were often framed in relation to ideas about gang violence.[63]
While Blair's observations widen the gap between the black and the
white community, silencing the former's vulnerability, *random* counters
such rhetoric that seeks to incriminate young black men by reinstating
the vulnerability of the black body in order to articulate an alternative
story to political and media discursive practices, thus offering an alternative possibility for response and action. Once more, the play's affective
fabric draws attention to the body as 'human waste' also evidenced in
the descriptions of Brother's body in the morgue, 'a chunk of him gone
/ now' and the small but fatal killer cut that 'punctured his ... / su'un –
important'.[64] Audiences thus bear witness to the aftermath of death,
which lies beyond mimetic representation. As Jenny Hughes argues, 'the
estranging, abject force of the live performance, and the terrible waste
of life that it dramatized' constitutes the play's force as '[i]t left behind
an invasive, tangible presence of waste and wasted life that was critically
resilient – that stayed after the performance was over'.[65]

Media stereotypes of black male youth are further undermined by
the sadness of his school friends leaving tributes at the murder spot
shrine, particularly the revelation that 'a hard-looking "hoodie" / [...]
under the cloak of Adidas / is a brotha / whose eyes don't stop flowin. /
Wet raw / with weepin'.[66] The image of the vulnerable hoodie who
grieves for the loss of his friend interferes with negative media representations and works towards humanization and recognition by
articulating an alternative story that often remains hidden from public view. It also helps to critically evaluate the processes of recognition
and silencing and appreciate that 'when a vulnerability is recognized,
that recognition has the power to change the meaning and structure
of vulnerability itself'.[67] Sister also resists the predominant media
portrayals of 'black on black violence' by emphasizing that Brother
was not part of a gang, an image often linked to the increase in the
murder of young black men, and pondering the arbitrariness of his
premature death. Her anger about the silence of witnesses that have
not come forward also implores audiences of the need for urgent
action to stop this 'cycle of shit'.[68]

That tucker green's play is both specific (a black family) and 'universal' (a family) is exemplified in a trajectory that takes audiences on a journey from a humorous account of a normal day to the emotional isolation of personal grief. The 'banal normality'[69] of a nuclear family – Mum, Dad, Sister, Brother – their mundane morning rituals as they wake up and set about their day, the randomness of Brother's murder, and the play's focus on their emotions and grief are some of the ways that tucker green moves the discourse beyond the specificity of racial issues.[70] Thus she interrogates the binary centre/margin, because, similarly to *stoning mary*, casting a black actress as Sister underlines a dual perspective in which the character represents both the specific and the general. Aleks Sierz's review suggests, for example, that 'although the family is black and the parents have been written as if they were migrants rather than British born, it is interesting that their grieving is so typically English'.[71]

Staging *random* in the Royal Court's main theatre is testament to the urgency of these concerns as a wider issue, not just for the black community. Thus, while the transfer of the production to the Royal Court's Theatre Local season in 2010 was framed as a way of reaching audiences within the community, particularly younger (black and working-class) spectators who might not usually attend the Sloane Square venue, tucker green deploys dramatic devices that work to break down associations with stereotypical perceptions of race.[72] This intervention is perhaps most pronounced in the way the (black) actress's body negotiates different genders, races and ages, becoming a vehicle for bridging the self and the Other, the private and the public, the individual and the collective.

Victims and perpetrators: *truth and reconciliation*

truth and reconciliation (2011), which takes its title and theme from the hearings held in post-apartheid South Africa, was directed by tucker green in the Royal Court's Theatre Upstairs, before moving to launch the Theatre Local Season at the Bussey Building, a former cricket bat factory in Peckham, now a thriving multipurpose arts venue. A global human rights agenda is explicit by the play being set in five different countries which have been sites of war, genocide and conflict – South Africa, 1998, Rwanda, 2005, Bosnia, 1996, Zimbabwe, 2007 and Northern Ireland, 1999. The projection of places and dates above each scene links tucker green's play to the real histories of conflict in these zones: the Sharpeville Massacre in South Africa in 1960, where the police opened fire on a group of black student protesters, killing 69; the Rwandan genocide in 1994, where long-standing tensions between Hutu and Tutsi tribes culminated in the mass murder of over half a million Rwandans; ethnic cleansing, genocide and the rape of women by Serbian armed forces during the Bosnian War from 1992 to 1995; and the Northern Ireland Troubles from the late 1960s until the late 1990s. As Fiona Mountford's review points out, these are 'all places where truth and reconciliation are longed for but desperately hard to come by, even in the most well-intentioned hearings'.[73] That many of these places have not undergone a formal truth and reconciliation process is a reminder that tucker green's play is an imagined response to residual issues in places where conflict has happened rather than a political docudrama. Despite the visibility of the local contexts, the play does not interrogate the reasons that have led to such conflicts or propose ways of reconciliation. Rather, tucker green foregrounds the complexities underpinning these conflicts and interrogates the very concepts of reconciliation and forgiveness.

The Truth and Reconciliation Commission hearings were established as part of a restorative justice process in South Africa after the end of apartheid. Formal tribunals publicly heard witness statements from the victims of violence and human rights abuses that occurred under apartheid; perpetrators would also testify as a way of achieving reconciliation or to be granted amnesty from prosecution for violence committed for political objectives.[74] In tucker green's play, victims and their families confront perpetrators of violence and abuse, opening up questions of responsibility and whether damage can be undone. Although these stories are not fully detailed accounts of each situation, the pain and suffering of the characters is palpable, which raises the question of whether the revelation of the 'truth' about what happened in the past can help the process of grieving and lead to forgiveness and reconciliation.

The emotional impact in the aftermath of conflict is expressed through the determination of the female characters who are seeking the truth about past human rights abuses of violence and genocide. Strong and defiant women push for answers about the truth of what happened to their loved ones, refusing to accept the role of passive victim; rather, they are assertive and outspoken, boldly confronting their communities and seeking a response for the abuse and loss of their families.[75] A South African Mum refuses to sit down until the man who killed her daughter 22 years earlier arrives at the hearing. A pregnant Bosnian Woman confronts the Serbian men who raped her. A Northern Irish Woman interrogates the mother of her son's killer. Stella, a Rwandan Widow (Tutsi) questions a Rwandan Man (Hutu) about how her husband was dressed, what his last words were, and whether he put up any resistance. Female defiance is exemplified in the fifth scenario in which a Zimbabwean Husband warns his wife about his inability to protect her from the consequences of speaking out against injustice – in the longest scene in the play, another woman rebukes the same husband for being 'weak' and failing to protect his wife.

Similar to her other plays, seemingly trivial, mundane or minor concerns gain significance in the characters' responses to trauma – where they sit, whether they can smoke, whether the chairs have cushions on them or not – and the play only hints at the horror of the various situations until it is captured fully in the final scene. Here, the young South African girl reprimands the officer who shot her several times in the back as she was running away and continued to shoot after she was already dead. The silenced (dead) victims of torture who appear as kinds of ghosts in the play do not seek mere visibility and recognition but 'witnesses to horrors beyond recognition'.[76] The Child's refusal to accept the Officer's justification for his past actions problematizes ideas about easy reconciliation, and, as this scene occurs at the end of the play, audiences witness his final reneging on an agreement to attend the future hearing and tell the family the truth about what he did to their child and where her body is buried. Similarly, a scene between Stella's dead husband Moses and the Man who tortured and killed him also shows difficulties with the concept of reconciliation. In his essay 'On Forgiveness' Jacques Derrida questions the very notion of forgiveness as something attainable and draws attention to the politics and power relations underpinning any reconciliatory acts carried out by third parties (who often serve their own interests) on behalf of the two conflicting sides. Derrida problematizes the universality of concepts such as 'human rights' and 'crime against humanity', which are determined by international law as erasing history and specificity.[77] Drawing attention to the Man lying about Moses's resistance during torture and his refusal to forgive, presents a sense of cynicism about whose needs are served by reconciliation hearings: 'I do not care for your regrets. I do not care for – your slippery words keep them – I can't be bothered with your ... ruefulness – can't be bothered with that reconciliatory bullshit. Keep it. I am not looking to be reconciled.'[78]

These confrontations also remind audiences of how individuals are personally affected by violent acts – the victims, those who have lost people, and the (mostly) military perpetrators (soldiers and policemen) who have to live with the guilt of the pain and loss caused by their extreme actions. Debates between the characters allude to the inherent complexities of passing judgement on these acts when the individuals underneath the uniforms are revealed. Ambiguous scenes in which perpetrators appear to be putting on a front, in denial, lying, guilty or haunted by their past misdeeds also create some empathy for them as individuals. The Rwandan Man's troubled past impacts on his daily life in the present – he seeks solace in alcohol and describes his family and friends as being fearful of him. His vulnerability is captured in stage directions describing him as tired and exhausted. In another scene, two Serbian ex-soldiers (selfishly) try to convince each other to admit to raping the pregnant woman, raising ethical questions about how we interpret their behaviour, then and now. Man 1, an ordinary family man with children and responsibilities, rationalizes that his single comrade has less to lose, while Man 2 argues that his life would be affected more because he has less external support from an extended family. As both men repeat 'I served my country' at the end of the scene, audiences are reminded of individuals whose own lives were potentially endangered during conflict and are now living with the consequences of their own atrocious war crimes.[79] A complex presentation of the positions of both victims and perpetrators demonstrates the difficulties involved in understanding these cruelties and of assessing where the responsibility of resolving conflict lies.

The production's publicity image, of three characters, each covering eyes, ears or mouth, brings to mind the proverb 'see no evil, hear no evil, speak no evil', a further suggestion of ideas about the West failing to respond to these global atrocities; but audiences are prevented from distancing themselves by a performance style that includes them as witnesses. The play does not intend to rewrite the historical narrative or provide solutions to these different cases in such a short time. Although its form departs from tribunal aesthetics, it is staged in such a way that the audience is explicitly involved as a witness to the aftermath of these conflicts. Names of real victims who have died in conflict are written on the walls of the stairs leading up to the theatre and are etched onto the hard wooden chairs used for the set and the audience's seating.[80] On entering the auditorium, spectators are instructed not to walk across the black-earthed floor, as though they are sacred ashes, or sit in any of the reserved chairs, which are labelled 'Witnesses' Family', creating a sense of anticipation and immediately including audiences as part of the tribunal gathering that is implied by the arrangement of the chairs on stage. The audience seating was intentionally positioned at a higher level from the stage so that they could have direct eye contact with the actors standing in the middle of the stage, while also evoking public galleries in courtrooms from which family members can observe trials.[81] Setting the production in the round further blurs the divide between audience and action, the effect accentuated by placing the actors amongst the spectators as 'witnesses' family' for some of the scenes. Thus the audience are often caught in the stage lighting and rendered witnesses alongside the characters that occupy some of these chairs throughout the play. At the Bussey Building in Peckham, noises from the trains arriving at the railway station next door added a further sense that these meetings were taking place in a non-specified yet sombre space where the pristine black-earthed set is gradually trodden in and across by the actors as a further symbolization of the effects of human desecration.

These stylistic elements seem to be a call to consider 'the real', wherein the play becomes a memorialization of the real human rights issues that these stories respond to. As director, tucker green insisted that 22 actors should be used to represent the different characters with no role doubling, leading to the largest primarily black cast ever at the Royal Court, which becomes a way of representing mass scale global suffering through a microcosmic world. As Claire Allfree's review astutely identifies, 'the voices of a few represent the unheard voices of thousands and thousands more'.[82] The production aesthetics evoke tucker green's politicized anger, a reminder of the need to understand the complexities of truth and reconciliation. As Charles Spencer's review concludes, the play 'nags away potently in the memory long after the performance is over'.[83] While tucker green does not prescribe what audiences should think or do, her continued provocative staging of such issues for predominantly white middle-class audiences at the Royal Court draws attention to injustice, highlights the difficulties of reconciliation, and by showing the impact of these issues seems to be imploring action.

Conclusion

tucker green's success as a black woman writing for the Royal Court is testament to the way she merges influences from black culture (particularly music and poetry) with British political theatre traditions. Her staging of human rights issues resonates with trends in contemporary British new writing that recognizes international contexts, which she intervenes in with a specific focus on (black) women and the foregrounding of 'black' urban language styles and experiences. By presenting 'black' and women's rights as 'human' rights, tucker green stages a claim for recognition of the specifics of their experience within concerns about 'universal' rights for humanity. Thus, while her plays are not issue-based in a conventional sense, using frameworks of 'witnessing' and 'vulnerability' to analyse them opens out a consideration of the particular impact of how they work to prick the moral consciences of (white) Western audiences about local and global issues.

tucker green's work promotes a politics of affect that alludes to Lehmann's 'aesthetics of response-ability', surprising the spectator with the dystopic realities represented. Witnessing further underscores an intention to implicate the audience into the collective experience of being held accountable and promote a response in the outside world. The process of witnessing as dramatized in her work also serves to frame attitudes towards 'what it means to be human', investing both victims and witnesses with the power to act in response to injustice; victims primarily seek to elicit a response from their witnesses in order to reverse the practices that have rendered their lives as a 'human waste' and gain the power to respond to the injustices inflicted upon them. At the same time, witnesses are also empowered as they are asked to respond, which suggests an incitement to response-ability and action.

In the wake of the fall of the Berlin Wall, Clive Barker makes a case for the efficacy of witnessing in the theatre: '[i]f times become hard and repressive [...] there is value in bearing witness. Whatever is happening in Britain and in the rest of Europe, people are starving and oppressed, and the dispossessed are being abused. In this world the theatre still has a role. The minimal role in protest is to stand up and be counted.'[84] tucker green's work extends the concerns that Barker signals beyond European borders, resonating with this need to 'stand up and be counted', although not through direct protest but by means of her politics of affect. Audiences touched by the heightened emotional impact of witnessing the pain of loss and anger can follow up on their feelings for tucker green's characters by seeking the understanding that precipitates direct action to stop such atrocities.

Notes

1. tucker green was also commissioned to write *monologue*, a five-minute piece produced as part of *The Laws of War*, 'Cries From the Heart' Human Rights Watch evening at the Royal Court in 2010.
2. *stoning mary* has been staged at the Schaubühne, Berlin (2007, dir. Benedict Andrews), Teatro Pradillo, Madrid (2008, dir. Marco Carniti), and SBW Stables Theatre, Sydney, by Griffin Theatre Company (2008). *born bad* opened at

Soho Rep, New York (2011, dir. Leah C. Gardiner). *dirty butterfly* premiered at Toronto Fringe Festival by Bound to Create Theatre (B2C) in 2012.

3. See, for example, Royal Court productions by Bola Agbaje (*Gone Too Far* (2007), *Off the Endz* (2010) and *Belong* (2012)), Levi David Addai (*93.2 FM* (2006) and *Oxford Street* (2008)), Roy Williams (*Lift Off* (1999), *Clubland* (2001), *Fallout* (2003) and *Sucker Punch* (2010)), and Kwame Kwei-Armah's trilogy of plays for the National Theatre (*Elmina's Kitchen* (2003), *Fix Up* (2004) and *Statement of Regret* (2007)).

4. See, for example, E. Aston, 'A Fair Trade? Staging Female Sex Tourism in *Sugar Mummies* and *Trade*', *Contemporary Theatre Review*, 18.2 (2008), 180–92, and D. Osborne, 'How Do We Get the Whole Story? Contra-dictions and Counter-narratives in debbie tucker green's Dramatic-Poetics', in M. Tönnies and C. Flotmann (eds.), *Narrative in Drama* (Trier: Wissenschaftlicher Verlag Trier, 2011), pp. 181–206.

5. H. Derbyshire and L. Hodson, 'Performing Injustice: Human Rights and Verbatim Theatre', *Law and Humanities*, 2.2 (2008), 191–211 (p. 196).

6. Derbyshire and Hodson, 'Performing Injustice: Human Rights and Verbatim Theatre', p. 195.

7. M. Luckhurst, 'Verbatim Theatre, Media Relations and Ethics', in N. Holdsworth and M. Luckhurst (eds.), *A Concise Companion to Contemporary British and Irish Drama* (Oxford: Blackwell, 2008), pp. 200–22 (p. 201).

8. Productions directed by the Tricycle's Artistic Director Nicolas Kent include: Richard Norton Taylor (ed.), *The Colour of Justice* (1999), *Justifying War: Scenes from the Hutton Enquiry* (2003) and *Bloody Sunday: Scenes from the Saville Inquiry* (2005), and Victoria Brittain and Gillian Slovo's *Guantánamo: 'Honor Bound to Defend Freedom'* (2004).

9. Kay Adshead wrote the play in response to the protest of the detained asylum seekers at Campsfield centre in Oxford for its abject living conditions ('Author's Note', in K. Adshead, *The Bogus Woman* (London: Oberon Books, 2001), p. 15). Caryl Churchill's pieces directly address the American–British invasion in Iraq in 2003 and the Israeli army's attack in the Gaza strip in December 2008.

10. E. Aston, 'Feeling the Loss of Feminism: Sarah Kane's *Blasted* and an Experiential Genealogy of Contemporary Women's Playwriting', *Theatre Journal* 62.4 (2010), 575–91 (p. 585, original emphasis).

11. J. Reinelt, 'The Promise of Documentary', in A. Forsyth and C. Megson (eds.), *Get Real: Documentary Theatre Past and Present* (Basingstoke: Palgrave Macmillan, 2009), pp. 6–23 (p. 12).

12. For a more detailed reference on the use of the term see L. Fitzpatrick, 'The Performance of Violence and the Ethics of Spectatorship', *Performance Research: A Journal of the Performing Arts*, 16.1 (2011), 64–5. Also, see H. Grehan's insightful discussion in '*Aalst*: Acts of Evil, Ambivalence and Responsibility', *Theatre Research International*, 35.1 (2010), 4–16.

13. C. Megson, '"This is All Theatre": Iraq Centre Stage', *Contemporary Theatre Review*, 15.3 (2005), 369–71 (p. 371).

14. K. Oliver, *Witnessing: Beyond Recognition* (Minneapolis and London: University of Minnesota Press, 2001), p. 16.

15. H.-T. Lehmann, *Postdramatic Theatre*, trans. K. Jürs-Munby (London and New York: Routledge, 2006), pp. 185–6.

16. E. Aston, 'debbie tucker green', in M. Middeke, P. P. Schnierer and A. Sierz (eds.), *The Methuen Drama Guide to Contemporary British Playwrights* (London: Methuen Drama, 2011), pp. 183–202 (p. 184).
17. P. Rae, *Theatre & Human Rights* (Basingstoke: Palgrave Macmillan, 2009), pp. 13–14.
18. Rae, *Theatre & Human Rights*, p. 20.
19. Grehan, '*Aalst*: Acts of Evil, Ambivalence and Responsibility', p. 10.
20. For a more detailed analysis see M. Fragkou, 'Precarious Subjects: Ethics of Witnessing and Responsibility', *Performing Ethos*, 3.1 (2013).
21. See Aston, 'A Fair Trade?' for a cogent analysis of the dynamics of the relationships between the women in this play.
22. K. Oliver, 'Witnessing and Testimony', *Parallax*, 10.1 (2004), 79–88 (p. 80).
23. d. tucker green, *stoning mary* (London: Nick Hern Books, 2005), p. 2.
24. Anon., *stoning mary* 'Education Resources' (London: Royal Court Theatre, 2005), 1–14 (p. 4).
25. K. Annan, 'Africa: Maintaining the Momentum', Commonwealth Lecture, London (2000), http://www.commonwealthfoundation.com/ (accessed 30 November 2011).
26. Cited in L. Gardner, 'I was Messing About: She's Won Awards and Acclaim but She is Still not Sure She is a Playwright', *The Guardian*, 30 March 2005, http://www.guardian.co.uk/ (accessed 10 July 2012).
27. *stoning mary* Post-Show Talk, Royal Court Theatre, London, 12 April 2005. Available at the British Library's Soundserver.
28. *stoning mary* 'Education Resources', 6.
29. *stoning mary* 'Education Resources', 4.
30. Z. Bauman, 'The World Inhospitable to Levinas', *Philosophy Today*, 43.2 (1999), 151–67 (p. 166).
31. Z. Bauman, *Wasted Lives: Modernity and its Outcasts* (Cambridge: Polity Press, 2004), p. 39.
32. Lehmann, *Postdramatic Theatre*, p. 184.
33. Cited in J. Thompson, *Performance Affects: Applied Theatre and the End of Effect* (Basingstoke: Palgrave Macmillan, 2009), p. 162.
34. tucker green, *stoning mary*, p. 23.
35. tucker green, *stoning mary*, pp. 52–3.
36. J. Butler, *Precarious Life: The Powers of Mourning and Violence* (London: Verso, 2004), p. 32.
37. tucker green, *stoning mary*, p. 48.
38. Oliver, *Witnessing*, p. 90.
39. tucker green, *stoning mary*, pp. 63–4.
40. tucker green, *stoning mary*, p. 73.
41. *stoning mary* Post-Show Talk.
42. Aston, 'Feeling the Loss of Feminism', p. 588.
43. Cited in S. Ahmed, *The Cultural Politics of Emotion* (Edinburgh: Edinburgh University Press, 2004), p. 175.
44. Ahmed, *The Cultural Politics of Emotion*, pp. 175–6.
45. Osborne, 'How Do We Get the Whole Story?', p. 188.
46. tucker green, *stoning mary*, pp. 61–3.
47. A. Jeffers, *Refugees, Theatre and Crisis: Performing Global Identities* (Basingstoke: Palgrave Macmillan, 2011), p. 153.

48. V. Segal, *The Sunday Times*, 10 April 2005.
49. D. K. Peacock, 'Black British Drama and the Politics of Identity', in Holdsworth and Luckhurst (eds.), *A Concise Companion to Contemporary British and Irish Drama*, pp. 48–65 (p. 60).
50. *stoning mary* Post-Show Talk.
51. *stoning mary* Post-Show Talk.
52. Thompson, *Performance Affects*, p. 129.
53. Cited in Thompson, *Performance Affects*, p. 129.
54. Evidence of such response can be found in relation to tucker green's earlier work; for instance, Lyn Gardner's review of *dirty butterfly* warned that the play 'will not suit those who [...] get irritated when characters stand around discussing their relationship rather than dialling 999 for the ambulance that is so clearly and urgently required', *The Guardian*, http://www.guardian.co.uk/ (accessed 10 July 2012).
55. I. Johns, 'Review of *stoning mary*', *Theatre Record*, 25.7 (2005), 424.
56. tucker green, *stoning mary*, p. 73.
57. *random* also toured to the Albany, Deptford and was adapted for radio (BBC Radio 3, 13 March 2010) and television (Channel 4, 23 August 2011).
58. See, for example, Roy Williams's *Fallout* (Royal Court, 2003) and Kwame Kwei-Armah's *Elmina's Kitchen* (National Theatre, 2003).
59. d. tucker green, *random* (London: Nick Hern Books, 2008), p. 2.
60. tucker green, *random*, p. 42.
61. K. Walker, 'Face the facts on knife crime, Blair tells black families', *The Daily Mail*, 12 April 2007, http://www.dailymail.co.uk/news/article-447925/Face-facts-knife-crime-Blair-tells-Black-families.html/ (accessed 19 October 2011).
62. P. Wintour and V. Dodd, 'Blair blames spate of murders on black culture', *The Guardian*, 12 April 2007, http://www.guardian.co.uk/politics/2007/apr/12/ukcrime.race/ (accessed 19 October 2011).
63. For detailed analysis of this public discourse around teenage murder see L. Goddard, 'Death Never Used to Be for the Young: Grieving Teenage Murder in debbie tucker green's *random*', *Women: A Cultural Review*, 20.3 (2009), 299–309.
64. tucker green, *random*, pp. 35, 37.
65. J. Hughes, *Performance in a Time of Terror: Critical Mimesis and the Age of Uncertainty* (Manchester: Manchester University Press, 2011), p. 27.
66. tucker green, *random*, p. 41.
67. Butler, *Precarious Life*, p. 43.
68. tucker green, *random*, p. 49.
69. A. Sierz, 'Review of *random*', *Theatre Record*, 28.6 (2008), 287.
70. For further analysis of the multiple perspectives of race and gender manifest in the performance style of this play, see M. Fragkou, 'Intercultural Encounters in debbie tucker green's *random*', in W. Huber, M. Rubik and J. Novak (eds.), *Staging Interculturality* (Trier: Wissenschaftlicher Verlag Trier, 2010), pp. 75–87.
71. Sierz, 'Review of *random*', p. 287.
72. Plays that have transferred as part of this outreach initiative are those that are thought to be of interest to communities other than the more typical Royal Court audience. Such pieces include Anupama Chandrasekar's *Disconnect* (2010), Rachel De Lahay's *The Westbridge* (2011), tucker green's *truth and reconciliation* (2011) and Bola Agbaje's *Belong* (2012).

166   *Contemporary British Theatre*

73. *The Evening Standard*, 6 September 2011. All *truth and reconciliation* review citations are taken from *Theatre Record* 31.18 (2011), 935–7.
74. See K. Avruch and B. Vejarano, 'Truth and Reconciliation Commissions: A Review Essay and Annotated Bibliography', *OJPCR: The Online Journal of Peace and Conflict Resolution*, 4.2 (2002), 37–76.
75. tucker green's commitment to focusing on the bereavement and traumatic experiences of strong women is echoed in *monologue* (2010), which distils some of the ideas articulated in *truth and reconciliation*. *monologue* focuses on a South African woman whose husband and children are killed by a neighbouring community. She places her identity as a woman, mother, wife and widow at the centre of the narrative in order to justify the fact that she will retaliate so as to achieve retribution for her family's murders.
76. Oliver, 'Witnessing and Testimony', p. 79.
77. J. Derrida, *On Cosmopolitanism and Forgiveness*, trans. M. Dooley and M. Hughes (London: Routledge, 2001), pp. 52–3.
78. d. tucker green, *truth and reconciliation* (London: Nick Hern Books, 2011), p. 71.
79. tucker green, *truth and reconciliation*, p. 31.
80. At the post-show talk for the play, Northern Irish actress Clare Cathcart stated that one of the names memorialized on the chairs is her cousin (Personal Notes, Royal Court Theatre, 21 September 2011).
81. Post-Show Talk, 21 September 2011.
82. *Metro* (London), 7 September 2011.
83. *The Daily Telegraph*, 7 September 2011.
84. C. Barker, 'Alternative Theatre/Political Theatre', in G. Holderness (ed.), *The Politics of Theatre and Drama* (Basingstoke: Macmillan, 1992), p. 38.

8
Children and the Limits of Representation in the Work of Tim Crouch

Helen Freshwater

In an article published in 2004 in *New Theatre Quarterly*, Mark Ravenhill identifies a direct link between the form and content of his early plays and his emotional response to the now-infamous killing of James Bulger; a link that he claims not to have been aware of until years after these plays were written. Looking back, he proposes that the killing in 1993 had a massive impact upon the national psyche, similar to the affective shift which occurred with the death of Princess Diana, four years later. He asserts that Bulger's murder became a focus both for private grief and public guilt about the greed and self-interest which characterized the final years of the Conservative government in the late 1980s and early 1990s. For Ravenhill, the murder resulted in an urge to write, and to find new forms. He states:

> Somehow [...] I felt that the existing plays just weren't right, that they wouldn't do any more. Not so much that they weren't good [...]. But somehow something had shifted, a tear in the fabric had happened.[1]

Ravenhill then goes on to offer a reading of his first three plays, *Shopping and Fucking* (1996), *Faust is Dead* (1997) and *Handbag* (1998), which draws out their shared preoccupation with the killing of the young by adults infantilized by the brutal logic of late capitalism. In this article, Ravenhill focuses upon the drama of the 1990s, speculating that James Bulger's murder may also have had a galvanizing impact upon other playwrights. He also claims that he eventually overcame his preoccupation with the murder, presenting 2001's *Mother Clap's Molly House* – which includes 'a baby doll [... that] is cared for rather than murdered or molested, and finally left behind as the game and the play concludes' – as evidence that he had laid this particular ghost to rest.[2] Ravenhill may have found closure but British culture – both popular and theatrical – continues to be haunted by anxieties about children and childhood. This chapter focuses on how this preoccupation manifests itself in the work of Tim Crouch.

Crouch started to write for the theatre in 2003, placing himself as a performer inside his own work. Before this date he trained as an actor, worked in film, television and theatre, and co-founded Public Parts Theatre with whom he produced a series of devised productions. His plays *My Arm* (2003), *An Oak Tree* (2005), *ENGLAND* (2007) and *The Author* (2009) have toured nationally and internationally, attracting numerous awards, and, in some cases, notoriety amongst audiences.[3] Crouch has also written plays for young audiences, including a series of monologues which focus upon Shakespeare's lesser characters: *I, Caliban* (2003), *I, Peaseblossom* (2004), *I, Banquo* (2005), *I, Malvolio* (2010) and *I, Cinna (The Poet)* (2012).[4] Scholarly engagement with Crouch's work has been developing alongside his reputation as a writer and performer, and the growing body of academic analysis of his plays includes examination of their development, form, reception and position in relation to contemporary theatre and other art forms.[5] But no one has yet observed that three of four of his plays for adult audiences published to date circle around narratives involving damaged, dead and abused children.[6] I argue below that the figure of the child is central to the exploration of the boundaries of representation in *My Arm*, *An Oak Tree* and *The Author*, and that Crouch's short play for young performers, *John, Antonio and Nancy* (2010) demonstrates his engagement with the political and cultural capital commanded by the child.

Sadly, this political and cultural capital has been most visible in recent years in the extensive media coverage which has accompanied the deaths of a small number of children. James Bulger's murder is just one particularly notorious recent event amongst several which focused the British public's attention upon the vulnerability of some children and the depravity of others. The murders of Sarah Payne, Holly Wells and Jessica Chapman, and the case of 'Baby P' all received blanket media coverage, which often appeared to be dedicated to stoking up moral panic about paedophilia, 'feral' children, neglectful or abusive parents, and inadequate child protection services. The media's apparent investment in the creation of this climate of fear and anxiety reached its nadir with the hysterical and all-pervasive coverage of the disappearance of Madeleine McCann in 2007. The way that this particular case regularly reappears in the media – as the McCanns continue to use the press in their campaign to find their daughter – is representative of many of these stories.[7] Even if the public only had an appetite for a fraction of this material, it would appear that many of us remain both appalled and fascinated by stories of the death, disappearance and abuse of children.

But anxieties are not limited to fear that children will be abducted, murdered by paedophiles, or commit violent crimes themselves. Threats to children and childhood seem to permeate every aspect of their existence, and parental anxiety over these threats has generated an extraordinary wealth of popular publications. Many authors publishing in this field focus upon children's exposure to marketing and the way in which they are being vigorously pursued as consumers. The metaphors deployed in titles such as *Candy from Strangers: Kids and Consumer Culture* (2005), *Consumer Kids: How Big Business is Grooming our Children for Profit* (2009) and *This Little Kiddy Went to Market: The Corporate Capture of Childhood* (2009) make it evident how high some writers consider the stakes to be, as they present the market as a manipulative sexual predator, intent upon abduction.[8] These fears about the effect of children's exposure to the full power of capital are closely related to concerns about the premature sexualization of children, which focus upon exposure to pornography, inappropriately early sexual activity and the selling of sexualized clothing.[9] Anxieties over twenty-first century childhood do not always take such concrete form, however. Some authors claim that the pace of modern life is 'toxic' to children; others that today's children are suffering from 'nature deficit disorder'.[10]

It is important to acknowledge that concerns about the modern world's deleterious effect upon children and the quality of childhood have been being voiced for many years. Neil Postman's *The Disappearance of Childhood* – which mourns the erosion of the distinctions between adult and child – was first published in 1982. David Elkind's *Hurried Child: Growing Up Too Fast Too Soon* (first published in 1981 and then reissued in 1998, 2001 and 2007) begins with the assertion that 'the concept of childhood [...] is threatened with extinction in the society we have created'.[11] And it can be argued that the behaviour of the young and the experience of youth was a source of anxiety long before childhood was recognized as a category in itself.[12] Nevertheless, anxiety about the experience of childhood in Britain seems to have intensified in the twenty-first century, and the pervasiveness of these anxieties leads Libby Brooks to conclude in her 2006 publication, *The Story of Childhood: Growing Up in Modern Britain*, that 'worries about children's well-being have been amplified to an excruciating pitch [...] Childhood has become the crucible into which is ground each and every adult anxiety – about sex, consumerism, technology, safety, achievement, respect, the proper shape of life. This is a time of child-panic.'[13]

Crouch is not alone in the formal and intellectual engagement with this 'child-panic'. Anxieties about children and childhood have been central to some of the boldest experiments in dramatic form on the British stage during the last 15 years. Several of the most innovative and productive British playwrights of the period return again and again to the figure of the child in their work. Dead, disappeared and dangerous children appear throughout the plays of Simon Stephens. *Bluebird* (1998) and *Sea Wall* (2008) circle around impact of the accidental death of a child; *One Minute* (2003) presents the distress and confusion of a mother whose child has disappeared. Stephens acknowledges that *Wastwater* (2011) – which explores child trafficking and sexual abuse – was written in direct response to the disappearance of Madeleine McCann.[14] *Herons* (2001), *Punk Rock* (2009) and *Pornography* (2007) include portraits of violent and disturbed children and teenagers.[15] Children have also played an increasingly important role in Martin Crimp's work. Threats are made to and by children in *Attempts on Her Life* (1997); much of the tension in *The Country* (2000) is generated by references to the offstage children; *Advice to Iraqi Women* (2003) plays upon the contrast between Western anxieties over children's well-being and the impossibility of protecting your child in a war-zone; and children are under threat from adults in Crimp's *Fewer Emergencies* (2005).[16] Children and memories of childhood are never far away in the work of Philip Ridley, too. Alongside his plays and books for children and young people, Ridley has produced several plays that focus centrally on the physical and sexual abuse of children. The controversial *Mercury Fur* (2005) – which Ridley's then publisher, Faber and Faber, refused to produce – asked audiences to contemplate the killing of children for sexual gratification; *Leaves of Glass* (2007) explores the toxic legacy of child abuse; while in *Shivered* (2012) children bear the brunt of exposure to both screened and viscerally real violence.[17] In all of these works, the figure of the child drives and focuses experiments with form.

These experiments are enabled by the extraordinary affective weight currently carried by the figure of the child and idealized fantasies of childhood. As Lee Edelman and Robin Bernstein have argued, these political and cultural investments – which insist that childhood innocence must be protected at all costs – amount to nothing less than a form of 'secular theology'.[18] And, as Edelman and Bernstein demonstrate, this framework of belief can be deployed to support a wide range of political positions, and has a significant impact on all members of society: even those who have little or no interest in children. It has also been argued that the conceptual or imaginary child proves so useful, and so powerful, as a political tool because children have long been thought of as blank pages, empty vessels or voids. For philosopher John Locke, and more recently, literary and cultural historian James Kincaid, children are available to be inscribed or filled with any meaning by adults. Writing in 1992, Kincaid argued that the child 'is not, in itself, anything but a cultural formation and an object of adult desire, a function necessary to our psychic and cultural life'.[19] Crouch's formal experimentation certainly utilizes the affective power of the blank and abstracted concept of the child; but his plays also demonstrate how the theatrical representation of the child can trouble and resist these forces of abstraction and idealization.

Crouch's first play, *My Arm*, revolves around detailed memories of childhood, but its emotional impact depends upon audiences' investment in the affective capital associated with the abstracted cultural concept of the child. This first-person monologue, delivered by Crouch, presents audiences with the curious history of its nameless protagonist and the consequences of his decision, at the age of ten, to raise his arm above his head and keep it there. He begins by relating the competitive endurance tests he indulged in with his brother as a child and his early experiments with 'self-determination' – holding his breath, refusing to speak for days – before exploring the consequences of his life-changing decision.[20] He then tells the audience about the medical, emotional and violent interventions that are made by his family, psychiatrists, doctors and strangers, in an attempt to convince him to lower his arm and return to 'normality', before revealing his celebration by the contemporary art world and subsequent conversion into a living (then abjectly dying) work of art by unscrupulous art dealers. The piece explores the consequences of choices made in childhood, the construction of childhood memory, and art's relations with the power of capital, problematizing the distinctions between subject and object, and the desire to find meaning and authenticity even where it is most vigorously denied.

These thematic preoccupations are all illustrated and advanced by the piece's form, most notably through Crouch's use of a collection of random small objects, gathered from the audience at the start of the show. Crouch positions these objects – keys, badges, toys and cosmetics – on a table on stage and live images of them are projected from a video camera onto a small television screen visible to the audience throughout the show. These objects are used by Crouch to 'stand-in' for people and things that appear in his story, and, as Stephen Bottoms and David Lane have demonstrated, greater imaginative investment is required to deal with the conceptual collision between the randomly selected object and the element of the story it represents.[21] Consequently, the use of these objects may serve to shift the spectator's relationship with the theatrical event. This shift is central to the kind of audience engagement Crouch is seeking.

Crouch asserts in interviews that his aim is to make work that is open, that leaves room for interpretation, and that hands over the role of author, in part, to audiences. In interview in 2010, he described the process as 'asking them to become an author with us' in the hope of realizing what he called 'a community of ownership'.[22] Other aspects of *My Arm* also function to generate the kind of active imaginative engagement and shared ownership that Crouch seeks. The non-representational minimalism of the scenography – in which the objects on the otherwise bare stage are either functional and unremarkable (a table, chair, television and screen) or randomly selected – provides ample space for audience members to engage imaginatively with Crouch's story. Moreover, there are no strong emotions on display during the performance. This deliberate reticence is both scripted and embodied. Crouch does not cry or physically present distress or discomfort, despite the emotional and corporeal extremity of the experiences he is describing for us. And, as he noted in an interview with Aleks Sierz, the script contains no adjectives.[23] The situation is described, and audiences are left to draw their own conclusions. The audience is also denied any satisfying psychological justification for the character's behaviour, as he rejects all of the attempts to explain his decision to raise his arm. Indeed, he refuses to assign any meaning to his actions, asserting that his gesture 'isn't for a moment about belief, or conviction, or integrity'. He refuses to link it with political protest, observing: '[i]f anything it was formed out of an absence of belief'.[24] He also rejects the idea that it could be interpreted as a response to his parents' shortcomings. As Crouch notes in his Introduction to the published script: '[t]he boy's action is more meaningful to others than it is to himself. His arm becomes the ultimate inanimate object onto which other people project their own symbols and meanings.'[25]

The piece also contains other gaps for audiences to fill and puzzles for them to unpick. One of the most convincing of these involves its provenance. For those audience members unfamiliar with Crouch and his work (as most would have been in 2003) it would not have been immediately apparent whether *My Arm* was his own story or not. Crouch's first-person narration and direct address to the audience certainly encourage audience members to view the story as his own. The narrator is never given a name that would distinguish him from Crouch, and the segments of grainy Super 8 Video home-movie footage which play at the beginning, middle and end of the piece appear to document scenes from the narrator's childhood and to offer an evocative visual representation of the personal history that is being related.[26] Consequently, it is not surprising that many audience members decide – at least to start with – that the life-story being related is 'true', and that it belongs to Crouch himself.[27] What is more remarkable is that some audience members still believe this at the end of the show, given all the evidence to the contrary. Crouch is not obviously ill; when he presents his back and hand for inspection at two separate moments in the performance, seemingly instructing audiences to look for a large scar and an amputated finger, his back and hand are clearly unmarked and whole. Most revealingly (and as the directions at the start of the play remind readers), he does not raise his arm above his head at any point in the performance. As Bottoms demonstrates, this 'gleeful scam' functions to highlight the dubious ethical position of the character of Simon Martin, the art dealer that the narrator has known since childhood. As the narrator tells us,

> Simon, then as now, was distinguished by a ruthless disregard for protocol [… and] operated by the rubric –
> *He writes laboriously on a placard.*
> 'Art is anything you can get away with'.[28]

As the stage directions inform readers, this sign remains visible to the audience throughout the rest of the show, pointing us both in the direction of *My Arm*, and the fictional Simon Martin's abuse of the narrator. As Bottoms argues, the piece provides an opportunity for spectators to reflect upon 'the way that the art world can be only too willing to buy into the sensationalized work of (con-)artists who may be more interested in turning a fast buck than in creating anything of beauty or redemptive value'.[29] It does not have to be this way, of course. As Bottoms notes in passing, Anthony – the narrator's brother – functions to provide an alternative vision of the transformative powers of art in *My Arm*. Simon Martin's cynical and parasitic acts of exploitation are contrasted with Anthony's growing political engagement. We are told Anthony produced an exhibition of photographs documenting the impact of the miners' strike, then that he is organizing an exhibition of artwork by refugees. The narrator's description of Anthony's artwork in the final lines of the play also demonstrates how the figure of the child is central to the space of creative questioning and imaginative engagement produced by the work. This description invites audiences to conjure up an image of the narrator's childhood. Relating a phone call to Anthony, the narrator recalls how they talked about their mother, and where they lived as children. He tells us that Anthony reported that he was painting: 'small canvases about his memories. He said he'd send me a portrait he'd done of me as a small boy. In it, he said, I was watching TV, plump and contented. With my arm around him.'[30] Critics attest to the affective impact of this ending. Despite the show's resolute refusal of sentiment, it is evident that the final evocation of this image of a moment of childhood memory works powerfully upon many who have heard it.[31]

The powerful affective cargo carried by the abstract concept of the child is also central to the impact of *An Oak Tree*. This two-hander shows us a father in the grip of overwhelming grief caused by the death of his 12-year-old daughter, Claire, in a car accident. The show stages the results of the father's efforts to meet and question the man that killed his daughter, who works as a hypnotist. In interview in 2008, Crouch notes that he equates the impact that the death of Claire has on her father with: 'the effect that World War I had on art – the idea [of ...] monumental loss making it no longer possible to trust the old, figurative ways of seeing'.[32] Here, Crouch – like Ravenhill – presents the loss of a child as motivating or requiring a reconsideration of form. *An Oak Tree* presents this reconsideration both formally and thematically. As Emilie Moran and Bottoms have noted, the piece engages with conceptual art's challenges to conventional artistic and cultural understandings of how representation functions – most explicitly in its reference to Michael Craig-Martin's 1973 work, *an oak tree*. Thematically, this is explored through the way in which grief brings the father to a radical revision of the relationship between subjects and objects. He describes how, unlike his wife, Dawn, he did not fixate on the conventional 'material evidence' of his daughter's existence in the first days after her death. Instead, he felt her presence in the material world around him:

> She was between lines, inside circles, hiding between angles. She was indentations in time, physical depressions, imperfections on surfaces, the spaces beneath the chairs.[33]

He then goes on to describe how he has changed a tree by the side of the road where the accident occurred into his daughter. The following scenes trace the disintegration of his marriage to Dawn, as she – like us – struggles to comprehend this transformation.

The investigation into the transformative power of the imagination is central to *An Oak Tree*. It provides spectators with very little by way of spectacle. The set is functional: eight chairs, stacked at the side of the stage; a piano stool; a microphone, sound system and speakers. The only nod to the referential representational economy of conventional, naturalistic theatre is the silver waistcoat worn by the hypnotist, played by Crouch. Indeed, the piece, like *My Arm*, is a tribute to the suggestive power of language. The hypnotist's act – in which the father is a willing participant – mirrors theatre's potential to immerse audiences in imaginative experiences of great emotional depth through the abstraction of the spoken word. The most remarkable and novel element of the production is the fact that the role of the father is taken on by a new actor – who has not seen the script before – every night. The script takes the second actor in and out of the role, showing the audience most (but not all) of Crouch's guidance to him or her, as the onstage encounter between the father and the hypnotist at one of the latter's shows is interspersed with scenes where the father is by the roadside, where his daughter was killed, and interacting with his wife. The piece's celebrated affective impact appears to be realized by and through watching this actor struggling to read the script and follow Crouch's instructions – some of which are delivered via headphones – as the glimpses of inevitable bewilderment or momentary uncertainty provided by this process effectively communicate the father's confusion.[34] Moreover, this strategy furthers destabilization of the relationship between performer and character which Crouch first explored in *My Arm*, and works with a similar tension between the extremity of emotional experience being explored and the limitations of its display, as the situation prevents the second performer from communicating the character's grief through the use of conventional gestures or physical signals.

The father's failure to present any conventional signs of grief also underpins his estrangement from his wife, made clear in a scene in which the hypnotist voices a distraught accusation from Dawn. She reproaches her husband for failing to grasp the reality of his daughter's death, and claims that he has always treated his family as abstractions:

> It's like some abstract intellectual fucking concept for you, isn't it. Claire's death. She never existed for you in the first place. She was just some idea. The idea of a daughter, just as I'm the idea of a wife. Marcy's the idea of a child. We don't exist for you, do we, not in flesh and blood.[35]

Crouch is clearly aware that this charge can be levelled at the piece itself. We are given very few details about Claire, and even fewer about Marcia, her younger sister. The play deals with this directly. The narrative breaks half way through for a scene in which the hypnotist answers questions about the show from the second performer. The second performer asks the hypnotist how old Marcia is supposed to be, and he replies: 'I don't know. Whatever you think.'[36] The second performer responds: 'about five?', and he comes back: '[f]ive's good. She's a bit underwritten.'[37] As critics and scholars have attested, this abstraction does not stand in the way of emotional engagement with the piece. Indeed, as Kincaid has argued, the abstraction of the figure of the child may actually enable a greater level of affective investment.[38]

The Author raises the affective stakes still further. Where *My Arm* leaves audiences with an image of childhood lost, and *An Oak Tree* asks them to consider the catastrophic emotional impact of the death of a child, *The Author* requires audiences to contemplate what is commonly considered to be the most depraved of crimes: the sexual abuse of a baby. Moreover, the play's form brings audiences into close proximity with the man who appears to be responsible for this outrage. This is the author of the play's title, a character named Tim Crouch, played by Crouch himself, who sits amongst the audience throughout. Crouch's risky decision to give this character his own name (and many other aspects of his personal history) and to place himself alongside audience members as the character confesses his guilt, forms part of *The Author*'s broader exploration of the ethical issues raised by the staging of violence. This exploration is realized through the play's slow and deliberate unpacking of the impact of a fictional Royal Court production upon its author Tim, the actors, Vic and Esther, who performed in it, and one of the people who saw it. The exact content of this play-within-a-play – which centres upon an abusive, incestuous father–daughter relationship – remains unclear, but the toll that making and watching it has taken becomes increasingly apparent during the show.

Crouch has acknowledged that his work on the play 'started with an idea of a culpable act of seeing'.[39] Its concern with the harm that our looking can do, both to ourselves and to others, is present throughout. Audience members are repeatedly instructed to 'look!' and asked whether they can 'see alright', particularly when what they are supposedly looking at is unpleasant or disturbing.[40] Crouch shares his preoccupation with the negative aspects of the gaze with many other artists, philosophers and scholars. Works such as Martin Jay's *Downcast Eyes* argue that anti-visual discourse is pervasive in the history of Western thought, whilst

Fredric Jameson sums up this suspicion in *Signatures of the Visible* which begins: '[t]he visual is *essentially* pornographic, which is to say that it has its end in rapt, mindless fascination'.[41] This suspicion is given a contemporary voice in Susan Sontag's 2003 publication, *Regarding the Pain of Others*, in which Sontag reassesses the conclusions she came to in *On Photography* in order to pick her way through the implications of the 'mounting level of acceptable violence and sadism in mass culture' and the resulting desensitization of spectators.[42]

The Author speaks of a similar unease and ambivalence about the consumption of staged violence and the passivity of audiences. This ambivalence is given a direct focus in the play's treatment of the character whose words 'I love this!' start the show. Played first by Adrian Howells at the Royal Court, and then by Chris Goode, this theatre-lover is, as Crouch puts it, 'theatre's worst enemy'.[43] A friend of the Royal Court, he admits to hanging around stage doors, entranced by what he perceives to be the glamour and romance of theatre. He is the ultimate passive consumer, going to see everything programmed and praising it all without discrimination. More disturbingly, the character is titillated by the spectacles of sex and violence which he sees on stage; and delights in the fact that most of the British population remains oblivious to what happens there. As he puts it: 'nobody out there knows, and nobody out there really cares'.[44] Commenting on this moment in the play, Crouch observed that it represents a 'desperate situation [in which ...] theatre is no longer an integrated cultural expression, but has become a separate voyeuristic specialism'.[45] For Crouch this character has been disempowered by the theatre he loves. He described him as 'a victim of theatre'; as being 'de-authorised by it'.[46] Ultimately, the fate of this audience member, and the company who perform the play he goes to see at the Royal Court, invites audiences to consider whether there is an ethical and moral equivalence between looking and doing, and whether one should watch spectacles of suffering when there is no possibility of making a direct intervention. It stretches these concerns about the harms that we may inflict on ourselves and others through looking beyond the theatre's walls, making connections between the kinds of looking that audiences do in the theatre and the looking that we do elsewhere: at videos, film, photographs, the Internet and in our everyday lives.

The figure of the child – or, more accurately, a baby – is central to the development of these connections. In the very final moments of the play Tim recalls the act that has led him to commit suicide. The script and Crouch's delivery leave audience members to decide for themselves whether Tim has only watched the sexual abuse of a baby on his computer, or whether he has actually touched Esther's baby son whom she has left asleep in the room with him. Tim insists that the 'baby stirs but it does not wake. It has no idea what is going on. It has no idea.'[47] There is no doubt about what Tim has watched, however. Contemplating his public humiliation following the discovery of his use of child pornography he tells the audience: '[y]ou won't forgive me, anyway. I know you. Look at you. You won't. You won't forgive me.'[48] He apologises, then leaves the theatre. This revelation functions as the challenging climax to the description of a series of 'culpable acts of seeing', which build in gravity throughout the play. In the first scene, Tim lasciviously describes the body of a young woman working at a floatarium, his comments capturing the casual objectification of the female body. Later he discusses footage of beheadings and executions he initially sought out on the Internet in the name of research, and then in an obsessive 'hunger to see what was going on'. His use of child pornography is figured, in part, as a product of his desire to encounter and absorb these 'images from the edges'.[49]

A combination of staging strategies enables the play to carry this challenging content. The performance notes at the beginning of the script make it clear that it should refuse to provide audiences with anything specific to look at. There is no spectacle – no set, no props, no stage: just two banks of seating from which audience members observe each other. There is nothing to see, apart from the other audience members and the performers who are seated among them. The style of acting adopted by the company, which echoes and develops that modelled by Crouch in *My Arm* and *An Oak Tree*, also supports the management of the play's combustible emotional cargo. The actors are undemonstrative, and their speech lacks conventional intonation. Lines are delivered directly, openly, almost cheerfully.[50] For Crouch, realizing and maintaining this style of delivery is key to the effects he is trying to create. He calls this style a 'lightness'; arguing that overly emotional delivery would close down the potential for audiences to invest in the work and interpret it in their own way. Describing the delivery of one of Esther's lines, in which she says: 'I suppose [I had] a bit of a breakdown, really', he observes:

> ... if she just gifts it, lightly, then everyone can have their own understanding of what that breakdown might have been [...] without the complication of representational emotion. There is emotion in the room, but the actors aren't demonstrating it for you. They are just presenting the story.[51]

This style – and other dramaturgical choices, such as the fact that the names of the characters are those of the performers playing them – also function to confound confident assumptions about the nature of the theatrical frame and the conventional contract between audience and performers, encouraging audiences to grasp their role in the creative construction of the piece, as in Crouch's earlier works. If anything, the piece places more emphasis upon the audience's interpretative agency. Discussing the contrast between *The Author* and his earlier plays, *An Oak Tree* and *ENGLAND*, Crouch observed that he had removed the reassuring explanation which introduces both of those pieces, noting that *The Author* is 'the most adult of my plays, because there is no guide to this experience'.[52] As audience members we are left to make up our own minds about whether the actors are in character or are effectively playing themselves; and we are also left to decide how to react to the regular invitations to respond to the questions which are directed at us by the cast.

   The play, however, breaks with one of the formal conventions it has established at a key moment. As discussed above, it resolutely refuses to provide spectacle: or rather, the only images it provides are the ones that spectators may produce in their imaginations. But there is one exception to this rule. About halfway through, the actress Esther asks us whether we would like to see a photograph of her son, Finn. On the two occasions I have seen the show this question produced an enthusiastic affirmative, and then audible 'ahs' as she shows the audience a photo of a smiling baby. This was then followed by an awkward silence as she continues to hold the image out in front of her, twisting and turning, seemingly ensuring that everyone has the chance to see him – despite the fact that most of the audience were obviously too far away to see. The significance of this ostensibly innocuous, if curiously lengthy, display is all too apparent by the show's conclusion. Commenting on the decision to use this image, Crouch noted that 'it might then come back to them at the end – it feels almost unbearable at times, when you know what's happening, it's unbearable'.[53]

   These revealing comments invite speculation. Is the moment unbearable for audiences, or for the performer? Crouch described how he felt during the Edinburgh run of *The Author*, seated amongst audience members with whom he has been chatting during the show, anticipating his final monologue in which he reveals the act of abuse for which he is now attempting to atone:

   ... almost always in Edinburgh half way through the show I would start
   to get a bit shaky, my legs would get a bit wobbly because I knew I was

going to have to say some stuff. And also almost every show I would start re-writing the final speech in my head. I have a very clear edit in my head that I could do, that would just bypass *the thing*.[54]

Of course, he never does bypass '*the thing*'. In fact, its voicing, and the fact that Crouch – as the author of *The Author* – risks being thought of as a paedophile by those audience members who may be struggling to differentiate between fact and fiction is central to what he is trying to achieve. But Crouch has every reason to be anxious about voicing '*the thing*'. He is describing viewing – and possibly participating in – behaviour which not only attracts the strongest expressions of public censure but also ferocious expressions of the most extreme hatred and disgust. And, as Erica Burman points out in *Developments: Child, Image, Nation*, this vilification has recently found physical form. A series of violent community attacks upon individuals suspected of being a paedophile or of having an association with one followed increasing public access to registers of identified 'sex offenders' in 2000. As Burman notes, '[a]ny spurious link could warrant direct, deadly action'.[55] Burman's analysis of the identificatory relations which underlie our affective response to babies also provides a measure of why a sexual attack upon an infant is considered so much worse than other crime. She notes that the image of the baby commands instant attention and extraordinary levels of affect, as the power of its symbolic connection with 'happiness, innocence, freedom from responsibility, [... and] being cared for' effectively 'occludes the ambivalence of our actual relations with children and childhood'.[56]

The Author is not unique in drawing on these connections. Theatre makers are well aware of the symbolic weight of an attack upon an infant and, as Crouch observed in interview, 'terrible things have happened to babies in the last forty years of new British writing'.[57] Moreover, the play's scripted insistence that it 'is set in the Jerwood Theatre Upstairs in the Royal Court Theatre – even when it's performed elsewhere' invites audience members with a working knowledge of the Royal Court's history to make the connection with the notorious attacks upon babies staged there in Edward Bond's *Saved* and Sarah Kane's *Blasted*.[58] Adrian's excited recall of the outrageous things he's seen done to babies at the venue drives the point home: 'I've seen a dead baby get eaten! That was great!'[59] Still, although Crouch's plays depend upon the strength of our cultural investment in children and childhood for their affective power, they are working both with and against the dominant cultural depiction of the child. Indeed, the children presented in *My Arm* are anything other than idealized. Rude, challenging and sexually aware, they have no interest in cooperating with adults and seem to feel no particular attachment to their parents. The narrator refuses to explain or justify his behaviour – or that of the other children he encounters – through revelations of abuse, neglect or mistreatment. Moreover, the childhood he depicts is resolutely ordinary in many ways. This is also true of the depiction of Claire and Marcia in *An Oak Tree*, and Finn the baby in *The Author*, where the sketchy details provided suggest nothing exceptional about these children. The plays also resist any straightforward positioning of child as victim and adult as aggressor. Though *My Arm* encourages audiences to deplore the objectification of the narrator, the play makes it quite plain that the original decision was his own, and that it is his passivity that makes his exploitation possible. And although the hypnotist is objectionable in many ways in *An Oak Tree*, it is never suggested that the death of Claire was anything other than an accident. *The Author* also resists presenting the most socially unacceptable behaviour in a reductive way. The slow build to Tim's shocking revelation encourages audiences to consider their own participation in the broader culture of display, exposure and objectification which has produced his ethical desensitization.

Nevertheless, some of the responses these plays have received indicate that cultural anxieties around the child remain strong enough to prevent intellectual engagement with their contents. In interview, Crouch recalled a woman who, as she walked out of *The Author* whilst it was playing at the Royal Court, announced: 'I'm a *mother*'.[60] In Brighton he was on the receiving end of an angry tirade from another audience member who announced that she would not have brought her pregnant friend with her had she known about the show's content, suggesting that the show's description of what authors might be driven to do to babies was unacceptably offensive for some audience members. It is important to acknowledge that the strong and sometimes disruptive responses the show received from volatile audiences during its run at the Edinburgh Festival in 2010 are not simply a product of its reference to child abuse. The reasons for these reactions no doubt vary between, amongst and within audience members, and are clearly produced, in part, by the way that the piece confounds desires to follow a 'social script' for participation in the show.[61] Yet some members of the audience obviously do object to the discussion of child abuse: objections which are hardly surprising in the broader context of the widespread 'child-panic' delineated by Brooks.

Politicians are well aware of this 'panic'. The welfare and well-being of children was central to New Labour's public policy. During their time in office from 1997 to 2010, the party introduced child tax credits, created the Sure Start early years scheme, made a statutory commitment to halve child poverty by 2010, and promoted their policies under the title 'Every Child Matters' initiative which led to the Children Act of 2004.[62] The impact of these policies – or their lack of impact – became the focus of political debate during the 2010 General Election campaign, and the rhetoric employed in these debates is indicative of the political weight carried by children and young people in contemporary politics.[63] Towards the end of their campaign, the Conservatives attempted to put over a more positive message. A week before the country went to the polls Shadow Secretary of State for Children, Schools and Families, Michael Gove, claimed that the Conservatives were 'fighting for our children's future'.[64]

Some of Crouch's most recent work brings children and contemporary politics into close contact. *John, Antonio and Nancy* (first performed at the Royal Court Theatre as part of the Rough Cuts season in 2010 and revived during 2012 at the Brighton Fringe) used three child performers. The children – wearing school uniforms – sit in a row, and address the audience directly. Their red, yellow and blue school ties, and the content of the phrases they present, enable audiences to identify them as John Brown, Antonio Clegg and Nancy Cameron: the children of the leaders of the three main political parties during the 2010 General Election. Speaking in turn, they report what their fathers have said during the election campaign in a series of ostensibly disconnected observations and platitudes. Cumulatively, these phrases capture the mixture of sentiment, aspiration and personal affidavits which characterize political debate before General Elections, as party leaders attempt to convince the country of their personal integrity, vision and responsiveness:

JOHN: My father has been shocked and sickened by what he saw.
NANCY: My father wants to create the big society.
ANTONIO: My father guarantees that he will work tirelessly for you.[65]

In performance, the piece had many of the formal characteristics of the plays discussed above. The children use the same denaturalized, unemotional style of acting that Crouch has developed, holding the audience's gaze through long pauses, as they work their way deliberately and dispassionately through the list of phrases. This style of presentation highlights the absurdity of political rhetoric deployed during the election, as the cultural association of children with hope and futurity foregrounds the cynicism of those who originally wrote and voiced these meaningless phrases. The children's distanced, deadpan delivery frustrates any attempt to sentimentalize. Any affect audiences feel will be a product of the value that individual children, and the idea of the child, holds for them personally and culturally. The child performers themselves do not invite this. Their abstraction is key.

Nevertheless, these children are available to be looked at, and the piece may appear, at first, to represent a significant departure from Crouch's earlier plays. *My Arm*, *An Oak Tree* and *The Author* trouble the spectatorial economy of conventional theatre formally, as well as thematically, by only providing limited or occluded images of children. Only those sitting close to Esther in *The Author* can actually see the photograph she displays; audiences see a boy running in a blurry family film and hear a report of a painting of two young boys in *My Arm*; Claire and Marcia in *An Oak Tree* are only ever represented in language. The affects these images of children produce do not depend upon their visual representation. *John, Antonio and Nancy* demonstrates that Crouch's strategy of invoking audiences' cultural attachment to the ideal of childhood innocence whilst resolutely refusing to idealize children does not depend upon this restricted view. Indeed, his latest experiments with child performers suggest that this combination of affective power can be achieved when children are there for all to see. This is achieved by providing audiences with the spectacle of what Kincaid, in his discussion of Dickens's child characters, calls 'the competent child'. These are children who 'do not brook being looked at but look straight back, thus foiling the voyeuristic game we play with children. These children are not on display. They gaze at us.'[66]

Crouch's use of child performers in *John, Antonio and Nancy* forms part of the broader invocation of the figure of the child in his work: an invocation which allows audiences to consider where the limits of representation lie, both in the theatre and in the wider world. The glimpses of the narrator's childhood provided in *My Arm* undoubtedly enable audiences to feel a greater sense of disquiet at his later objectification and exploitation, and *An Oak Tree* uses the death of a child to explore the nature of our attachment to subjects and objects, or people and things. In *The Author*, the emotional leverage produced by invoking the violation of an infant brings the ethical issues raised by the display of violence and abuse into sharp relief. The appearance of child performers in *John, Antonio and Nancy* explicitly directs attention towards political, as well as artistic, forms of representation. As Bottoms notes in his introduction to Crouch's collected plays, his work asks 'questions about the things that we *value* – both culturally and personally'.[67] And, one might add, the figure of the child provides the link between cultural and personal value in Crouch's work.

Notes

1. M. Ravenhill, 'A Tear in the Fabric: the James Bulger Murder and New Theatre Writing in the Nineties', *New Theatre Quarterly*, 20.4 (2004), 305–14 (p. 309).
2. Ravenhill, 'A Tear in the Fabric', p. 310.
3. For discussion of the strong responses *The Author* received, see T. Crouch, 'Response and Responsibility', *Contemporary Theatre Review*, 24.1 (2011), 416–22.
4. Crouch performed in all of these productions, apart from *I, Cinna (The Poet)*. His other plays include *Kaspar The Wild* (written for primary school children to perform in 2006); and *Shopping For Shoes* (which was commissioned by the National Theatre's Educational Department and first performed at St Ursula's School, Greenwich in 2003), as well as adaptations and original works for radio.
5. See the collection of essays by S. Bottoms, H. Freshwater, C. Goode, H. Iball, a smith and Crouch himself in *Contemporary Theatre Review*, 24.1 (2011); also S. Bottoms, 'Authorizing the Audience: The Conceptual Drama of Tim Crouch', *Performance Research*, 14.1 (2009), 65–76; T. Crouch, 'Darling you were Marvellous', in C. Svich (ed.), *Out of Silence: Censorship in Theatre and Performance* (Roskilde: Eyecorner Press, 2012), pp. 99–106; E. Morin, '"Look Again": Indeterminacy and Contemporary British Drama', *New Theatre Quarterly*, 27.1 (2011), 71–85. Interviews with Crouch include '*The Author*: Tim Crouch in Conversation with Helen Freshwater', *Performing Ethos*, 1.2 (2011), 181–96; 'Tim Crouch', in P. O'Kane (ed.), *Actors' Voices: The People Behind the Performances* (London: Oberon Books, 2012), S. Ilter, 'A Process of Transformation: Tim Crouch on *My Arm*', *Contemporary Theatre Review*, 24.1 (2011), 394–404; C. Svich, 'Tim Crouch's Theatrical Transformations', 2006, HotReview.org, http://www.hotreview.org/ (accessed 24 June 2012); 'Tim Crouch interview with Dan Rebellato', 2009, http://rhul.mediacore.tv/media/tim-crouch-interview-with-dan-rebellato (accessed 24 June 2012).
6. This chapter was completed in the summer of 2012.
7. The McCann family's campaign to find their daughter receives regular media attention, as news stories appear illustrated with digitally created age-progression photographs designed to enable recognition. Images of Jon Venables and James Thompson (James Bulger's killers) return periodically to screens and newspaper covers as news of their release, the controversy over the protection of their identities, and Venables' return to custody in March 2010 enabled journalists to revisit the story. Venables' re-imprisonment also fuelled debate over whether it is appropriate to describe children as intrinsically evil and if rehabilitation is possible, and became the focus of a political row between the Children's Commissioner Maggie Atkinson and Ed Balls (the then Children's Secretary) over the age that children should be held criminally responsible. Sarah Payne's murder has stayed in the

public eye since her death in 2000 as a result a high-profile campaign by the tabloid *News of the World* for 'Sarah's Law' – which would give parents access to information about sex offenders – and the staggered introduction of the resulting Child Sex Offender Disclosure Scheme between 2008 and 2011. The image of Holly Wells and Jessica Chapman, taken shortly before their deaths in 2002, appeared in the papers again in 2011 with the news that the anonymity granted Maxine Carr (who provided their killer, Ian Huntley, her then boyfriend, with an alibi at the time of the murders in 2002) would be extended to cover Carr's child. Reporters expressed outrage at the cost to the taxpayer of providing Carr with anonymity, 'round-the-clock police protection' and a 'new life'. See 'Madeleine McCann: Police Issue Image of Girl Aged Nine', BBC News, 25 April 2012, http://www.bbc. co.uk/ (accessed 23 June 2012); A. Gabbatt, 'Balls rejects call to raise age of criminal responsibility', *The Guardian*, 15 March 2010, http://www.guardian. co.uk/ (accessed 23 March 2010); 'Children's Chief apologises for Bulger killers comment', BBC News Online, 17 March 2010, http://news.bbc.co.uk/ (accessed 23 March 2010); G. O'Shea, 'Huntley's lover Carr "becomes a mother"', *The Sun*, 31 October 2011, p. 7; D. Collins, 'Maxine Carr's Baby to Live a Secret Life; Soham Liar's Tot will never know Mum's Real ID', *The Mirror*, 31 October 2011, p. 22; 'Shamed Maxine has Baby', *Daily Record*, 31 October 2011, p. 9.

8. S. Beder, W. Varney and R. Gosden, *This Little Kiddy Went to Market: The Corporate Capture of Childhood* (London: Pluto Press, 2009); E. Mayo and A. Nairn, *Consumer Kids: How Big Business is Grooming our Children for Profit* (London: Constable, 2009); S. Dale, *Candy from Strangers: Kids and Consumer Culture* (Vancouver: New Star Books, 2005).

9. The popular parenting website Mumsnet launched an effective campaign, 'Let Girls Be Girls', in 2010 that led to a government commissioned report on the commercialization and sexualization of childhood, and the adoption of a voluntary code of practice by British clothing retailers. This was followed by governmental recommendation of further voluntary action on the part of advertisers in 2012. See http://www.mumsnet.com/campaigns/let-girls-be-girls (accessed 23 June 2012); R. Bailey, *Letting Children Be Children: Report of the Independent Review of the Commercialisation and Sexualisation of Childhood*, Department of Education, June 2011; *Responsible Retailing: BRC Childrenswear Guidelines* (London: British Retail Consortium, 2011).

10. S. Palmer, *Toxic Childhood: How the Modern World is Damaging Our Children and What We Can Do About It* (London: Orion, 2006); R. Louv, *Last Child in The Woods: Saving Our Children From Nature-Deficit Disorder* (London: Atlantic Books, 2010).

11. D. Elkind, *The Hurried Child: Growing Up Too Fast, Too Soon* (Cambridge, MA: Da Capo Press, 2007), p. 3.

12. See L. Brooks, *The Story of Childhood: Growing up in Modern Britain* (London: Bloomsbury, 2006), p. 5.

13. Brooks, *The Story of Childhood*, p. 16.

14. Simon Stephens noted: '[t]he very first initiating moment [for *Wastwater*] was reading the news stories of May 2007 about the abduction of Madeleine McCann'. S. Stephens and K. Mitchell in discussion with O. Animashawun, 18 March 2011, 'Wastwater podcast', http://www.royalcourttheatre.com/ (accessed 22 June 2012).

15. Others have noted this tendency in Stephens's work. After meeting Stephens and hearing him offer 'heartfelt tributes to his wife and three children', journalist Andrew Dickson asked: '[c]an this really be the man who has written several plays lingering on the death of children, and another [*Motortown* (2006)] that contains the cold-blooded murder of a 14-year-old girl?' See 'Playwright Simon Stephens: "The same old agonies return to haunt you"', *The Guardian*, 8 April 2011, http://www.guardian.co.uk/ (accessed 22 June 2012).

16. As A. Sierz notes: '[a]lthough they rarely appear onstage, they are often present, sometimes insistently present. And, even when they are not, their absence attracts attention.' A. Sierz, *The Theatre of Martin Crimp* (London: Methuen Drama, 2006), p. 136.

17. For a discussion of the controversy over *Mercury Fur*, see P. Ridley and A. Sierz, '"Putting a New Lens on the World": the Art of Theatrical Alchemy', *New Theatre Quarterly*, 25.2 (2009), 109–17; for a discussion of the way in which the play's form encourages ethical engagement with the issues raised by witnessing staged violence, see A. Harpin, 'Intolerable Acts', *Performance Research*, 16.1 (2011), 102–11.

18. L. Edelman, *No Future: Queer Theory and the Death Drive* (Durham and London: Duke University Press, 2004), p. 12. See also R. Bernstein, *Racial Innocence: Performing American Childhood from Slavery to Civil Rights* (New York and London: New York University Press, 2011).

19. J. Kincaid, *Child-Loving: The Erotic Child and Victorian Culture* (New York and London: Routledge, 1992), p. 5.

20. T. Crouch, *My Arm* (London: Faber & Faber, 2003), p. 17.

21. See D. Lane, 'A Dramaturg's Perspective: Looking to the Future of Script Development', *Journal of Media Practice*, 30.1 (2010), 127–42 (pp. 131–3); Bottoms, 'Authorizing the Audience: The Conceptual Drama of Tim Crouch', 73–6.

22. 'The Author: Tim Crouch in Conversation with Helen Freshwater', 184.

23. T. Crouch in conversation with A. Sierz, 'Writer and Actor Tim Crouch on *An Oak Tree*', *Theatre Voice*, 23 February 2007, http://www.theatrevoice.com/ (accessed 10 July 2012).

24. Crouch, *My Arm*, p. 14.

25. Crouch, 'Introduction', *My Arm*, p. 9.

26. As the script indicates, this footage actually belonged to a friend of Crouch, Chris Dorley-Brown. Crouch, *My Arm*, p. 10.

27. Bottoms attests to the fact that he was 'hoodwinked' ('Authorizing the Audience', p. 74). As the critic for *The Herald* noted: '[a]t first glance, you could easily mistake this first-person narrative for autobiography'. 'Give a big hand for the man making waves', *The Herald*, 4 August 2003, p. 13.

28. Crouch, *My Arm*, p. 26.

29. Bottoms, 'Authorizing the Audience', p. 75.

30. Crouch, *My Arm*, p. 37.

31. J. Macmillan [*The Scotsman*, 2003]: 'the wonderful final image of this show is so straightforwardly moving that it left many members of the audience, including me, close to tears', cited in http://www.timcrouchtheatre.co.uk/ (accessed 11 July 2012); and D. Cavendish: 'creeping up on your emotions, the show becomes an elegy for lost childhood, while deconstructing the

ways in which we mythologise our past', 'Arms and the Man', *The Daily Telegraph*, 9 August 2003, p. 18.
32. Quoted in Bottoms, 'Authorizing the Audience', p. 69.
33. T. Crouch, *An Oak Tree*, in *Tim Crouch: Plays One* (London: Oberon Books, 2011), pp. 49–106 (p. 89).
34. Bottoms notes that he found moments in *An Oak Tree* 'harrowingly moving'. See 'Authorizing the Audience', p. 66. The notes for the second actor, published with the script, acknowledge the potential emotional impact of the show and caution: 'the story of *An Oak Tree* concerns the loss of a child; if this experience is personally close then we would advise against you getting involved'. Crouch, *An Oak Tree*, p. 55.
35. Crouch, *An Oak Tree*, p. 98.
36. Crouch, *An Oak Tree*, p. 93.
37. Crouch, *An Oak Tree*, p. 93.
38. See J. Kincaid, 'Dickens and the Construction of the Child', in W. S. Jacobson (ed.), *Dickens and the Children of Empire* (Basingstoke: Palgrave Macmillan, 2000), pp. 29–42 (p. 37).
39. T. Crouch interviewed by H. Freshwater, 30 September 2010.
40. T. Crouch, *The Author*, in *Tim Crouch: Plays One*, pp. 161–204 (p. 182).
41. M. Jay, *Downcast Eyes: The Denigration of Vision in Twentieth Century French Thought* (Berkeley: University of California Press, 1993), p. 221; F. Jameson, *Signatures of the Visible* (London and New York: Routledge, 1992), p. 1.
42. S. Sontag, *Regarding the Pain of Others* (London: Penguin, 2003), p. 90.
43. '*The Author*: Tim Crouch in Conversation with Helen Freshwater', p. 195.
44. Crouch, *The Author*, p. 193.
45. '*The Author*: Tim Crouch in Conversation with Helen Freshwater', p. 195.
46. '*The Author*: Tim Crouch in Conversation with Helen Freshwater', p. 195.
47. Crouch, *The Author*, p. 202.
48. Crouch, *The Author*, p. 203.
49. Crouch, *The Author*, p. 177.
50. T. Schmidt provides a useful discussion of the quality of speech in Crouch's work in Chapter 2 of his unpublished PhD thesis, 'The Politics of Theatricality: Community and Representation in Contemporary Art and Performance' (Queen Mary, University of London, 2011).
51. '*The Author*: Tim Crouch in Conversation with Helen Freshwater', p. 193.
52. '*The Author*: Tim Crouch in Conversation with Helen Freshwater', p. 184.
53. Tim Crouch interviewed by Helen Freshwater, 30 September 2010.
54. '*The Author*: Tim Crouch in Conversation with Helen Freshwater', p. 186.
55. Burman recalls, 'a paediatrician in Wales was attacked because her professional title bore a resemblance to the term paedophile'. E. Burman, *Developments: Child, Image, Nation* (London and New York: Routledge, 2008), p. 133. For further details of the attack, see R. Allison, 'Doctor Driven Out of Home by Vigilantes', *The Guardian*, Home Pages, 30 August 2000, p. 1.
56. Burman, *Developments*, p. 146.
57. T. Crouch interviewed by H. Freshwater, 30 September 2010.
58. Crouch, *The Author*, p. 164.
59. Crouch, *The Author*, p. 192.
60. T. Crouch interviewed by H. Freshwater, 30 September 2010.
61. See Crouch, 'Response and Responsibility'.

62. This act created the role of Children's Commissioner and was designed to facilitate coordination between the agencies with responsibility for child protection.

63. Theresa May (then Shadow Secretary of State for Work and Pensions), highlighted the Labour Party's failure to meet their commitment to halve child poverty by 2010. David Cameron made reference to the recent sentencing of two brothers, aged 11 and 12, who had subjected two other young boys to a violent and prolonged attack in Edlington in Doncaster the previous year at an election campaign event. Cameron asserted that the attack was indicative of a 'broken society'. Linking the case to a series of notorious killings involving children and young people, he proclaimed: 'I don't think it is right every time one of these events takes place to say that it is just some isolated incident of evil that we should look away from and regret. [...] Are we going to do that every time there is a Jamie Bulger or a Baby Peter or a Ben Kinsella or a Garry Newlove or what has happened in Doncaster?' See T. May, 'Labour's Failure on Child Poverty', *The Guardian*, 27 March 2010, http://www.guardian.co.uk/ (accessed 24 June 2012); P. Walker and M. Wainwright, 'Edlington Brothers Jailed for Torture of Two Boys', *The Guardian*, 22 January 2010, http://www. guardian.co.uk/ (accessed 24 June 2012); A. Stratton, 'Case is symptom of a "broken society", says Tory leader', *The Guardian*, 23 January 2010, p. 5. Two men and the mother of 'Baby Peter', or Peter Connolly, were jailed for causing or allowing the death of a child in 2008. Sixteen-year-old Ben Kinsella was stabbed to death by other teenagers in 2008. Gary Newlove was murdered by a group of teenagers in 2007 after remonstrating with them for vandalizing his car.

64. M. Gove, 'Fighting for our Children's Future', 29 April 2010, http://blog. conservatives.com/ (accessed 24 June 2012).

65. T. Crouch, *John, Antonio and Nancy* (unpublished manuscript, 2010).

66. Kincaid, 'Dickens and the Construction of the Child', pp. 37–8.

67. S. Bottoms, 'Introduction', *Tim Crouch: Plays One*, pp. 11–20 (p. 16).

Index

Printed and bound by CPI Group (UK) Ltd, Croydon, CR0 4YY